BOOKS AND THEIR WRITERS

BOOKS AND THEIR WRITERS

BY

S. P. B. MAIS

Essay Index Reprint Series

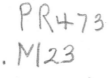

BOOKS FOR LIBRARIES PRESS
FREEPORT, NEW YORK

First Published 1920
Reprinted 1968

LIBRARY OF CONGRESS CATALOG CARD NUMBER:
68-54359

PRINTED IN THE UNITED STATES OF AMERICA

TO
MY WIFE

CONTENTS

PART III: BOOKS IN GENERAL

PREFACE

LET me make it quite clear at the outset : I have laid no claims to be thought a literary critic : the following papers are not studies in literature. While other men were more healthily and patriotically employed in digging up their allotments and gardens, for physical reasons I was forced to confine myself to the garden of my mind, by no means a fruitful soil : I have but little creative genius : abandoning this barren task I then began to dig in the gardens of other men's minds : this book is the result. All I have sought to do has been to convey some of the pleasure I have gained from desultory reading of all kinds during the last few years, to those who take the trouble to turn these pages : the art of criticism is not mine. I have not obtruded my own personality more than was absolutely necessary. I have merely walked about prolific vineyards and orchards and plucked a cluster of grapes here, a plum there, to entice you to share some of my golden pleasures. That I have missed some of the best will be obvious to any one who looks at the chapter-headings ; that I have included much unripe and indigestible, or over-ripe and putrid fruit I beg leave to deny. There was so much that was very good that I could have filled another volume with ease. Some of these essays have already appeared in print. For permission to include them in this volume I wish to thank the editors of *The Fortnightly Review* and *To-day*.

PART I

NOVELISTS AND NOVELS

" *Oh, it's only a novel . . . only some*
work in which the greatest powers of
the mind are displayed, in which the
most thorough knowledge of human
nature, the happiest delineations of
its varieties, the liveliest effusions of
wit and humour, are conveyed to the
world in the best chosen language."

I

INTRODUCTORY

I HAVE lately read a book by W. L. George (who appears to write with equal facility about everything) on the Modern Novel. I remember to have been astounded at his selection of authors : now that I, in my turn, find that I want to say something about the novel I can already hear the critic saying, " What an amazing selection." It is quite impossible to make a class list. It is like the competition of finding out which is the best of Keats' five *Odes,* or Shakespeare's greatest tragedy. I have no favourite author. The last time I dared to write generally of the modern author I was taken to task for omitting to mention Charles Marriott. It never struck my critic on that occasion, I suppose, that there are writers who dare not talk about some things because the temptation to fill volume after volume would be so strong. There are moods when Marriott's are the only novels I can rely on to restore me to mental health : I know no man who can make the other sex live as he makes it live : do you remember the passage in *Mrs Alemere's Elopement* where Dick meets Evelyn again, loving her body, she loving him not at all : " She must despise him for his self-restraint when she was under his protection " ? It is a terribly merciless rending of the veil. I love Marriott for his epigrammatic style, his vivid grasp of essentials both in scenic descriptions and in analysis of character : I love him for his " all-round-

13

ness." He is as much at home with successful business men, scientists, architects, engineers, and miners as he is with artists and philosophers. I love him for his cleanness, his mental sanity, his gospel of " To take by leaving, to hold by letting go." It is certainly a mote, a blemish that he should so persistently dwell on drunkenness in women, and the necessity for divorce in the life of every man, but I like a man who can courageously rush into the market-place with a gospel of this sort : " There is a free love which is neither the ludicrous complication of marriage generally understood by the term, nor a foolish denial or cowardly evasion of sex." I love him for his sense of beauty and goodness, his gentleness and kindly humour . . . but I daren't pick him out as a subject for a special article. It would occupy too much space. I have instead made a quite arbitrary selection : I could have lamented at great length on the disappearance of the Arnold Bennett who gave us *The Old Wives' Tale*, and the appearance of the expert journalist who gave us *The Pretty Lady* and *The Roll-Call*, both of which exhibit great talent, but no genius whatever. I could have pined (for pages) for the Wells of *Mr Polly*, *Kipps*, and *Love and Mr Lewisham*, and become angry that so great a humorist should have devoted to the Deity, politics, sex, and education, what should have been devoted to scientific prophecy and the comedy of the draper's assistant : I could have used up my vocabulary of eulogies on the trilogies of J. D. Beresford and Oliver Onions, and wondered sorrowfully why the former should have condescended to *God's Counterpoint*, and the latter to write reconstruction novels like *The New Moon*.

I very nearly decided to give Alec Waugh an article to himself, but I am almost alone in not considering *The Loom of Youth* a book of surpassing genius. *The Prisoners of Mainz* is ever so much better ; the former was all stale news to me as I am a schoolmaster : it shows great powers of observation, but I get quickly tired of descriptions of games and caricatures of masters. Arnold Lunn and St John Lucas are much more artistic in their pictures of school life : they are so much less heavy. But it would be hard to exaggerate the importance of Alec Waugh : he has made education almost as popular a subject as spiritualism, which is all to the good . . . and by writing it he cleared the way for himself. He now has acquired humour, lightness, geniality, and self-confidence.

I could have written much on the childlike *naïveté* of Irene McLeod : *Graduation* is one of the few novels of the present time which exalts love in its simplest, most honourable sense. Miss M. Fulton, too, is a new writer who achieved in *Blight* such a success that I would willingly call attention to its merits at greater length. Then there are Middleton Murry with his very modern minute psychological study of moods and thoughts in *Still Life*, and Hugh Walpole, the eclectic, who lives entirely in and for his art. I suppose if I were really compelled to place my candidates in order of merit I should hesitate for a long time before deposing Hugh Walpole from the premier position, partly because he is interested in the things that interest me more than any others. In *Mr Perrin and Mr Traill* he started a fashion whereby it was no longer considered impossible to include schoolmasters in a novel. In *The Dark Forest* and *The Secret City* he made me even more anxious to know something of that fascinating enigma, Russia, than I had been, after labouring for years among its native writers. *The Secret City* is, after *Forti-*

tude, the modern novel I would select for my desert island. Walpole's pictures of Russian cities, of Russian home-life, of the revolutions, are masterpieces and remain as concrete images in the mind long after the book is read. And . . . who can depict so well the problems that after all matter so much more to us than anything else in the world . . . our relations with our fellows ? "It's no use trying to keep out of things. As soon as they want to put you in—you're in. The moment you're born, you're done for." He realises the price at which a man achieves freedom : how one delivers one's soul over to another human being and is thenceforward lost. "Love's always selfish, always cruel to others, always means trouble, sorrow, and disappointment. But it's worth it, even when it brings complete disaster. Life isn't life without it." Nothing worth having can be achieved without paying enormously . . . and I love Hugh Walpole because he can both face the fact and reckon the cost, and yet count love as worth the horrors it brings. He sees life simply as a training-ground for the immortal soul. "The secret of the mystery of life is the isolation that separates every man from his fellow—the secret of dissatisfaction, too ; and the only purpose in life is to realise that isolation, and to love one's fellow-man because of it, and to show one's own courage, like a flag to which other travellers may wave their answer . . . life is a tragedy to every Russian simply because the daily round is forgotten by him in his pursuit of an ultimate meaning. We in the West have learnt to despise ultimate meanings as unpractical and rather priggish things." Hugh Walpole realises, as few other writers realise how the power of passion sweeps away all obstacles in its frenzy to achieve its object : he has

penetrated to the secret city which is in every man's
heart : " I love him so that I am blind for him and
deaf for him and dead for him. . . . Before it is too
late—I want it, I want him, I want happiness."
Such is the poignant cry of the Russian woman un-
happily married, who finds in the stolid Cambridge
" Rugger Blue " the firmness and solidity and power
which every woman worships more than anything
else in the world. I could write at length of John
Galsworthy's sensitive heart, of Miss G. B. Stern's
insight into the problems of the sexes ; I should like
to extol Ralph Straus's strong, trenchant, healthy
point of view, and Joseph Conrad's Romantic realism.
Leonard Merrick's sad irony should receive its due
share of praise, and Sheila Kaye Smith's masterly
pictures of Sussex should not pass unnoticed. . . .
I suppose there are not less than fifty writers
whose books one eagerly devours year by year. At
one moment we are intrigued by the queer artistry
of James Joyce; the next, and Gilbert Cannan's
clear, hard, polished intellect seems to us the most
desirable art in the world. The war is over, and those
domestic problems which once seemed very small
when compared with the immanence of death and
the grandeur of male friendships, now loom as large as
ever. One thing only we require of those who write,
that they shall be as Tchekov says, " humanists to
the very tips of their fingers." They must find life
interesting, they must be insatiably curious, they
must write of people and things as they see them.
They must have a point of view, and they should
inspire us with courage and enable us to face our
own difficulties. There would appear to be a sharp
cleavage between the novels that matter, those which
make us think, and attempt to present us with a

picture of actualities, and those myriads of others
which don't pretend to do more than amuse.   There
is no question that the world is made the better by
those energetic spirits who feel called upon to commit
to paper the thoughts that surge through them, the
experiences through which they or their imaginations
pass.   Novel-writing is no easy task : and few things
make one so speechless with rage as the stupidity of
those blind readers who write " vulgar rubbish "
across a page of Swinnerton, or " the man with the
muck-rake " on the title-page of Galsworthy.   Writers
have to dive deep into the bed of humanity and
bring up whatever they find : it is only the exception
who returns with the pearl.   But it requires courage
to dive.   The text on the cover of the *Quarterly* has
been made the excuse of every mud-flinger for the
last hundred years.   It is time we realised that the
best kind of criticism is pityingly silent over poverty
of thought and diction, and lavish of praise where
praise can honestly be given.   There is so much that
is good that we need never read anything else.   It
is obvious that we are not by any manner of means
unanimous in our definition of what is good, but
everybody (except George Moore) finds some reward
in reading Shakespeare, so I maintain that 90 per
cent. of those who read this book will be rewarded
if they read the works of the authors mentioned in
it.   They are not all easy.   It is as hard to concentrate on to Dorothy Richardson as it is on to a piece
of Latin or Greek unseen, but the reward is great
(sometimes) in proportion to the labour we bestow.
It costs but little effort to follow the Baroness Orczy,
and the recompense is slender ; Conrad and Henry
James demand the same mental alertness in their
readers as they themselves are possessed of.

II

THE GENIUS OF COMPTON MACKENZIE

IN *Sylvia Scarlett* Compton Mackenzie carries on
his Balzac scheme of economical selection by
continuing the histories of men and women
whose acquaintance we have already made in
earlier books. In attempting, therefore, a general
survey of his work one is bound to come to the
conclusion that his first book, *The Passionate Elopement*, was simply a magnificent *tour de force*, an
exquisite "essay in literary bravura," a piece of
loveliness thrown off by the artist as a young man
while he was feeling his way.

The six novels which followed it all deal with the
same little coterie of principals, and there is no
reason why the number should not be extended in-
definitely. He himself computes it at thirty.

There is no question of our getting tired of them,
once we take into account certain definite limitations
that are peculiar to Mackenzie's genius. In the first
place, he possesses a memory which is almost Macau-
layesque. I know of no author who can re-create
our earliest years so accurately or so sympatheti-
cally : unfortunately this leads him into the error
of believing implicitly in a gospel he has made
his own : "Childhood makes the instrument, youth
tunes the strings, and early manhood plays the
melody."

"I very much doubt if any impressions after
eighteen or nineteen help the artist," says Guy.

19

" All experience after that age is merely valuable for
maturing and putting into proportion the more vital
experiences of childhood."

Wordsworthian, but not true. Nevertheless, Mackenzie believes it, and so we have to listen to an
interminable noise of hammering at the instrument
followed by an extravagantly long tuning-up before
the play begins. In spite of the accuracy with which
he reveals to us again the golden hours of our infancy,
the thick-sighted ambition of our youth, with its
quick-changing rhapsodies, and the unhealthy imagination of our adolescence, we get bored. The curtain-
raiser is too long : the adventure is all prelude.

His second limitation is even worse ! He seems
quite unable to create a decent man. Alan can at
least play cricket, but none of his other " heroes "
has any positive virtue. Maurice is as unstable as
Reuben : Jenny's exquisite character crystallises
itself into " commonness " in his eyes when he
attempts to get her into proper perspective by leaving her : Guy is so inert that he allows trifling debts
to destroy one of the most perfect idylls in fiction :
he is molluscous, jejune, made up of shreds and
patches of other men's clichés : " I must be free if
I'm going to be an artist," he repeats, parrot-like,
to Pauline, understanding not a whit what he means.
This is, if you please, the man who was talked of as
" the most brilliant man of his time at Oxford."

There are many absurdly impossible incidents in
all these novels, but there is nothing quite so farcically
surprising as Michael Fane's " First " in History.
Much might be forgiven him if he had brains ; he has
nothing but a maudlin affection for Don Quixote, an
unhealthy taste for the more licentious classics and
low life, a sentimental attitude to religion, and an

astounding ignorance of life. We are led to believe
that Sylvia in the end settles down after her picar-
esque life with this nincompoop for her husband :
if our guess is correct she might just as well have
remained with her " thoroughly negative " Philip
(also an Oxford man).

It is as if Mackenzie definitely set out to prove
that a University turned out all its pupils cut to
pattern . . . and what a pattern it is ! " Shallow,
shallow ass that I am," plaintively bleats Maurice
with his usual insincere self-depreciation, " incom-
petent, dull, and unimaginative block." That exactly
describes them all. One other trait they have in
common which finally places them beyond the pale
of our favour. They are, without exception, incor-
rigible snobs. One could forgive their interminable
empty chatter, their futility, even their woodenness ;
but their appalling self-complacency destroys any
possible interest on our part in their welfare. They
have money, therefore they are the salt of the earth.
I have seen Mackenzie compared with Thackeray, for
what reason I cannot fathom. But this gallery of
callow undergraduates might well be included in the
modern *Book of Snobs.*

Lastly we come to the limitation of label. It is
customary to classify all modern authors. Mackenzie
has been hailed as the leader of the " realistic "
school. This is no place to enter into a discussion
on the connotation of critical labels, but if " realistic "
is meant to be synonymous with " actual," Mackenzie
is no more a realist than Dickens was. He has the
comic spirit much too fully developed (thank God
he possesses what none of his heroes has, a sense of
humour) to depict life as he sees it. With a gorgeous
abandon he gives his nimble wit free play to carica-

ture : he has no gospel to preach, no point of view to present : he merely strives to entertain . . . and that he is the most diverting prestidigitator and mirth-provoking showman of our age *Poor Relations* convincingly proves.

Unfortunately, we don't expect Lord George Sangers to be artists. Compton Mackenzie is an artist to the finger-tips, and he has therefore been persistently misunderstood. Disappointment lies in store for those befogged critics who think that Compton Mackenzie is of the family of Hugh Walpole, J. D. Beresford, or Gilbert Cannan.

Is it after all a limitation not to belong to the introspective school ? The riddle of the universe is not necessarily to be solved by the novelist. . . . Is it a crime to revert to the tradition of *Tom Jones* ? Mackenzie is in the direct line of Fielding. Is not that enough ? Why complain that he falls short of an achievement which he never set out to attain ?

So much for limitations. What has this wayward genius, then, to offer if he has no gospel, and can't paint an endurable well-bred man ? In the first place, he is a consummate architect. Young modern novelists for the most part are so taken up with analysing their emotions, and sifting their psychological experiences, that they have eliminated form and technique altogether. They rather pride themselves on their lawlessness. Mackenzie plans on a colossal scale, but rarely makes a mistake : his edifice is not only beautiful (few living writers have quite such a feeling for the best word : his sentences are exquisitely balanced, pellucidly clear, and rhythmical), but it is utilitarian. He has great inventive powers ; he is always deeply stirred by beautiful things, and can convey the essence of an impression

more economically and surely than most of his contemporaries.

Guy and Pauline is so beautiful that we are almost
drugged by the sweetness of it. Every season of the
year, every flower, and every changing light is seized
and put on to paper perfectly. When he sets out
deliberately to paint a landscape, whether it be of a
Cotswold village with its cobbles overgrown with
grass, of Cornwall in December with its blue and
purple veronicas and almond-scented gorse, or Ana-
sirene with its anemones splashed out like wine upon
the green corn, and red-beaded cherry-trees throwing
shadows on the tawny wheat, we sit dumb as before
a picture by a great master.

It is the presence of beauty that never fails to show
Mackenzie at his best. He is one of Nature's great
interpreters—and I am not sure that he is not woman's
best interpreter. Jenny is not the only pearl to be
cast before swine. Pauline, Sylvia, each in her own
individual way, is equally precious and adorable.

We have seen two of the inimitable trio giving up
their boundless maiden treasures, in each case to a
puppet—and in each case so deftly and delicately
has their passion been portrayed that we can
think of no parallel outside the pages of *Richard
Feverel.*

Mackenzie has an uncanny insight into the hearts
of his heroines. Women do shower their love on to
the most undeserving men. It is quite true that
Pauline will never forget Guy ; she is like the nymph
on the Grecian Urn . . . : it was quite in keeping
with passionate, heart-broken Jenny's temperament
that she should give herself to a dirty rotter when she
found Maurice wanting, though I can never reconcile
myself to her marriage ; I was not at all surprised

at Sylvia Scarlett becoming a temporary prostitute after leaving Philip.

It is partly because they are so virginal in character, partly because they so hate men to make love to them, that (when the flame is kindled) these heroines descend a little lower than conventional angels on being scorned. Mackenzie is never happier than when he is transcribing the dialogues of his women : one can hear their very accents (if we are not snobs they do not grate on our polished ears), and we fall desperately in love not with their physical beauty so much as with their wonderful vivacity, never-failing spirits, and extraordinary bonhomie.

The tang of bitterness on Sylvia's tongue adds to her charms. These are the lips we wish to hear at carnival-time (when we drop the mask of our respectability) whispering " Viens donc . . . je t'aime." We need no second invitation. From the crowd of Pierrots we draw our lily-white Columbine, and cease from banging other roysterers on the head with bladders : we set out on an amazingly incredible crusade, and mix with the wives of lavatory-attendants, decadent artists, maniacs who think that they are inside out, Treacherites, priests, murderers, harlots, pseudo-Emperors of Byzantium, chorus-girls, and procurators . . . we are whirled from the Fulham Road through Granada, Morocco, Brussels, the United States, to Buenos Ayres ; from the sylvan quiet of Plashers' Mead to the ugly filthiness of Leppard Street : we meet a fresh romance at every turn in the road. If we tire of one set of companions we can shake them off by taking the first 'bus that passes.

We are swept along so fast that we no longer feel any astonishment at meeting Maurice in the heart of Africa, Arthur Madden in a third-rate hotel in Sulphurville, U.S.A., or think it strange that Sylvia, Lily, and Michael should find one another again at a skating-rink dance.

Her mother *would* go mad on the very day that Jenny gave herself to Danby : the young wife of seventeen in such a world may well know her Petronius and Apuleius, and give her judgment on Aristophanes. The secret is that these are not real people : Mackenzie's is not the world as we know it. Everything is possible on the cinema, and *Sylvia Scarlett* is the finest film I have ever seen. We go to the pictures to get away from realities, to indulge our senses in a riotous phantasmagoria. " Let the young enjoy theirselves," is the ever-recurring cry of the old in all these books.

" If you could break loose yourself sometimes," cries Sylvia in desperation to her pedantic husband, " you'd be much easier to live with."

The syrens call ; like Fra Lippo Lippi we begin to tear our sheets into ropes to let ourselves down from our prison. . . . We, too, want to join the laughing nymphs who sing to the guitar beneath our window. Transported for the moment into golden asses, we try our hand at the game only to be rebuffed sadly in our search for the real Sylvia—we meet no daughters of joy, but *filles de joie*, no " lazy, laughing, languid Jenny," but only some desperately dull drab whose sole resemblance to our dream-heroine is that she actually calls us " soppy date " and bids us " ching-a-ling " if our purse is too attenuated to glut her desires.

No—the wise man will be content to take Compton Mackenzie at his own valuation.

Exquisite figments of our imagination, Sylvia, Pauline, and Jenny, dream-heroines all, we love you far, far better than Michael, Guy, and Maurice ever could—but we are no Pygmalions—we prefer such Galateas in the marble.   You can never come to life however hard we pray—and we are realists enough in our soberer moments to breathe quite candidly, " Who cares ? "

Compton Mackenzie is our vicarious adventurer, our vicarious gallant : we owe him much for our vicarious escapades : they leave no nasty taste in the mouth.

III

NORMAN DOUGLAS

W HEN I last dared to give voice to my personal tastes in modern fiction, I was taken to task by many correspondents for having omitted to mention the favourites of others. In many cases they certainly coincided with mine : my excuse for not having publicly proclaimed my affection for these was simply due to lack of space. There are so many novelists writing to-day whose works I infinitely prefer either to those of Thackeray or Dickens that it would be impossible in the length of one essay to maintain my separate reasons for them all. I tried last time to show what my favourite authors had in common : this time I propose rather to let each one manifest his good qualities individually, no longer as members of a school, but as a fresh delineator of life, relying on no precedent, following in the footsteps of no greater contemporary. First among these is Mr Norman Douglas, who in *South Wind* has produced a book totally unlike any other that I have ever read, inimitably humorous, packed full of philosophy, rich with irony, and interesting throughout. That it completely mystified the critic of *The Daily Mail*, who self-complacently asserted that he could not understand what it was all about, may be in itself a recommendation. After all, what is it all about ? An island, called Nepenthe, famous for its lobsters, girls, and sirocco, which last plays quaint tricks on the temperaments of all who visit it or live there, is the setting. The characters are all eccentric in so far as they do not conform to the common standards of life.

The book opens with a description of the landing thereon of a sea-sick colonial bishop and a philandering priest. We are then invited to follow a delicious biography of the local patron saint, Dodekanus, so called, perhaps, because he met his death by being sawn asunder into twelve separate pieces while bound between two flat boards of palmwood : another current legend has it that he owed his name to a missive containing the two words *Do dekanus* ; give us a deacon. The grammar is faulty because of the natives' rudimentary knowledge of Latin : they had only learnt the first person singular and the nominative case. A certain Mr Ernest Eames was at that time making it his life-mission to bring up to date a full history of the island and its legends. Of him we learn that " it was not true to say that he fled from England to Nepenthe because he forged his mother's will, because he was arrested while picking the pockets of a lady at Tottenham Court Road Station, because he refused to pay for the upkeep of his seven illegitimate children, because he was involved in a flamboyant scandal of unmentionable nature and unprecedented dimensions, because he was detected while trying to poison the rhinoceros at the Zoo with an arsenical bun, because he strangled his mistress, because he addressed an almost disrespectful letter to the Primate of England, beginning ' My good Owl '—for any such like reason ; and that he now remained on the island only because nobody was fool enough to lend him ten pounds requisite for a ticket back again."

I can picture the face of *The Daily Mail* critic,

fed on a constant diet of Guy Thorne and William
le Queux, worrying over this passage, vainly searching for a plot. The colonial bishop fresh from con-
verting Bitongos (who had taken to the Gospel like
ducks to water, wearing top-hats at Easter) and
M'Tezo (who filed their teeth, ate their superfluous
female relations, swopped wives every new moon,
and never wore a stitch of clothes) fell quickly in
love with Nepenthe. He indulged in arguments over
educational reform with Mr Keith, who advocated
the introduction of sociology and jurisprudence into
the school curriculum, and the abolition of practically
all the existing subjects ; he revelled in the endless
colour-schemes with which the island provided him,
houses of red volcanic tufa, windows aflame with
cacti and carnations, slumberous oranges glowing in
courtyards, roadways of lava—pitch-black, skies of
impenetrable blue. He met Freddy Parker, the
Napoleonic President of the local club, who swindled
every one right and left ; Count Caloveglia, who had
" faked " an antique, the Locri Faun, that he sold
for thirty-five thousand francs ; the Duchess, who
was not a duchess at all ; Miss Wilberforce, invariably
clad in black, who indulged immoderately in strong
drink and denuded herself of her clothes on frequent
occasions ; Denis and Marten, young rivals for the
love of Angelina, who was as pretty as she was
sexual. . . . Each and all of these chatter at random
as the mood takes them, sometimes satirically about
our national vices of the deification of strenuousness,
our failure to elevate the mind, our ridiculous struggle
with the elements, and incessant bother about the
soul.

Denis and Marten on the subject of chastity (" a
man needn't handle everything dirty in order to be

doubly sure about it ") or Ruskin (" Good God ! he's
not a man : he's an emetic ") make glorious reading.
The conflict between the idealist and the brutalitarian
is superbly told.

One delicious trait of Norman Douglas is his
habit of returning to a subject when he thinks that
it can still amuse us. For instance, we learn later
in the book with regard to Mr Eames that " it was
not true to say of him that he lived on Nepenthe
because he was wanted by the London police for
something that happened in Richmond Park ; that
his real name was not Eames at all, but Daniels ;
that he was the local representative of an international
gang of white-slave traffickers ; that he was not a
man at all, but an old boarding-house keeper who
had very good reasons for assuming the male disguise ;
that he was a morphinomaniac, a disfrocked Baptist
Minister, a pawnbroker out of work, a fire-worshipper,
a Transylvanian, a bank clerk who had had a fall,
a decayed jockey who disgraced himself at a subsequent period in connexion with some East-End
Mission for reforming the boys of Bermondsey, and
then, after pawning his mother's jewellery, writing
anonymous threatening letters to society ladies about
their husbands and vice versa, trying to blackmail
Cabinet Ministers, and tricking poor servant-girls out
of their hard-earned wages by the sale of sham
Bibles, was luckily run to earth in Piccadilly Circus,
after an exciting chase, with a forty-pound salmon
under his arm, which he had been seen to lift from the
window of a Bond Street fishmonger. All these
things, and a good many more, had been said. Eames
knew it. Kind friends had seen to that."

This conscientious historian had had a lapse from
grace in his earlier days on the island, and that was

to fall in love after the fashion of a pure-minded gallant gentleman with an exuberant, gluttonous dame with volcanic eyes, heavy golden bracelets, the soupçon of a moustache, and arms as thick as other people's thighs. She was known as the *ballon captif.* She had nearly seduced Mr Eames into marrying her when her husband turned up, and Mr Eames luckily was saved.

Of a love theme there is but little in the book. One of Mr Marten's many escapades in this direction may be taken as typical.

" O ego te amare tantum ! Nemo sapit nihil. Duchessa in barca aquatica cum magna compania. Redibit tardissimo. Niente timor. Amare multissimo ! Ego morire sine te. Morire. Moriturus. Capito ? Non capire ? Oh, capire be blowed," Denis heard him murmur, " tremolo agitato, con molto sentimento " to Angelina in the Cave of Mercury. There is more about drink than love in this Rabelaisian medley. The picture of Miss Wilberforce singing to the night-wind, " Oh, Billy had a letter for to go on board a ship," unlacing and unbuttoning the while, sticks in the memory more forcibly. There is shrewd philosophy strewn hither and thither for those who patiently allow the author to pursue his own path and do not hurry him.

" Do not swim with the crowd. They who are all things to their neighbours, cease to be anything to themselves. Even a diamond can have too many facets. Avoid the attrition of vulgar minds, keep your edges intact. A man can protect himself with fists or sword, but his best weapon is his intellect. A weapon must be forged in the fire. The fire, in our case, is Tribulation. It must also be kept untarnished. If the mind is clean, the body can take

care of itself. Delve deeply : not too deeply into
the past, for it may make you derivative ; nor yet
into yourself—it will make you introspective. Delve
into the living world and strive to bind yourself to
its movements by a chain of your own welding," he
says in one passage ; in another, " What is the
unforgivable sin in poetry ? Lack of candour."
Again, " When I take up a subject this is what I
do : I ask myself : ' What has this fellow got to say
to me ? ' "

Occasionally we chance upon a brilliant summing
up of the defects of some great man, as, for instance,
this, on Samuel Butler : " Anything to escape from
realities—that was his maxim. He personifies the
Revolt from Reason. He understood the teachings
of the giants, but they irked him. To revenge himself he laid penny crackers under their pedestals.
His whole intellectual fortune was spent in buying
penny crackers. There was something cheeky and
pre-adolescent about him—a kind of virginal ferocity.
He lacked the male attributes of humility, reverence,
and sense of proportion. The tail of a cow was just
as important to him as the tail of a comet : more
important, if it could be turned into a joke. Look
at the back of his mind and you will always see the
same thing : horror of a fact."

A little time ago I applied the adjective Rabelaisian to the humour revealed in this book, without,
perhaps, sufficient justification. In chapter xvi, however, in the list of the many fountains of Nepenthe,
we find that same love of cataloguing that is so
prominent a characteristic of Rabelais.

" The so-called ' Old Fountain ' of subacidulate and
vitriolique flavour, chalybeate and cataplastic, was
renowned for removing stains from household linen.

Taken in minute doses, under medical advice, it gave relief to patients afflicted with the wolfe, noli me tangere, crudities, Babylonian itch, globular pemphlegema, fantastical visions, Koliks, asthma, and affections of the heart."

Of another we learn that it was renowned for its calming influence on all who suffered from abuse of lechery or alcohol, or from ingrowing toe-nails.

One of the most successful chapters in the book is that which tells of the " good old Duke," Nepenthe's most famous ruler. His method of collecting taxes was a marvel of simplicity. Each citizen paid what he liked. If the sum proved insufficient he was apprised of the fact next morning by having his left hand amputated : a second error of judgment was rectified by the mutilation of the remaining member.

He had a trick of casting favourites into dungeons and concubines into the sea that endeared him to his various legitimate spouses. " Nothing," he used to say, " nothing ages a man like living always with the same woman."

His theories on education, too, were unorthodox : he limited the weekly half-holidays to five, and sold to the slave-markets of Stamboul and Argier by weight, and not by the piece, all those boys and girls who talked or scribbled on blotting-pads during school hours. " Nose after ears " was one of his blithest watchwords. " A good salute is worth a good soldier," apropos of the fact that the firing of a gun was attended with some considerable danger.

The discussion on theology between the Bishop and Mr Keith is peculiarly delightful by reason of the imaginary conversation that takes place on the
· subject of the Ten Commandments between Moses (the kindly old fellow who likes people to have as

much harmless amusement as possible) and Aaron (the sour-faced Puritan, the dyspeptic old antediluvian who was envious of his neighbour's pleasure, and so counted all pleasure as sin).

A comparison between the Russian temperament and the English leads to the following acute observation :

" The Russian has convictions, but no principles. The Englishman has principles, but no convictions, he obeys the laws : a criminal requires imagination. He prides himself on his immunity from vexatious imposts. Yet whisky, the best quality of which is worth tenpence a bottle, is taxed till it costs five shillings ; tobacco which could profitably be sold at twopence a pound goes for fivepence an ounce. Englishmen will submit to any number of these extortions, being persuaded that such things are for the good of the nation. That is an Englishman's method of procuring happiness : to deny himself pleasure in order to save his neighbour's soul."

To return for a moment to individual characterisations it is pleasant to envisage the person of Mrs Parker, wife of the infamous Freddy, from the following description : " She possessed that most priceless of all gifts : she believed her own lies. She looked people straight in the face and spoke from her heart ; a falsehood, before it left her lips, had grown into a flaming truth." Catholics had been known to cross themselves at the fertility of her constructive imagination. Her death leads to some aphorisms on the subject of mortality on the part of Mr Keith, which I find it hard to refrain from quoting. But I must hurry on, past the story of the marrowfats and the reason why so many American women are as flat as boards, in front and behind (a hundred guesses

would leave you as far as ever from the truth here);
past the murder of Muhlen (yes, things do happen,
even on lotus-eating Nepenthe), and the amazing
speech for the defence of the supposed criminal by
Don Guistino ("He had a mother: he had no
mother") to St Eulalia, patroness of Nepenthean
sailors. St Eulalia, like St Dodekanus, arrests our
attention. She was born in 1712, took the vow of
chastity at the age of two years and eleven months,
never washed, nor changed her underwear: she put
baskets of sea-urchins in her bed, and as a penance
forced herself to catch the legions of vermin that
infested her brown blanket, count them, separate the
males from the females, set them free once more, and
begin over again. She died at the age of fourteen
years and two months. Her corpse forthwith became
roseate in colour, exhaled a delicious odour of violets
for twenty weeks, and performed countless miracles.
On dissection, a portrait of St James of Compostella
was discovered imbedded in her liver.

For twelve days did the colonial bishop remain on
this amazing island in a kind of merry nightmare.
There was something bright and diabolical in the tone
of the place, something kaleidoscopic—a frolicsome
perversity. Purifying, at the same time. It swept
away the cobwebs. It gave you a measure, a standard, whereby to compute earthly affairs. He had
carved out new and round values: a workable, up-
to-date theory of life. He was in fine trim. His
liver—he forgot that he ever had one. Nepenthe had
done him good all round.

And so, if we read this book in the right spirit,
our visit to Nepenthe will do us good all round.

England, after the tingling realism of that Mediterranean island, may well seem parochial, rather dun,

fireproof, seaworthy; but we may cease to be so horrified at the extreme and the unconventional. Our visit, if it does nothing else, ought to make us more tolerant.

On one reader, at any rate, it has had the effect of wishing for more so strongly that, in spite of the generous fare of 464 closely printed pages given in this volume, he prays night and day that Mr Douglas may continue for the rest of his life to write down all that he knows about his Treasure Island. For surely its treasure is inexhaustible. This book has no beginning and no end. It just stops when the author thinks he has said enough for the moment. But let him not imagine that he said enough for all time. I for one could go on reading about Nepenthe were the book as long as the *Encyclopædia Britannica*, but then I am fond of humour, and humour in our literature is rare indeed.

IV

FRANK SWINNERTON

MR SWINNERTON has already nine novels to his credit, all of them masterpieces of style, and is still comparatively unknown. Yet he is as well able to reproduce the atmosphere of life in the successful and unsuccessful suburbs of Weybridge and Kennington as Stephen McKenna is in the aristocratic world of Mayfair and Kensington ("where the dialect songs come from "). He is far more alive than Mr McKenna : his vision is larger, his sympathies broader.

In *Nocturne,* a wonderful *tour de force,* in which the whole action is confined to six hours, we actually share every minute of the young milliner's experiences. The small house in Kennington Park, where laughing, loving, passionate Jenny lives with her paralysed " Pa " and jealous Martha-like sister " Em," is put before us perfect in every detail : we see " Pa's " appetite for romance satisfied in the shape of murder and sudden death in the newspaper, as his appetite for food is by mountainous apple-dumplings. " Em's " yearnings are reserved for the insipid " Alf," who " walks out " with Jenny, while Jenny's may be gauged from this extract : " She wanted to go out in the darkness that so pleasantly enwrapped the earth, back to the stir and glitter of life somewhere beyond. Her vision had been far different from this scene. It carried her over land and sea right into an unexplored realm where there was wild laughter

37

and noise, where hearts broke tragically and women in the hour of ruin turned triumphant eyes to the glory of life, and where blinding, streaming lights and scintillating colours made everything seem different, made it seem romantic, rapturous, indescribable. From that vision back to the cupboard-like house in Kennington Park, and stodgy Alf Rylett, and supper of stew and bread-and-butter pudding, and Pa, and this little sobbing figure in her arms, was an incongruous flight. It made Jenny's mouth twist in a smile so painful that it was almost a grimace.

"'Oh, lor!' she said again, under her breath. '*What* a life.'"

Pa was something like an old beloved dog, unable to speak ; it was Emmy who best understood the bitterness of his soul ; it was Emmy who was most with him, and Emmy who felt sometimes as if she could kill him in her fierce hatred of his helplessness and stupidity. Emmy was harder than Jenny on the surface, but weaker below. Jenny was self-sufficient, self-protective, more happy-go-lucky, more humorous than Emmy. We see these sisters (who love one another deeply) first quarrelling over Alf. He prefers Jenny, and she treats him like dirt, while Emmy is furiously jealous.

"He's all right in his way," admitted Jenny. " He's clean. But he's quiet . . . he's got no devil in him. Sort of man who tells you what he likes for breakfast. I only go with him. . . . Well, you know why, as well as I do. But he's never on for a bit of fun. That's it : he's got no devil in him. I don't like that kind. Prefer the other sort."

A knock at the door interrupts the sisters' tart arguments, and Alf appears armed with seats for the theatre ; before he has the chance to invite Jenny (in her sister's presence), she makes it clear that she thinks he has come to take Em, and forces him to do so. While Em, who is overjoyed, goes out of the room to dress, Jenny and Alf have a heart-to-heart row which reveals their naked souls to the reader in a way that almost shocks one, so real does it sound. It is as if we were held by a vice in the room, compelled to listen to confidences of the most private sort. Eventually Alf and Em go, and Jenny is left at home to look after Pa and work out in her mind exactly what she has done, gradually rising into a frenzy of rebellion at the dullness and slavery which is her life. While she is lost in reverie there is another knock at the door, and she opens to find a large car, a chauffeur, and a letter for her from a sailor she had met some months before, requesting her to come to supper on his yacht. After a sharp conflict with her conscience she leaves Pa and drives off in an intoxication of bliss. Keith, her dream-lover, meets her on board and takes her down to the cabin. " She had never before seen such a room. It seemed, because the ceiling was low, to be very spacious ; the walls and ceiling were of a kind of dusky amber hue ; a golden brown was everywhere the prevailing tint. In the middle stood a square table ; and on the table, arrayed on an exquisitely white tablecloth, was laid a wondrous meal. The table was laid for two ; candles with amber shades made silver shine and glasses glitter. Upon a fruit-stand were peaches and nectarines ; upon a tray she saw decanters : little dishes crowding the table bore mysterious things to eat such as Jenny had never before seen . . . everywhere she saw flowers similar to those which had been in the motor-car."

It is noticeable that Mr Swinnerton knows how to

make our mouths water with a description of food,
thereby confirming Alec Waugh's evidence that for
a book to be successful one necessary ingredient is the
actual description of rich meals. Coming as we do from
the stew and bread-and-butter pudding of Kennington
we are all the more likely to succumb, as Jenny does, to
the soup, whitebait, trifle, peaches, almonds, and wonderful red wine which Keith had so cunningly prepared.
The love-making that follows the meal is astoundingly
real : Jenny, loving him with all the force of her
passionate nature, yet struggling with herself all the
time, believes that it is all no use as he didn't
love her as she wanted him to. In the end he tells
her quickly the story of his life. " I picked up a
girl in London when I was twenty—not honest, but
straight to me. It was no good. She went off with
other men because I got tired of her : I told her she
could stick to me or let me go. She wanted both.
Then I got engaged to a girl—married to her when
I was twenty-three—and she's dead. After I'd been
with her for a year I broke away. . . . I haven't got
a very good record : I've lived with three women,
all of whom knew more than I did. I've never
done a girl any harm intentionally : the last
of them belongs to six years ago. You're the girl
I love."
     " What I'm wondering," said Jenny, " is, what
you'd think of me if I'd lived with three different
men ? " On and on runs the argument between them,
Keith trying to make her believe that he would love
her always, marry her on his return from the voyage
just due to begin, Jenny knowing her absolute love
for him, yet holding back, distrust of him looming
large before her : ultimately she capitulates and
returns home at midnight to find that in her absence

Alf and Emmy have agreed to get married, and Pa
has had a bad accident.

Having at last got into bed she begins to judge her
own conduct. " She was Keith's : she belonged to
him : but he did not belong to her. To Keith she
might, she would give all, as she had done : but he
would still be apart from her. Away from him,
released from the spell, Jenny knew that she had
yielded to him the freedom she so cherished as her
inalienable right. She had given him her freedom :
for her real freedom was her innocence and her desire
to do right. She could not forgive herself. She
struggled to go back to the old way of looking at
everything. In a forlorn, quivering voice she ventured : " What a life ! Golly, what a life ! " But
the effort to pretend was too great. She threw herself on the bed : " Keith . . . oh, Keith. . . ." The
subtle analysis of a young girl's mind has never been
better done.

Shops and Houses is a novel of quite another sort.
Here we are shown the narrowness of suburban
society. " One would think that a quite special
piece of righteousness had been dealt out to each of
the Beckwith ladies at birth by a benign fairy. Living in Beckwith is like living upon glass. It is both
slippery and brittle. Nearly all the women suffer
from aimlessness, an insatiable egomania." The
Vechantors, who lead this society, are, however, above
this pettiness : it is of Louis Vechantor and his
fortunes that the book treats. Mr Swinnerton is
exceedingly bitter in his irony about this suburb of
his. " Nothing ever happened at Beckwith. It was
like a backwater. Only time was consumed. That
was the secret, terrible aim of dwellers in Beckwith.
To eat a day and look forward to the next with

insatiable appetite. Little concerts in half-warmed
church rooms, little amateur theatricals and dances
in the shabby Town Hall—anything to destroy the
danger that lurks in unoccupied time. Restlessness
demands an outlet, not in constructive action, nor in
clear thinking, nor in real festivals or in the cultiva-
tion of growth ; but solely in the destruction of time
and the resuscitation of exhausting excitements." But
the greatest excitement comes in unexpectedly. A
certain William Vechantor, cousin to *the* Vechantors,
takes over a grocer's shop in the town, and society
is horrified, aghast. Louis Vechantor can't see why
his family are so upset, and says so, whereupon his
father turns on him with fierce comments about
shallow democratic snobbery.

Louis is suddenly diverted from the problem about
the cousin-grocers by being made the confidant of a
weak young man called Eric Daunton, who has
become engaged to an " impossible " girl. Louis
advises him to marry her in spite of all opposition,
and then does something himself which sets the wheel
of fate in motion for him ; he calls on his cousins
and meets Dorothy, the grocer's daughter, completely
different from the Beckwith girls, who were tough, and
superficially emotional, who seemed to live for excitement and to make it for themselves out of nothing.
He begins to ruminate over the curious anomalies in
the other sex, the insensitive cruelty of Veronica
Hughes, who could gloat over the agony of a bleeding
bird. Dorothy was not at all Beckwithian : she was
not devout, she took nothing on trust. He meets
her by accident again one day in a train at London
Bridge, and in spite of her rudeness to him manages to
rouse her to talk, and recognises something real and
vital about her that he could admire, as different

as possible from Veronica. A spying gossip, by name Miss Lampe, sees Louis and Dorothy getting out of the train together, and spreads malicious rumours, and Louis is tackled by Veronica for going about with " that common girl." Worse—the customers of the Vechantors drop off, one by one. The gossip even reaches the ears of his father and mother, and he is told to cease from seeing any more of his cousins ; he refuses and leaves home in consequence. He has an abortive interview with Veronica, and then Daunton comes to lament over his failure to cut loose from his traditions.

" In Beckwith they swaddle you all up, and you're bound to break out on the quiet ; and then—no, they don't beat you, or shut you up ; they cast you out. It's the *punishment* they're keen on. It satisfies their cruelty : Veronica, for instance, if she got hold of a man who'd cut all meetings in the dark, all the hysterical little smothered kisses and cowardly secrets, she'd very likely fall in love with him and be a woman." Dorothy meanwhile had fallen more and more in love with Louis now that he had cast off his fetters and left home. " It gave her life new signifi-cance, as though she had been groping blindly, with-out any clear aim. Ah, if Louis loved her : even that did not matter, if she could only be important to him ! " It was a beautiful time to her, in spite of the shop, in spite of the houses filled with unhappy and ill-disposed people which she passed each day. It was enough to live and love. As time passed she became fearful : no one seemed to have heard any-thing of Louis : Dorothy was in a panic lest he should be ill. Then came the night of the concert when she discovered that Veronica was also in love with Louis, and was betrayed by her emotion into calling Miss

Lampe " a venomous beast of a woman." She then becomes maddened with jealousy, gets ill, only recovering on the reappearance of Louis. Ultimately they, of course, fall into each other's arms . . . but it's Beckwith that we are mainly concerned with in this novel, not the love lyrics. " I've been thinking," says Dorothy, " whether perhaps Beckwith—that it isn't altogether a place at all. I mean, whether it isn't a sort of disease. If you live in London you hardly know your neighbours—you have your own friends. Nobody else cares twopence about you. But London isn't England. I've been wondering if, directly you go to *England* to live, you don't find Beckwith. Isn't Beckwith any small town in England? Isn't the choice between London—that's heartless—and Beckwith, where your life's everybody's business? Lovely Beckwith—poor—poor people—shut up in their houses and their shops, and never seeing outside—I think I hate stupidity worse than anything on earth, because it frightens me and crushes me." In order to press the moral home Mr Swinnerton favours us with an epilogue in the shape of a conversation between Miss Lampe and other typical Beckwithians after Louis and Dorothy had escaped from their toils. " While they were here I felt all the time that they were spoiling our little Cranford." Cranford ! a community spending its time in a venomous search for the weakness of other people, watching, envying, scratching.

V

STEPHEN McKENNA

M R McKENNA leapt into fame with *Sonia* : it was no compliment to him. He had already written novels before this which apparently no one read, which were nearly as good as, if not better than, the one over which the public chose to rave. He is a born raconteur : but there is very little depth in him : most of his work scintillates with an obvious harshness : he indulges in epigrams : like Oscar Wilde he does not seem even to realise that there are any classes of society other than the aristocracy : his horizon is bounded by Half-Moon Street on the one side and Clarges Street on the other : he has a gift of wit which in *Ninety-six Hours' Leave*, a book that couldn't have taken more than ninety-six hours to write, is thoroughly adapted for readers of *The Bystander* and undergraduates generally. It is as well that there should be novelists who exactly suit convalescents. The authoress of *Elizabeth and Her German Garden* is one of the best of these : Stephen McKenna is another. . . . I cannot think him a genius : talented ? yes. Admirable for reading in a train or when the brain is tired. And this is not to depreciate his value. There are very few really satisfactory novels which can hold our attention and yet not probe into the problems of life. You may say that in *Midas and Son* he has attacked a very grave problem, that of immense wealth and its dangers, but most of us would be willing to accept all the responsibilities of vast riches quite light-heartedly if any sportsman were to be forthcoming with the offer of them.   The problem of poverty as seen by George Gissing gives genius full scope, but genius regards the problem of Midas as quite a good joke.   We thank God for Stephen McKenna because he occupies our very necessary hours of ease.   It is so delightful to find that he knows his job.   There are scarcely any people in his pages who are not titled : the joy of discovering that they do actually talk as titled people do talk—that is, like every one else above the local grocer—is a very real one.   Most novelists have a special vocabulary for dukes : they move stiffly in their presence : it is hard even for an Honourable to unbend.   I like characters who make it a rule never to see suffering : for whom suffering and poverty do not exist.   " When the world is simply crowded with beautiful things to see, to hear, to smell, to touch, to taste, it is nothing but perverted ingenuity to go in search of squalor and pain and hunger : the only suffering I know is that which comes over me when I reflect on the transitory nature of it all, and between ourselves I don't let that distress me as much as an artist in life should."   I feel drawn to people who keep engagement books of this sort : " April 30th, oysters go out of season ; " who make epigrams like " Man cannot live by Aubrey Beardsley alone, at least not after he's five-and-twenty " ; " To speak seriously argues an arrested temperament " ; or the more sober statements of men like Lord Darling- ton, " You can't get a wife without working for her, and you can't work without a wife " ; or the Oxford don " who used to say that the worst of bachelor parties was that you missed the exquisite moment when the ladies left the room."

And having written so far I am troubled.   I don't want to cross it all out because it is in some measure true. But it is not the whole truth. Let me test it by taking *The Reluctant Lover* as an example of his art at its best. There are few more readable books on the market : there is a rattling good plot, unexpected *dénouement*, human characters, adorable heroines, quite a number of them : Mr McKenna has the deftest touch in limning the features and probing the minds of attractive young girls : his dialogue is always clever, if at times unnaturally artificial and stilted : he is a master craftsman in avoiding loose ends and polishing rough edges. In some ways this story of the selfish, but entirely lovable boy, Cyril Fitzroy, is the story of the development of every man : " He affects to study women as he studies men, in the light of specimens : and sometimes as works of art by an inspired hand. From a sexual point of view he is completely indifferent and extraordinarily cold-blooded." But he is doomed to fall when the exquisite Myra Woodbridge, piqued by his indifference, sets her **cap** at him. The description of Lady Delaunay's ball, where the pair first meet and dance together for six hours in succession, is inimitably told : the intellectual sparring between the two is a watered-down Meredith, and therefore more like life as we know it than it is in Meredith. This is not to suggest that Mr. McKenna can compare in any way whatever with this or any other genius : I still maintain that he has no genius : but his talent is unmistakable. I could find it in my heart to wish that he would quote less Latin, and not hark back so frequently to Oxford experiences. He writes like the elderly uncle he pretends to be in *Sonia*. Even as an undergraduate he must have been very like a don. Still quite a young man, like Cyril Fitzroy, he yet talks academically and in the tones of sophisticated, disillusioned middle age. Not for him the follies and extravagances of youth. One reads something of himself in the character of Rodney Trelawney, the young Oxford don prematurely aged and world-weary, knowing little of sympathy, inexperienced in life, a little crabbed, a little inhuman, a little lonely, yet immensely complacent and self-satisfied. He must have his Oxford lunch of dressed crab, quails, green peas, marasquino jelly, *croustade au parmeson*, strawberries, and iced hock cup; his clothes must fit him perfectly, and there must always be the white silk pyjamas; there must be a persistent dredging of the waters of the memory to recall old Oxford " rags," old Oxford tales discreditable to Balliol, upholding the prestige of The House. . . . But all this, again, is a trifle unkind and only partly true. There is plenty of intellectual stimulus, and very little beating about the bush, no morbid psychology here : on the other hand, there is some very straight talk at times, as in this illuminating passage : " Give a thing for nothing, and it will be valued at nothing : give poor people free education, and they regard it as value-less. If Rodney [it is Myra speaking] gives me the whole-hearted adoration you speak of—and I don't have to struggle for it—I shall count it as valueless, and in course of time it will die of neglect. Which is not a good condition for ' sickness and health, weal and woe,' for life. The remedy is to find some one who attracts me and force him to love me whether he wants to or not. And when I have won his love I shall value it, and when he has had to part with it with a struggle he will see the value I put upon it, and know it is in good hands, and he will honour me for the fight I have fought and the victory I have won." She is thinking, of course, of Cyril, who is neither primitive (the body-hunter) nor in the second stage of civilisation (the heart-hunter, the philanderer), but the soul-hunter, the connoisseur of rare emotions. The battle-royal between Myra and Cyril when he shows his hand is a masterpiece of analysis. He tries to show her the unwisdom of setting one's affections on anything or any one in the whole world other than oneself.

" I suggest that happiness only comes to the man who has strangled all affections and trodden every appetite under foot. If you marry, you are giving a hostage to misfortune in your wife and every one of your children. If you grow fond of a cat or a book or a house . . . the cat may die, the book may be lost, the house burnt down."

" For the man who cannot take pleasure in the sight and scent of a rose because he knows it must soon die, there is no hope," quotes Myra. Later Cyril is brought to book by a member of his own family. " It's better to cultivate and cherish a rose and to enjoy its scent and beauty, even if it ultimately dies, than to be content with a wax flower which never fades, but never gives you a moment's gratification in a lifetime. We've all got to die, Cyril, and my complaint against your philosophy is not that it is rottenly unsound, not that it is going to make yours an unhappy life, but simply that you play the game of life and don't want to obey the rules. . . . You're going to die probably before your work—whatever it may be—is finished. So am I. Well, do the best you can in the interval. If you love your wife and she dies before you, well—so much the worse for you, and make the most you can of the time you're together. For heaven's sake don't imagine that you're entitled to a special Providence which is going to insure you against all risks free of

charge, and don't have a grievance when death lays
hands on your most cherished possessions." But he
is not won over even when, in a third great scene,
Myra shows her love for him and is prepared to
marry him : he sees too clearly : he loves her, but
he is afraid of himself. " Before a man marries he
must feel that his wife is indispensable to him, and
that he could not go on living without her. I don't
feel that. I've always boasted of not being dependent
on any one for my happiness, and I've grown to
believe it." The strange couple agree to a secret
engagement for two years to test Cyril's idea that
it may only be an infatuation. Cyril goes abroad
with his sixteen year-old ward, Violet, another charming girl. Rodney, a rejected lover of Myra's, again
returns to the attack and fails, and at length the
time of probation comes to an end, Myra having
discovered without the help of the gods the one man
for whom she would sacrifice everything in the world ;
then suddenly Violet falls ill and nearly dies of
diphtheria, while Cyril and Myra talk interminably
(quoting the classics freely) in a way calculated to
shock the careless reader. Cyril then saves Violet's
life by risking his own, and to his astonishment finds
that his ward on her recovery is in love with him,
and he marries her, but Myra has the last word.
" I'm too independent for you, Cyril : you want
somebody who will look up to you and depend on
you and need your help and support. That's why
you and Violet are going to be very well suited and
very happy together."

This really is the secret of Mr McKenna's limitations : all his heroes and heroines are good only in as
far as they are well suited and happy together. It is
time he deserted his Sonia and returned to Violet.

VI

THE CENTENARY OF JANE AUSTEN

I

AS a callow undergraduate I remember being roused out of an apathetic stupor while attending a lecture on the history of the English novel by these startling words on the subject of Jane Austen's readers : " Rabbits cannot be expected to take an interest or see anything humorous in the sight of other rabbits performing their ludicrous antics."

Was the reason that I had failed to appreciate the subtlety and charm of Jane Austen solely due to the fact that I was dull of mind and of as commonplace a character as some of the dramatis personæ of her works, and therefore unable to see the comic side of her delineation ? I returned home determined to find out exactly where her power lay, what claims she really had to be called the feminine counterpart to Shakespeare.

I found that the mistake I had made was not entirely due to my own ineptitude, but that I had read her too fast. I had hurried over page after page in order to reach the story, to get the hang of the plot, to find some exciting incident, for all the world as if I expected some lurid " film " drama. I had to revise my method of reading. I had to learn the hard lesson that Jane Austen was not " Aunt Jane " of the crinoline era moving stiffly in an artificial circumscribed area, speaking correctly in an old-fashioned, effete, precise English, but a genial, kindly, yet caustic genius who wrote with her tongue in her cheek, and, like Chaucer, was not averse from pulling her readers' "legs" unless they exercised care. Instead of a "bookish blue-stocking" I found a woman with an almost uncanny depth of insight into human character, one who realised that although life was far more important than literature, yet the true novelist exercised the function of displaying the greatest powers of the mind, and that novels are works "in which the most thorough knowledge of human nature, the happiest delineation of its varieties, the liveliest effusions of wit and humour, are conveyed to the world in the best-chosen language."

In other words, I found that new, hitherto un-dreamt-of, vistas were being opened up to me, vistas which helped me to understand this complex, intricate tangle which we call the art of living. As a result of my re-reading I first felt a sense of shame at having allowed myself to be so blind to her greatness, and then a sense of mystery as to how a woman who lived so simple and secluded a life could ever have achieved so stupendous a task.

Here was a girl who only lived for forty-two years, the daughter of a country parson, who never went abroad, to London but rarely, whose greatest excitement was a visit to Bath or Lyme Regis, who may or may not have suffered disappointment in love, but certainly had no grand passion, who lived through the French Revolution, Waterloo, and Trafalgar, and yet makes no mention of those stirring times, leaving behind her a sequence of novels which within their own limitations are unapproachably perfect. She lived for the most part in the depths of the country at a time when rural society was even more vacuous than it is to-day. Small-talk, knitting, filigree-work, and backgammon occupied the leisure hours of her sex, while men shot and hunted in moderation, but were always ready to accompany the ladies on their shopping excursions or to a local dance.

This is the life that Jane Austen set out to describe, knowing no other. That she succeeded in imbuing this with eternal interest makes one wistfully regret that she had not Fanny Burney's chances of mixing with the great men and women of her time, and yet . . . we have her own word for it that she could not have undertaken to deal with any other types of men and women than those among whom her lot was cast.

"I could no more write a romance than an epic poem. I could not sit down seriously to write a serious romance under any other motive than to save my life ; and if it were indispensable for me to keep it up and never relax into laughing at myself and other people, I am sure I should be hung before I had finished the first chapter."

When the Prince Regent's librarian suggested that she should delineate the habits of life of a clergyman, she replied :

"The comic part of the character I might be equal to, but not the good, the enthusiastic, the literary. Such a man's conversation must at times be on subjects of science—philosophy, of which I know nothing ; or at least be occasionally abundant in quotations and allusions which a woman, who, like me, knows only her mother tongue, and has read little in that, would be totally without the power of giving. A classical education, or at any rate a very extensive acquaint-ance with English literature, ancient and modern, appears to me quite indispensable for the person who would do any justice to your clergyman ; and I think

I may boast myself to be, with all possible vanity, the most unlearned and uninformed female who ever dared to be an authoress."

It is not surprising in the light of this to find that she has nothing in common with a great moral teacher like Dostoievsky ; her religion never obtrudes itself into her writings ; she has no formal gospel to propagate.

She was neither Pantheist, Monotheist, Agnostic, nor Transcendentalist ; that she hated Evangelicalism while recognising its good points we know. Heartlessness is the only crime that she finds it in her heart to condemn unsparingly.

We do not go to Jane Austen for descriptions of natural beauty ; she has neither Hardy's nor Wordsworth's passion for scenery ; she does not use hedgerow delights nor grim mountain peaks as a background for her characters, any more than she treats of man in his relation to his environment. In other words, she has no poetry ; she avoids the heroic, the romantic, and the ideal.

She does not probe the human soul for motives, nor does she seek to illuminate or display them as later novelists have done ; as Mr Warre Cornish says, she has no need to construct her characters, for they are there before her, like Mozart's music, only waiting to be written down.

She does not use her narrative power as Fielding did to tell a story and create situations, but simply as a means to an end, the unfolding of character. That is, she belongs to the school of Richardson rather than to any other of her predecessors, the school which has received such an impetus in our own day in the work of Arnold Bennett.

She paints in every detail with meticulous care ;

with the true artistic temperament she refuses to pass
any tendency to the slovenly, but with deliberation
and exactitude sketches in every trait which will
help to make the portrait life-like.

Like all geniuses she recognised both where her
true *métier* lay and how she achieved her self-imposed
task. Every one remembers her phrase about " the
little bit (two inches wide) of ivory on which I work
with so fine a brush as produces little effect after much
labour."

Her pellucid vision gave her two eminent characteristics which at first sight would seem to be
contradictory : her capability for seeing through all
pretentiousness led her to denounce all false romanticism, as we see in her counterblast to *The Mysteries
of Udolpho. Northanger Abbey* gave the death-blow
to the hysteria caused by Mrs Ann Radcliffe ; her
irony seems almost at times to descend to acerbity
. . . and yet at the same time her collateral sense of
humour made her kindly disposed and magnanimous
in her sympathies to creatures whom other artists
would have condemned without mercy. That is, she
seems to combine, as Andrew Lang said, gentleness
with a certain hardness of heart, which are difficult
to reconcile until we have made a close study of her
methods.

No greater mistake could possibly be made than to
imagine her as a soured old maid, though the bust
erected to her memory in the Pump Room at Bath
goes a long way to give that impression.

On the contrary, she was distinctly pretty, sunny-
natured, gay even to frivolity, an accomplished con-
versationalist, a singer and a musician, possessed of
a natural aptitude for and skill in games, extraordinarily well-balanced and sane in her outlook . . .

an ideal wife, one would suppose, for any cultured man of the world. It is only by understanding these facts about her that we realise the meaning of what Professor Saintsbury calls the " livingness " of her work. She writes as one who has, as Lady Ritchie puts it, " a natural genius for life." That she enjoyed her forty-two years to the full we cannot doubt. She was no Shelley, a genius of moods, alternately in heaven or hell ; she pursued an even path of placidity and content, neither troubling herself overmuch with the perplexities that obsess the mind of the social reformer nor harassed with religious doubts.

Suffering does not make her suicidal, nor has she any of that divine discontent which we usually associate with our best writers. How many of our famous men of letters were able to work in the midst of domestic interruption and make no sign of impatience ? It is a small point, but quite an illuminating one.

She had no private study. As she worked with the others in the common sitting-room she would sometimes burst out laughing, go to her desk and write something down, and then go back to her work again and say nothing.

It is worthy of notice that her geniality was not of that vapid sort that proceeds from ignorance or wilful blindness to human fatuity and vice, that sings to the shallow, optimistic tune that " all is for the best in the best of all possible worlds." It is to her everlasting credit that although she was under no delusions as to the state of humanity, she neither condemned it nor sneered at it ; she had nothing of the cynic in her temperament. There have, of course, been critics who have appended that libellous label to her, but they belong to the same category which stigmatises Thackeray and Swift as possessing the same trait. How any one with her genius for laughter and affection, her interest in mankind, or her clear-sightedness could be accused of cynicism, which is a property of the owl and bat and donkey in humanity, I do not understand. She is a master of irony and satire, it is true ; but these are incompatible with misanthropy, the touch-stone of cynicism ; of this she had not a trace. She is not of those who were disillusioned by the fever and the weariness and the fret of life. She was no pessimistic Teuton philosopher ; she was too busy taking notes on the people with whom she came into contact to spend time in moralising. She was essentially of a happy nature, and kept a strong curb on her emotions ; that she felt deeply is probable, that she ever gave full vent to her feelings we instinctively know to be untrue. Her love tragedy, if she had one, was not allowed to spoil her life ; she may very well have passed through the depths, but she emerged from the conflict victorious, having battered down the forces of darkness, and continued to irradiate sweetness and light in her books as well as in her life.

Other authors might easily have been discomfited by the reception given to their work by publishers if a first manuscript had been rejected by return of post as hers was in the case of *Pride and Prejudice*. Not so Jane Austen ; she continued to write almost until the day of her death, sure of the verdict of posterity, the only judgment upon which genius really relies. She knew that her appeal was universal and not liable to grow dim with the passage of years. Her satire and humour are as fresh to-day as ever they were, and as an antidote to the horrors of our time no other author can compare with her.

II

We commonly find that if we want to test the truth about an author, a perusal of his or her correspondence is of the greatest value to enable us to decide how far the judgments we have formed from their serious work are accurate. In their letters we take them off their guard; they are in undress, no longer the mouthpieces of divine inspiration, but flesh and blood like ourselves.

Jane Austen's almost racy letters to her sister shed a flood of light on her character and help us still further to dot the " i's " and cross the " t's " of criticism.

They are for the most part compositions of a quite light and trivial nature, dwelling on topics such as might interest any country-bred girl. Dress looms large, and so does small-talk about the everyday round of work and amusement, people met, dances, and the like. But all through them we see the same shrewd, Puck-like spirit darting hither and thither, we hear the silvery laughter of the girl who painted Mr Collins and Mrs Jennings; they are obviously written by a girl who cannot help seeing the funny side of everything, who is vividly interested in people and their idiosyncrasies; the deeper things in life are not discussed, not because she was shallow, but because there are some things which language is incapable of expressing, where silence is the only true speech. Those traces of bitterness which occasionally disturb us in her novels appear again here.

" Only think of Mrs Holder being dead! Poor woman, she has done the only thing in the world she could possibly do to make one cease to abuse her," may stand as a typical example out of many;

but no one could contend that such phrases are
deliberately cynical ; at the worst they are but
thoughtless witticisms, and really hurt no one. Jane
Austen was entirely devoid of malice. She suffered
fools more or less gladly ; she would try the barb of
irony to laugh them out of their folly, but they were
not like those others, at the opposite end of the scale,
" pictures of perfection," which she confesses made
her sick and wicked.

The puzzle is that so highly gifted and all-seeing
a genius should have adopted such a detached,
tolerant attitude towards humanity. There have
been many who have found fault with her for not
waxing indignant at the follies of society. These
assert that she has no moral sense, but surely to
instil into us the necessity for mutual tolerance and
unfailing humour in our dealings with our neighbours
is in itself a moral act of the highest order.

The first thing that strikes any one who has tried
to read Jane Austen's novels aloud is the dramatic
power displayed in the conversations. No novelist
ever made his or her characters express themselves
so simply or forcibly in their parts as she does. It
would seem that we have lost in her one of our
greatest playwrights. The unfolding of character in
dialogue has not been better done by any of our
dramatists, and has certainly not been approached
by any other novelist. No novels make so immediate
an appeal when declaimed as hers do. Even youthful
audiences who are popularly supposed to be incapable
of appreciating the subtlety of her wit are quickly
entranced.

Think for a moment of that famous second chapter
in *Sense and Sensibility*, where Mr John Dashwood
is converted by his wife with regard to his ideas as

to their duty to his widowed sister and her daughters. It is conceived and executed with an exactness of phrase and economy of words that calls to mind that parallel scene in *King Lear* where the old man is deprived of his retinue.

With what deft strokes are we shown the whole of a person's character in one short, ironic sentence.

" Mrs Jennings was a widow, with an ample jointure. She had only two daughters, both of whom she had lived to see respectably married, and she had now, therefore, nothing to do but to marry all the rest of the world."

The vulgarity of the Steele family is shown in their use of " prodigious," " vast," " beau," and the like words, in omitting the personal pronoun in their correspondence ; we recognise the type at once. That is the secret of Jane Austen's power : she has seized upon the salient, ineradicable characteristics of the type which is always with us ; the unstable lover, the gossiping, scandal-mongering old dame, the young impressionable girl who could not bear the thought of her sister marrying a man with so little " sensibility " that he could not read the poets with understanding or fire, the staunch, sound, unselfish heroine who bears her own tragedy without any outward sign, but spends herself in sympathising with weaker natures in their misfortunes ; the pedant, the snob, the haughty, the supercilious, the impertinent . . . all are here drawn with unerring accuracy.

I know nothing in our literature to compare with the concluding paragraphs of *Sense and Sensibility.* Ninety-nine out of every hundred authors would have made Marianne a tragic heroine, but Jane Austen realised that she was not great enough for that ;

she was audacious enough to risk an anticlimax in order to secure verisimilitude.

" Marianne Dashwood was born to an extraordinary fate. She was born to discover the falsehood of her own opinions, and to counteract by her conduct her most favourite maxims. She was born to overcome an affection formed so late in life as at seventeen, and with no sentiment superior to strong esteem and lively friendship, voluntarily to give her hand to another !—and that other a man who had suffered no less than herself, under the event of a former attachment, whom, two years before, she had considered too old to be married, and who still sought the constitutional safeguard of a flannel waistcoat ! "

As for the villain, Willoughby, we read that " he lived to exert, and frequently to enjoy himself. His wife was not always out of humour, nor his home always uncomfortable ; and in his breed of horses and dogs he found no inconsiderable degree of domestic felicity."

The opening sentences of *Pride and Prejudice* might almost be taken as a test of our ability to appreciate Jane Austen. She has a knack of beginning in an exhilarating, startling way on most occasions, but it may well be doubted whether any novel starts quite so happily as this :

" It is a truth universally acknowledged that a single man in possession of a good fortune must be in want of a wife "—after which delightful touch of irony we are immediately introduced to Mr and Mrs Bennet, who proceed to squabble over their daughters' chances of securing the rich young stranger's hand and purse in a dialogue which touches the top note of humour.

Elizabeth Bennet is Jane Austen's as she is nearly every one else's favourite heroine.

"I must confess," she writes to her sister, "that I think her as delightful a creature as ever appeared in print." On her Jane Austen has lavished the best of her own inimitable humour, high spirits, gaiety and courage, so that she takes high place among the great women in fiction, and becomes no mean companion for even Clara Middleton or Clarissa Harlowe.

The alternate attraction for and repulsion from Darcy which Elizabeth felt is drawn with the sure hand of the great creator ; and then, while we are still absorbed in the swaying fortunes of the principals, there quietly creeps upon the scene one of the most famous characters in comedy, Mr Collins. His interview with Elizabeth when he formally proposes to her is in Jane Austen's richest and happiest style. So long as humour lasts that chapter cannot fail to bring joy to the human heart. It is as universal in its appeal as the "Bottom" scenes in *A Midsummer Night's Dream* (Bottom was, after all, only Mr Collins in one stage of society as Dogberry was Mr Collins in another) or the Falstaff episodes at Gad's Hill and Eastcheap.

Lady Catherine de Bourgh, who "if she accepted any refreshments seemed to do it only for the sake of finding out that Mrs Collins's joints of meat were too large for her family," is another character over whom the Comic Spirit sheds its harmless but mirth-provoking rays. The whole novel abounds in rich personalities without whom the world would be the poorer, but we are most of all concerned with the happiness of Elizabeth, who, like others of Jane Austen's heroines, finds that true love which is all-powerful can spring from "the cold fountain of grati-

tude no less than from the volcano of passion."
Jane Austen's lovers are remarkably free from
passion.

After *Pride and Prejudice*, in popular estimation,
comes *Mansfield Park*. Tennyson, for one, preferred
the latter, but the general run of readers know their
Pride and Prejudice well and *Mansfield Park* not at
all. There is, of course, more emotion and drama in
the earlier of the two, but *Mansfield Park* is freer
from exaggeration and contains the never-to-be-
forgotten impertinent and meddlesome Mrs Norris.
In no novel do we so quickly pick up the thread of
the plot ; by the third page, as Mr Cornish says, we
are quite at home, know everybody, and even begin
to look forward to the final event.

After the ill-natured Mrs Norris, who will not extend her hospitality to Fanny Price because " I
should not have a bed to give her, for I must keep
a spare room for a friend," Jane Austen probably
hated her sister, Lady Bertram, more than most of
her other odious characters.

" She was a woman who spent her days in sitting
nicely dressed on a sofa, doing some long pieces of
needlework, of little use and no beauty, thinking more
of her pug than her children, but very indulgent to the
latter when it did not put herself to inconvenience."

In this novel we see strongly brought out a trait
that is particularly noticeable in all Jane Austen's
novels, the mutual confidence and sincerity of feeling
displayed between brother and sister : she never
tires of emphasising this side of life.

Emma is the most consistently cheerful of all the
novels. E. V. Lucas considers it to be her best, her
ripest, and her richest, the most " readable-again "
book in the world. Comedy reigns supreme, with

never the vestige of a cloud to spoil the serenity and the joy. No one is very wealthy or very poor : the whole action takes place in the village of Highbury among a set of people who meet daily. The gradual dawn and growth of love between Knightley and Emma, who makes matches for every one but herself, is uncannily well brought home to the reader, and their final love-scene is one of the happiest in literature. The vulgar and patronising Mrs Elton and talkative Miss Bates are a joy for ever, particularly the latter, who, though " neither young, handsome, rich, nor married, without beauty and cleverness, was yet happy and contented. She loved everybody, thought herself a most fortunate creature and surrounded with blessings."

Northanger Abbey is most interesting because of its historical value as an attack on the artificial school of romanticism which was so popular among young girls of that time. Catherine Morland's discovery of the roll of paper which she is convinced are love-letters is one of the most successfully satiric studies in the whole range of Jane Austen's work.

" Darkness impenetrable and immovable filled the room. A violent gust of wind, rising with sudden fury, added fresh horror to the moment. . . . Human nature could support no more. . . . Groping her way to the bed, she jumped hastily in, and sought some suspension of agony by creeping far underneath the clothes. . . . The storm still raged. . . . Hour after hour passed away, and the wearied Catherine had heard three proclaimed by all the clocks in the house before the tempest subsided and she unknowingly fell fast asleep. She was awaked the next morning at eight o'clock by the housemaid's opening her window-shutter. She flew to the mysterious manuscript. If the evidence of sight might be trusted, she held a washing-bill in her hand."

No longer could the Catherine Morlands dare to put any faith in the style of literature made popular by *The Castle of Otranto*, or *The Mysteries of Udolpho*. By this one blow did Jane Austen clear the ground for the manly, healthy, historical romance of Scott and disperse the whole gang of foolish frighteners of youth who filled the minds of young girls with unimaginable horrors and sentimental tomfoolery.

Persuasion, the last of her novels, begins with as famous a sentence as that which I quoted from *Pride and Prejudice*, describing the joy which Sir Walter Elliot took in "the Snob's Bible," the Baronetage, and is famous for the fact that it contains about the only memorable incident recorded in any of her work : the accident that befell Louisa Musgrove on the Cobb at Lyme Regis. Here, too, occurs one of those rare descriptions of natural scenery, of which, as a rule, Jane Austen is so sparing. She shows that she could observe, when she wished, inanimate objects in Nature with as acute an eye as she usually brought to bear on humanity. It was only that her fellow-men interested her more than Nature did. She watches them lynx-eyed, and, as her biographer says, "she never drops a stitch." The reason is not so much that she took infinite trouble, though no doubt she did, as that everything was actual to her, as in his larger historical manner everything was actual to Macaulay.

In all her gallery, as Macaulay noticed, she left scarcely a single caricature, and it is in this that Jane Austen approaches most nearly to the manner of Shakespeare. To be humorous, it has often been pointed out, it is necessary to exaggerate abundantly.

E

Jane Austen has gone a long way to refute what else
might seem an irrefutable argument.

Scott and Tennyson both spoke of her work in
glowing terms, and from their day to this she has
had no detractors among the greatest critics (with the
sole exception of Charlotte Brontë), but only increased
the circle of her readers.

Her plots, like Shakespeare's, were not in a high
degree original or ingenious ; her work is almost devoid
of incident : she repeats, not only her situations, but
in a lesser degree her characters.

But, as G. K. Chesterton says, no other woman
has been able to capture the complete common sense
of Jane Austen. She knew what she knew, like a
sound dogmatist ; she did not know what she did
not know, like a sound agnostic : she knew more
about men than most women, in spite of the fact
that she is commonly supposed to have been protected from truth. If that was so, it was precious
little of truth that was protected from her. When
Darcy says, " I have been a selfish being all my life
in practice *though not in theory*," he approaches the
complete confession of the intelligent male.

Womanly foibles have never before been so merci-
lessly exposed ; compared with her astringent tonic
properties, the satire of Addison or Steele is as barley
water is to ammonia. Her pen has the point of a
stencil and the sharpness of a razor-edge : there is
nothing in her work of the vague or the shadowy ;
every character stands out like a cameo, every sentence
was true to the ordinary speech of her day, and yet
possesses that unfathomable universal quality which
makes it ring as fresh and as true after a hundred
years as it did on the day when it was first written.

VII

CLEMENCE DANE

MISS CLEMENCE DANE in *Regiment of Women* has startled me more than any writer on education whose work I have ever read. Why the book was not censored I cannot understand. Those of us whose prime care in life it is to see a wholesale reform in education must owe her a very considerable debt, for she has attacked the existing system with an amazing insight into its weakest and most vulnerable places. I have spent many years in trying to prove that our great stumbling-block was the lack of interest in intellectual and artistic occupations, and that all would be well if we could once stimulate the youth of the country to care about learning in the same degree that it cares about athletics—and now a self-confessed amateur comes along and knocks all my pet theories down and tells us that the problem is quite different.

To put it tersely, it is not the brain, but sex that is wrongly developed and neglected. Every schoolmaster knows that one of the most perplexing features of boarding-school life lies in the question of boy-friendships. We of the public schools rigorously keep boys of sixteen and over apart from the juniors. In spite, however, of the harshest rules (perhaps because of them, in some instances) irregular friendships are formed, hideous scandals take place, and wholesale expulsions follow.

On the face of it there would appear to be little

harm in these friendships, and if these led to nothing
more than friendships we should encourage rather
than hinder them. But strange as it may sound to
the uninitiated, these friendships rapidly develop into
love-affairs, and the element of passion is introduced.
We talk of boys " being keen " on each other, of
girls having " a craze " for one another. If we could
dismiss these cases as mere ebullitions of " sloshy "
sentiment we might perhaps have cause to complain
that they were a waste of time, but we could scarcely
condemn them as pernicious.

I do not wish in a paper on the art of the novel to
introduce a disquisition on unnatural vice, but I never
met an author who dared even to suggest the prevalence of this poisonous habit in schools. We have
bound ourself in a conspiracy of silence to the detri-
ment of all progress. It is quite time we started to
enlighten the parents of our charges. But while
we professionals funk the problem, a mere outsider
throws the bomb with complete assurance and leaves
us aghast . . . not because she joins with our un-
spoken thoughts, and decides that the imagination
of a child's heart is unclean, but because she wishes
to make all of us—schoolmasters and mistresses—sit
up and take stock of our own position in the matter.

It is we who are to blame, it seems. Instead of
keeping to our rôle of stern autocrat, unapproachable
despot, we choose to descend from our daïs, become
friendly and companionable and inspire hero- and
heroine-worship, quite without meaning to. A kindly
word here, encouragement over a piece of work, an
inspired talk about History or Mathematics or
Divinity (even the dullest of us is inspired sometimes), and we are regarded as only a little inferior
to the Deity : our lightest word is regarded as a

dictum straight from Heaven, our ill-considered judgments as the voice of God. I quite grant at the outset that I cannot seriously bring myself to believe, even after fifteen years' experience, that I have ever caused any boy of any age to regard me with any feeling in any way related to hero-worship. I have been regarded as slightly mad, slack, a martinet, impartial, grossly unfair, an impractical idealist, shockingly material, a human companion, an inhuman beast, almost everything except a god. Most schoolmasters among my very varied acquaintance would confess to much the same experience. Girls may be more inclined to bestow their affections passionately (I was going to say unhealthily) on their mistresses than boys do on their masters, but no one in his senses would conclude from this that a boy is less passionate than a girl : to whom then does he turn, failing his masters ? On his companions, not usually of the same age. Here lies the danger of bringing up boys of all ages from thirteen to nineteen together. There is no question that such companionships lead to terrible situations and unmentionable crimes.

The point is how to avoid them. By far the best thing to do to begin with is to read Clemence Dane. *Regiment of Women* is an astounding novel to launch on the world as one's initial effort. It requires courage to attempt to interest a public, nourished on love-stories, a public exceedingly conservative in its tastes—in the daily round of a girls' school. Yet she grips our attention at once and never for a moment loses it.

All the characters are drawn with an almost diabolic insight into the human mind. The most important person is a mistress, Clare Hartill, whose one aim in life is to surround herself with youthful protégés and make them submit themselves wholly to her influence, alternately fawning upon them and neglecting them. She it is who is chosen to exemplify the force of John Knox's judgment that " the monstrous empire of a cruell woman we knowe to be the onlie occasion of all these miseries " ; the miseries being inflicted on an imaginative lonely child of thirteen who commits suicide because her mistress alternately pets and bullies her, and a young assistant mistress who has to choose between her devotion to the same tyrant and her love for a man.

Miss Dane puts her case with a force which is undeniable, emphasising each incident with such care and full detail that the *dénouement* is quite inevitable, and there is no trace of the machinery, no noise of engine or whirring of wheels as one would expect after hearing the bare outlines of the story.

It is inevitable that the pretty, young, enthusiastic, simple-minded Alwynne should fall a prey to Clare Hartill's carefully-spread net, and just as inevitable that the lonely thirteen-year-old Louise should respond to Clare's attentions.

That Louise should be precocious in her reading, acting, and thinking is no anomaly. Every schoolmaster and mistress must know of hundreds of cases where a quite young child shows æsthetic appreciation of a most advanced and mature kind while he or she retains the most childlike attitude to many of the problems of life which are no longer problems to the adult, either because they are solved or shelved *sine die*. Louise, for instance, can talk glibly about Meredith, but is completely woebegone when she finds that **her** mistress is ignorant of the Bible and will not commit herself to any positive assertions about God. It is hard for a child to understand that when we grow

up we are either completely sure or magnificently
careless about immortality and a Deity.

There are critics who rebel against the suicide
incident :. they deny that any small girl could feel
so depressed at the harshness of a beloved mistress
as to kill herself. But Louise, to me at least, rings
true no less in her death than in her life. She is exceptionally impressionable and came under a ghoulish
influence : taking the part of Arthur in *King John* had
unsettled her completely. Her failure to satisfy, her
inability to fathom, the shallows of Clare's mind, led
her to destroy herself rather than continue an existence which had suddenly, inexplicably, become un-
bearably hateful. After all, boys and girls at school
have committed suicide in real life before now, not
solely because they failed to pass examinations.
There are more ways than one even of killing a
child.

It may be urged, not unreasonably, that Miss Dane
is altogether too bitter : that she feels deeply is
evident on every page, that she is extremely sensitive
even to the least sinister usage must be plain to
every one. Sensibility and depth of emotion lead
to bitterness, if not cynicism, when thwarted, and it
is possible to be thwarted objectively. How else
account for such a passage as this ?

" Henrietta Vigers was forty-seven when she left.
She had spent youth and prime at the school, and
had nothing more to sell. She had neither certificates
nor recommendations behind her. She was hampered
by her aggressive gentility. Out of a £50-salary she
had scraped together £500. Invested daringly it
yielded her £25 a year. She had no friends outside
the school. She left none within it. Miss Marsham
presented her with a gold watch, decorously inscribed,

the school with a handsomely bound edition of Shakespeare. Heaven knows what became of her."

Miss Dane obsessed by the failure of the segregated
system advocates by indirect means the co-educational
policy as a solution. It is at this point in her story
that we feel a legitimate complaint. Her book is one
of those very rare examples of propagandist art : she
interests us enormously in her destructive mood ; she
is not so successful in convincing us about the practical
results of adopting her Utopia. That is the first
blow : the second is her failure to satisfy us with
her hero. Roger is a first-class prig, quite impossibly
wooden. The amazing thing is that Alwynne seems
to realise the enormity of the system to which she had
given her life-blood when she attempts to construct her
story anew for his sake. Talking of Louise's passion
for Clare she hits at last on the truth. " If she had
been grown-up it would have been like being in love."
The appalling tragedy of the child's suicide, which
had gone far to destroy her mental balance, could
apparently be dispelled by Roger's " all-understanding
sympathy." To me it seems rather that the gloom
is dispelled and the ghost raised by Alwynne's own
sexual impulses being stimulated : she meets for the
first time in her life a man who is interested in her :
from that moment the conflict is entirely one-sided.
We know that the call of Nature will be more insistent
than the barren unnatural cry of the lacerated selfish
ell-woman (ell-woman is the nearest word I can get
to define what has no adequate definition, but if we
could imagine the " wretched wight " in Keats' poem
to be a woman, then Clare Hartill is a perfect example
of *La Belle Dame sans Merci.* After all, " vampire "
is Elsbeth's own word for her, and she had known
her longer than any other person in the book). It is

perhaps Miss Dane's greatest triumph that she can
make us almost sympathise with the bloodsucker
when we see her outwitted by Nature : she puts up
a splendid fight against overwhelming odds, but all-
powerful Nature has only to produce the dullest type
of man and all the elaborated schemes of the spiritual
pervert fall to pieces.

The difficulty with *Regiment of Women* is that the
reader gets so thrilled with the excitement and novelty
of the idea that he is inclined to forget the artistry.
It is only on a third or fourth reading that one begins to
realise the consummate compactness of the language :
here are no loose trimmings, no irregular irrelevancies.
Slow but inexorable are the wheels of fate, and good
artist as she is, Miss Dane presents her impression
of life and leaves it to each of us to draw his own
conclusions, if conclusions are necessary.   I can fore-
see many worthy schoolmistresses, imbued with the
purest ideals, enthusiastic, morally and spiritually
energetic, pulling themselves up sharp and asking
themselves whether they are not liable to fall into
this most insidious of all temptations : " In the
effort to control the spirit of a pupil, to make our
own approval his test, and mould him by the stress
of our own pressure—in the ambition to do this, the
craving for moral power and visible guiding, the
subtle pride of effective agency, lie some of the chief
temptations of a schoolmaster's work."   It is hideous
to think that those who are keenest over their work,
most anxious to produce noble citizens, may all un-
consciously find themselves so far tampering with
human souls as to drive them to ruin.   The natural
corollary of Miss Dane's book would seem to prove
that no teacher can afford to try to win that human
companionship or affection from the young, which

is one of the most precious joys in life . . . but I am overstepping my limits as a critic. The worst of books like *Regiment of Women* is that they insidiously lead us to argue about their point of view and their novel doctrines rather than to confine our attention to their merits as pure literature.

VIII

DOROTHY RICHARDSON

THERE is no question about Miss Richardson's genius. As novel follows novel in rapid succession, all dealing with the development of Miriam Henderson, we feel more and more certainly that the authoress has justified her peculiar method of presentation. She has definitely cut loose from tradition : she relies on no incident to rouse our interest : there is neither beginning nor end : there is no reason why the series should not be continued to infinity. We are concerned entirely with the mind of the heroine. Her thoughts and impressions take up the whole of the book. She doesn't analyse : she doesn't explain : she does not narrate : she simply unfolds the workings of a girl's mind. As a result she gets closer to actualities than any writer outside the Russians. And yet—the mere male is filled with apprehension : Miss Richardson seems to be attempting the impossible : she is trying to deny passion, sex, the whole domain of man. There arises a suspicion that her novels are the outcome of repressed sexuality. "There will be books," she writes in *The Tunnel*, "with all that cut out—him and her—all that sort of thing. The books of the future will be clear of all that."

At any rate in her books there is no "him and her" : but most of us find that such ruthless pruning cuts out the greater part of life : few of us can rise superior to the insistent call of sex. 'Tis not only woman's

whole existence : it is rapidly becoming man's too :
there are cynics, of course (but Miss Richardson is no
cynic, she takes an extravagant joy in life), who would
deny this and hold themselves aloof. But one begins
to feel sometimes that the obsession of sex is not
so baneful as the deadly fear of becoming obsessed
with it.

But once remove from your mind the thought that
passion is necessary in a novel and you will give
yourself up with unending enjoyment to Miss Richardson's views of life. There is so much that one wants
to say about them all. In order, however, to confine
oneself to the limits of a chapter it is necessary to
concentrate. I will, therefore, take only *The Tunnel,*
a novel in which, as usual, nothing happens. Miriam
escapes (her whole life is a series of escapes : she is
a dreadful coward) from the Mornington Road. We
are first shown the effect on this extraordinary girl of
living free and alone in lodgings on a pound a week.
" All the real part of your life has a real dream
in it ; some of the real dream part of you coming
true. You know in advance when you are really
following your life. Coming events cast *light.* It
is like dropping everything and walking backwards
to something you know is there. . . . I am back now
where I was before I began trying to do things like
other people. . . . Twenty-one and only one room to
hold the richly renewed consciousness, and a living to
earn. . . . There was no *need* to do anything or think
about anything. . . . No interruption, no one watching or speculating or treating one in some particular way
that had to be met. . . . Reading would be real. . . .
I should never have gone to Mornington Road unless
I had been nearly mad with sorrow. . . . Following
advice is certain to be wrong. When you don't

follow advice there may be awful things. But they are
not arranged beforehand. . . . I will never again be
at the mercy of people, or at all in the places where
they are. That means keeping free of all groups. . . .
I run away from them because I must. They kill
me. . . . How frightfully happy I am." She finds
silly conversation of casual friends whom she can
pick up and discard exhilarating, real, and satisfying.
. . . But—"What a hopeless thing a man's consciousness was. A man could never be really happy
with a woman unless he could also despise her. Any
interest in generalities, any argument or criticism or
opposition would turn him into a towering bully. All
men were like that in some way. If a woman opposed
them they went mad." It will be noticed that Miss
Richardson indulges freely in generalisations, and, of
course, goes wrong. It is a pity that she generalises so
insistently upon man. She always fails to understand
him. It is a pity, too, as *The Spectator* reviewer says,
that she should be so anxious to be thought ultra-
modern. Her whisky and her cigarettes seem to be a
necessity. We envisage her as ridiculously aping the
male she so much despises. Then we forgive her at once
because of her wonderful eye for observing details. No
one has ever brought home an atmosphere so exactly
as she does. Take this picture of a dentist's office.
" Miriam swept from the bracket table the litter of
used instruments and materials, disposing them
rapidly on the cabinet, into the sterilising tray, the
waste basket, and the wash-hand basin, tore the
uppermost leaf from the head rest pad, and detached
the handpiece from the arm of the motor drill while
the patient was being shown upstairs. Mr Hancock
had cleared the spittoon, set a fresh tumbler, filled
the kettle and whisked the debris of amalgam and

cement from the bracket table before he began the scrubbing and cleansing of his hands, and when the patient came in Miriam was in her corner reluctantly handling the instruments, wet with the solution that crinkled her finger-tips and made her skin brittle and dry. Everything was in its worst state. The business of drying and cleansing, freeing fine points from minute closely adhering fragments, polishing instruments on the leather pad, repolishing them with the leather, scraping the many little burs with the fine wire brush, scraping the clamps, clearing the obstinate amalgam from slab and spatula, brought across her the ever-recurring circle . . . the exasperating tediousness of holding herself to the long series of tiny careful attention-demanding movements . . . the punctual emergence when the end was in sight of the hovering reflection, nagging and questioning, that another set of things was already getting ready for another cleansing process. . . . The evolution of dentistry was wonderful, but the more perfect it became the more and more of this sort of thing there would be . . . could God approve of this kind of thing . . . was it right to spend life cleaning instruments . . . all work has drudgery . . . blessed be drudgery, but that was housekeeping, not some one else's drudgery . . . and no one knew what it cost. . . . It was keeping to that all day and every day, choosing the most difficult, tiresome way in everything that kept that radiance about Mr Hancock when he was quietly at work. . . . I mustn't stay here thinking these thoughts . . . it's that evil thing in me, always thinking thoughts, nothing getting done—going through life like—a stuck pig. If I went straight on things would come like that just the same in flashes . . . bang, bang, in your heart, everything breaking into light just in front of you, flowers and light stretching out. Then you shut it down, letting it go through you with a leap that carries you to the moon—the sun, and makes you bump with life like the little boy bursting out of his too-small clothes, and go on choking with song to do the next thing deftly. . . . I can't be easy till I've said it in my mind, and I'm sad till I've said it somehow . . . and sadder when I have said it. But nothing gets done. I must stop thinking from now and be fearfully efficient."

But she doesn't : she thinks aloud all through the book. Some people, most, I fear, will be put off by countless pages like that which I have quoted. But it is not for the story, but for the impression which life makes on the mind of a young girl that one reads this book. To put her novel down and go out into the street or on to the common is necessary very frequently in order to keep in touch with that life which most of us value very highly because we have compromised at an early age and allowed ourselves to descend into that arena to fight, but it is equally refreshing to return to the rarefied atmosphere of *The Tunnel* and watch Miriam's fugitive and cloistered virtue remaining aloof from the dust and heat. For one thing, by so doing she has kept her virgin soul intact and is able to say things about music, painting, and literature which we recognise to be true and fine and totally beyond our power of expression.

" Somebody had said that all good art, all great art, had a sensuous element . . . it was dreadful, but probably true. Mr Hancock was ' put off ' by sensuousness, by anybody taking a delight in the sun on rice-fields and the gay colours of Japan . . . perhaps one ought to be ' put off ' by Hearn. . . ."

Or this about reading : " There ought to be clear
enunciation. Not expression—that was like commenting as you read ; getting at the person you were
reading to . . . reading with expression really hadn't
any expression." Or this about Zola : " Wandering
back to her room she repeated the phrases in her
mind in French : they seemed to clear up and take
shelter—somehow they were terse and acceptable,
and they were secret and secure—but English people
ought not to read them in English. It was outrage-
ous. Englishmen, . . . the Frenchman had written
them simply . . . French logic . . . Englishmen were
shy and suggestive about these things—either that
or breezy . . . ' filth,' which was almost worse." Or
this about Eden Phillpotts : " There was something
about the name : soft and numb, with a slight chatter
and hiss at the end, a rainstorm, the atmosphere of
Devonshire and the mill-wheel." Even her friends
comment on Miriam's " extraordinarily sharp sense
of right and wrong." Everybody else seems to
be blunting her senses all the time by " going in
amongst the crowd " (a Hendersonism for " married "),
or mixing " naturally " with others. I say " her "
advisedly. Men's senses in Miriam's eyes are already
blunted beyond all hope of repair. Miss Richardson
seems to me to be most paradoxical : she calls our
existence (yours, mine), the sheltered life : her idea
of complete emancipation is to be able " to turn up
on Sunday morning in your knickers with your
hair down " far from " sheltered " women and
" complacent abominable " men. Miss Richardson
has got a bee in her bonnet about us as a sex.
She can't use the word " man " without losing her
temper. She is more reasonable on the things of the
mind.

" You ought not to think in words—I mean—you can think in your brain by imagining yourself going on and on through it, endless space."

" You can't grasp space with your mind."

" You don't GRASP it, you go through it. . . . There is no such thing as eternal punishment. It makes God a failure and a fool. It's a man's idea. Sitting on a throne judging everybody and passing sentence is a thing a man would do."

Again, on the eternal subject of " Man " :

" Old men seemed to have some sort of understanding of things. If only they would talk with the same conviction about other things as there was in their tone when they said those personal things (my beauty, my sweet, you sweet girl, etc.). But the things they said were worldly : generalisations, like the things one read in books that tired you out with trying to find the answer, and made books so awful—things that might look true about everybody at some time or other, and were not really true about anybody—when you knew them. All the things the old men said about life and themselves and other people were sad : ' Make the best of your youth, my dear, before it flies.' If it all ended in sadness and envy of youth, life was simply a silly trick. *Life* could not be a silly trick. That is the simple truth . . . a certainty. Whatever happens, whatever things look like, life is not a trick." Life is not a trick to Miriam simply because she is always ecstatically happy. " To toss all the joys and happiness away and know that you are happy and free without anything." " Why do lovely things and people go on happening ? " Harking back to the subject of words : " Whether you agree or not, language is the only way of expressing anything, and it dims everything. So the Bible is

F

not true : it is a culture.   Religion is wrong in making
word-dogmas out of it.   Christ was something.   But
Christianity, which calls Him divine and so on, is
false.   It clings to words which get more and more
wrong. . . . Then there's nothing to be afraid of
and nothing to be quite sure of rejoicing about.   The
Christians are irritating and frightened.   The man
with side-whiskers [Huxley, a special object of
Miriam's hatred] understands something.   But."
Her defence of women talking shamelessly at
concerts and chattering on a mountain-top in the
presence of a magnificent panorama would have
rejoiced the heart of Rupert Brooke :   " Then men
mustn't treat them as works of art : it was perfectly
reasonable that the women who got that sort of
admiration from men should assert themselves in the
presence of other works of art."   One of the frighten-
ing things about Miss Richardson's genius is the way
that she sends her thoughts out in all sorts of queer
directions.   " Miriam figured them in a flash coming
down the road to the house : their young men's talk
and arguments, their certainty of rightness and com-
pleteness."   Or this of music :   " The player's air of
superiority to other music was insufferable : her way
of playing out bar by bar of the rain on the roof, as
if she were giving a lesson, was a piece of intellectual
snobbery.   Alma's horrible holding back of the third
note for emphasis where there was no emphasis . . .
it was like . . . finding a *wart* at the end of a fine
tendril.   Why are the English so awful about music ?
They are poets.   English people ought never to play,
only to listen to music.   They are not innocent enough
to play.   They cannot forget themselves."   Or this
on Shakespeare :
" Women always despise men under the influence

of passion or fatigue : did a man *ever* speak in a
natural voice—neither blushing, nor displaying his
cleverness, nor being simply a lustful slave ? To
pretend one did not see through a man's voice would
be treachery. Harshness must go—perhaps that was
what Christ meant. . . . The knowledge of woman
is larger, bigger, deeper, less wordy and clever than
that of men. Men have no real knowledge, but of
things ; a sort of superiority they get by being free
to be out in the world amongst things ; they do not
understand people, ' a civilisation can never rise above
the level of its women.' Perhaps if women became
lawyers they would change things. Women do not
respect law. Portia ? She had been invented by a
man. There was no reality in any of Shakespeare's
women. They please men because they show women
as men see them. Shakespeare's plays are ' universal '
because they are about the things that everybody
knows and hands about, and they do not trouble
anybody. They make every one feel wise."

To revert to men for the *n*th time : " In speech with
a man a woman is at a disadvantage, because they
speak different languages. She may understand his.
Hers he will never speak nor understand. In pity,
or from other motives, she must therefore, stammer-
ingly, speak his. That's the truth about life. Men
and women never meet. Inside the life-relationship
you can see them being strangers and hostile : one
or the other, or both, completely alone." A sentiment immediately followed by her usual song and
caper of well-being. " I am frantically, frantically
happy," presumably because there are no males at
hand to bother. But this mood doesn't last : in the
next chapter she is at it again, hell-for-leather, attacking the man-made world.

" If one could only burn all the volumes ; stop the publication of them. But it was all books, all the literature in the world, right back to Juvenal . . . whatever happened, if it could all be avenged by somebody in some way, there was all that . . . the classics, the finest literature—' unsurpassed.' Education would always mean coming into contact with all that. . . . There was no getting away from the scientific facts . . . *inferior* ; mentally, morally, intellectually and physically . . . her development arrested in the interest of her special functions . . . reverting later towards the male type . . . old women with deep voices and hair on their faces. . . . Woman is undeveloped man : if one could die of the loathsome visions . . . if by one thought all the men in the world could be stopped, shaken, and slapped. There *must*, somewhere, be some power that could avenge it all. . . . It will go on as long as women are stupid enough to go on bringing men into the world. . . . There is no pardon possible for man. The only answer to them is suicide ; all women ought to agree to commit suicide. . . . There was nothing to turn to. Books were poisoned. Art. All the achievements of men were poisoned at the root. . . . Religion was the only hope. . . . But no future life could heal the degradation of having been a woman. . . . Christ was a man. If it was true that He was God taking on humanity—He took on *male* humanity. . . . Life is poisoned, for women, at the very source." It becomes after scores of such pages rather pathetic : it is obviously her great obsession. It is pleasanter to· leave this topic and turn again to her general style. *The Spectator* critic, confessedly an elderly male, finds an affinity with jazz-music and other modern diablerie in such thought-waves as this : " Last night's soapy

water poured away and the fresh poured out ready
standing there all night, everything ready. . . . I
must not forget the extra piece of string . . . Je-ru-
sa-*lem* the gol-den, with-milk-and-hun-ney-blest . . .
sh, not so much noise . . . beneath thy con, tem,
pla, tion, sink, heart, and, voice, o, ppressed.

I *know* not, oh, I, know, not.

Sh . . . sh . . . hark, hark, my soul angelic songs
are swelling O'er earth's green fields, and ocean's
wave-beat shore . . . damn—blast, where are my
bally knickers ?—Sing us sweet fragments of the songs
above.

" The green world everywhere, inside and out . . .
all along the dim staircase, waiting in the dim cold
kitchen. No blind, brighter. Cool grey light, a
misty, windless morning. Shut the door.

They STAND *those* HALLS *of* ZI-ON
ALL JUBILANT *with* SONG."

I, on the other hand, can follow every note of this :
it is all exactly right, one's mind does work just in
this strange, jerky, inconsequent sort of way. This
is the work of an artist who not only thinks, but
remembers what she thinks. The question, is if one
discards incident, which thoughts are revelant and
which put in because they happen to recur to the
memory ? For, after all, art is selection, not entirely
observation. We are to see the development of the
girl's mind. It is open to question whether this
method of presentation always succeeds in showing
us this development. We forgive her her frequent
use of that odious word " serviette " ; we forgive her
her love of reproducing completely idiotic conversation, it is harder to forgive her diseased attitude to

the male sex, hardest of all to forgive her for running
away from life . . . and yet at the end of all, she
does interest us. *The Tunnel* is no easy book to read.
Quite nine-tenths of those who take it up will not
have the patience to work out the rich ore contained
in it, for there is rich ore, as I have tried to show,
and concentration is certainly needed if we are to
profit by the experience of ploughing through it.

May Sinclair sees in Miss Richardson's novels an
art and method and form carried to punctilious perfection. There is, it is true, no drama, no situation,
no set scene. Nothing happens. It is just life going
on and on. In identifying herself with this life, Miss
Richardson, in May Sinclair's eyes, gets closer to reality
than any other novelist. No other writers use their
senses so purely or so intensely. This intensity is
the effect of an extreme concentration on the thing
seen or felt. So her novels are of an extraordinary
compression, and of an extenuation more extraordinary
still. One does not differ from May Sinclair lightly :
what she says, she means . . . and it is obvious that
she regards Dorothy Richardson as a profoundly
significant phenomenon. I would not deny that, but
I withhold complete adoration on grounds that I
have already tried to make plain.

PART II

POETRY AND POETS

I

INTRODUCTORY

MR G. S. STREET has some shrewd comments
to make on the enormous output of verse
during the last few years. It was obvious, of
course, that all the young poets were in the Army;
to be a poet at all connoted that one was of military
age, as one commonly writes verse in the first flush
of youth rather than in a ripe old age : it is equally
obvious that in moments of great stress or emotion
men do write poetry, or at any rate formulate it
so that it may be recollected in tranquillity, but
most war poetry is remarkable for its reticence on
the subject of the deeper emotions ; the moods
evoked are those called into being by weariness,
comradeship, country scenes, and so on. Now Mr
Street's theory is that these thousands of verses were
hammered out in the mind at a time when paper
and pen were not available, on the march, in the
trench, on duty of some sort. Thoughts would flit
through the minds of these men, pleasant enough or
vivid enough to make them want to write them down :
as this was impossible they had to commit them to
memory. What greater aid to memory than rhythm
or rhyme ? This seems to me a most likely solution.
The planning of a sonnet in his head, with its intricate
rhyme-scheme would certainly enable a man to retain
an impression, and the search for the best word and
the necessary rhymes would certainly heighten the
effect of the thought and make it of infinitely greater

value than if it had been hastily written down in loose prose.

This theory would explain the absence of *vers libre* among the soldier-poets, perhaps the most popular form of writing poetry before the war.

Ford Madox Hueffer certainly still indulges in it, but it is significant that he takes special pains in his preface to defend his use of it. In 1913 it almost needed a defence if one dared to rhyme or scan. Now Hueffer even makes his *vers libre* rhyme ! The war has driven the poet back from fanciful experiment to tradition : the long, lonely hours have led to silent thought, but not silent writing : the silent thought has become crystallised in the old classical form, and we have poetry in the true succession of the Philip Sidneys and the Lovelaces of old.

But this is, after all, but a slight matter. The war has done more than drive the *vers librist* back to saner channels in which to float his argosy. As Arthur Waugh has well pointed out, the younger school of poets, headed by Rupert Brooke, stood for individualism against the tyranny of convention, honestly striving to present life as they saw it ; they failed through an incurable spirit of selfishness. Incurable, that is, but for the war. The poet back from the trenches still retains his individuality, but it has ceased to be introspective : all our sympathies have become extraordinarily widened : no longer do we speak glibly as the Victorians did of the ennobling glories of war : we have discovered it to be an unspeakable horror, paralysing the very soul : it becomes the mission of a Sassoon " to strip the tinsel from Bellona's robes " and reveal to us the stark and chattering skeleton beneath. By a quaint paradox individualism has expanded into a passion for companionship.

Think of the interchange of letters in verse between Graves, Sassoon, and Nichols. Multiply that a million-fold . . . read any soldier's poetry : his work is brimful of warmth and tenderness for others. The most self-centred generation in history has been transformed into the most sympathetic and humane.

To go back a little. It is not my purpose to take in detail any of those " Georgians " who were famous before the war : it is necessary, therefore, for the purposes of continuity to sum up their achievement. They scorned the amorous pessimism of the decadent nineties : they refused to be obsessed by the passions : they would not allow themselves to get drunk on the superb melodies of Swinburne : they prided themselves on their sincerity and fought under the banner of realism. Now realism has been made to connote as many different meanings as that overworked word romantic.

To the early Georgians it meant stark nakedness, frank brutality. Luckily it extended its scope to include the mysticism of Evelyn Underhill, the para-doxical balladry of Chesterton, the all-embracing sympathy of Ralph Hodgson, and the quaint humour of Harold Monro (who endows apparently inanimate objects with reason and life), as well as the Billingsgate colloquialism of Masefield's long narrative poems. In a word, these poets refused to specialise : they all overstepped the prescribed boundaries, and poetry became infinitely more human, and consequently humorous. Lascelles Abercrombie relies on intellec-tuality; De la Mare on a most seductive wizardry; D. H. Lawrence, almost a fanatic on one subject, and that thoroughly unpleasant, owing to the unruly turbulence of his surcharged emotions, relies entirely on sex. The introduction of the dramatic element, at once bizarre, awkward, and hyper-intellectual, owes much to Donne, who, it is significant to add, has come into his own after three hundred years' neglect.

" Half an hour's roaming about a street or village or railway station shows so much beauty that it's impossible to be anything but wild with suppressed exhilaration.   And it's not only beauty and beautiful things.   In a flicker of sunlight on a blank wall, or a reach of muddy pavement, or smoke from an engine at night, there's a sudden significance and importance and inspiration that makes the breath stop with a gulp of certainty and happiness. . . . I suppose my occupation is being in love with the universe—or (for it's an important difference) with certain spots and moments and points of it."

That is the very spirit of Donne reincarnated in Brooke : the Brooke of *Grantchester*, and *Heaven.* That is what enabled him to say with perfect sincerity, " There is nothing in the world like friendship.   There is no man who has had such friends as I, so many, so fine, so various, so multiform, so prone to laughter, so strong in affection, and so permanent, so trustworthy, so courteous, so stern with vices and so blind to faults or folly, so apt to make jokes and to understand them."

At times in his letters and his poems he reminds us of Compton Mackenzie's rather hard but brilliant heroine, Sylvia Scarlett : then the beloved poet of Grantchester emerges once more, the lover of England.

" Plymouth—was there ever so sweet and droll a sound ?   Drake's Plymouth, English Western Plymouth, city where men speak softly, and things are sold for shillings, not for dollars ; and there is love and beauty and old houses . . . and beyond which are little fields, very green, bounded by small piled

walls of stone : and behind them the brown and
black, splintered, haunted moor. By that the train
shall go up : by Dartmouth, where my brother was—
I will make a litany ; by Torquay, where Verrall
stayed ; and by Paignton, where I have walked in
the rain : past Ilsington, where John Ford was born,
and Appledore, in the inn of which I wrote a poem
against a commercial traveller ; by Dawlish, of which
John Keats sang ; within sight of Widdicombe, where
old Uncle Tom Cobley rode a mare ; not a dozen
miles from John Galsworthy at Manaton ; within
sight almost of that hill at Drewsteignton, on which
I lay out all one September night, crying . . ."

" I've never been quite so happy in my life," he
wrote when he learnt that he was to go out to the
Dardanelles, " not quite so pervasively happy : I
suddenly realise that the ambition of my life has
been to go on a military expedition against Constantinople." The immense popularity of Brooke may
owe much to his personal beauty, his intellect, his
deft humour, the tragedy of his death, or a hundred
causes, but most of all he will be remembered and
loved for his unfailing zest for life, his universal, all-
embracing love.

> This one last gift I give : that after men
> Shall know, and later lovers, far-removed,
> Praise you, " All these were lovely " ; say, " He loved."

W. H. Davies is another of those who come outside
the scope of my paper except as an influence. It is
easy to poke fun, as J. C. Squire does, at the childish
simplicity of his theme : like Brooke he is carried
off his feet by the most ordinary objects of everyday
life. He is content to feel and to translate his rapture
on to paper without moralising :

But riddles are not made for me,
My joy's in beauty, not its cause :
Then give me but the open skies,
And birds that sing in a green wood
That's snowbound by anemones.

He is content to sit still in the hedgerows and drink
in the beauties of his surroundings and pour out his
thanksgiving in simple melodies :

Sing for the sun your lyric, lark,
Of twice ten thousand notes :
Sing for the moon, you nightingales,
Whose light shall kiss your throats ;
Sing, sparrows, for the soft, warm rain,
To wet your feathers through :
And, when a rainbow's in the sky,
Sing you, cuckoo : " cuckoo."

It would be unfair, however, to pass on to my
choice of individuals without reflecting briefly on such
work in Edward Marsh's *Georgian Poetry*, 1916–1917,
as is worthy of special mention. The previous
volumes I have dealt with elsewhere.[1]

Following upon the khaki-bound volume of 1911–
1912 and the blue of 1913–1915, we have now the
emerald green of 1916–1917 to complete a series of
poetry as interesting as any in our shelves. Nine out
of the eighteen poets represented here are new ;
consequently the work of the " older inhabitants " is
restricted in order to make way for a sufficient number
of poems from the unknown writers.

I propose to follow Mr Marsh's own order of
reversing the alphabetical order in this instance, for
the purpose of bringing the new blood to the fore.

First on the list comes Mr W. J. Turner.

[1] *From Shakespeare to O. Henry*, Grant Richards.

In his opening poem, *Romance*, he dwells upon the effect of exotic names on the boy-mind :

> When I was but thirteen or so,
> I went into a golden land ;
> Chimborazo, Cotopaxi,
> Took me by the hand.

The death of father and brother, the presence of masters and boys at school, affected him but dimly :

> The houses, people, traffic seemed
> Thin fading dreams by day ;
> Chimborazo, Cotopaxi,
> They had stolen my soul away !

In *Ecstasy* he essays a subject which is too hard for him. In formless metre, which does not even rhyme, he tries to depict the effect produced upon his mind after seeing " a frieze on whitest marble drawn of boys who sought for shells along the shore." The effect was that

> The wind came and purified my limbs,
> And the stars came and set within my eyes,
> And snowy clouds rested upon my shoulders,
> And the blue sky shimmered deep within me,
> And I sang like a carven pipe of music.

It is all stiff and wooden, never galvanised into the true stuff of poetry.

I like him better when he returns to the magic of place-names, as he does in *The Hunter* :

> I met thee first long, long ago,
> Turning a printed page, and I
> Stared at a world I did not know,
> And felt my blood like fire flow,
> At that strange name of Yucatan.

After finishing the twelve pages allotted to him

in this anthology I come to the conclusion that I
prefer Mr Turner as a dramatic critic in *Land and
Water*.   He has colour, and, when he wishes it, music,
but he is careless of prosody.

It is delightful to turn over and find that James
Stephens has returned from his vague twitterings to
give us again songs at once eager, musical, and
birdlike.   He has never been in happier vein than
in *Fifteen Acres* :

>   I stoop and swoop
>   On the air, or loop
> Through the trees, and then go soaring, O :
>   To group with a troop
>   On the gusty poop
> While the wind behind is roaring, O :
>   I skim and swim
>   By a cloud's red rim
> And up to the azure flooring, O :
>   And my wide wings drip
>   As I slip, slip, slip
> Down through the raindrops,
>   Back where Peg
>   Broods in the nest
>   On the little white egg,
> So early in the morning, O.

The touch, too, in *Check*, about night creeping on
the ground :

>   I heard the rustle of her shawl
>   As she threw blackness everywhere,
>   Upon the sky and ground and air,

is wholly delightful and unmistakably his own.   But
the ingenuous *naïveté* of an innocent can be overdone,
and no longer can we find charm in such phrases as
" Her face was awful white " or " It flew down all

crumply and waggled such a lot," even from children, in poetry.

It is delightful to find that Harold Monro has really come into his own at last, and in the extracts from *Strange Meetings* given here we get a very fair idea of that philosophy for which we used to search in vain in his work. It is plain enough now to see that he is trying to link up the organic with the inorganic worlds :

> Since man has been articulate . . .
> He has not understood the little cries . . .
> Has failed to hear the sympathetic call
> Of crockery and cutlery . . . the stool .
> He sat on, or the door he entered through :
> He has not thanked them, overbearing fool !

He then proceeds happily to illustrate the various means which our inanimate friends employ to call attention to our neglect of them :

> The rafters creak : an empty cupboard door
> Swings open ; now a wild plank of the floor
> Breaks from its joist and leaps behind my foot.

The bed sighs, the kettle puffs tentacles of breath, the copper basin tumbles from the shelf, the gas flares and frets irascibly, " reminding me I ought to go to bed."

> The putty cracks against the window-pane,
> A piece of paper in the basket shoves
> Another piece, and toward the bottom moves.

Pencils break their points . . . :

" There is not much dissimilarity " (he concludes) :

G

> Not much to choose, I know it well, in fine,
> Between the purposes of you and me,
> And your eventual Rubbish Heap and mine.

Week-End is a delightful sonnet series, containing ten stanzas dwelling on the same theme :

> There you are waiting, little friendly house . . .
> Your homely floor is creaking for our tread . . .
> The key will stammer, and the door reply,
> The hall wake, yawn, and smile . . .
> There's lovely conversation in this house :
> Words become princes that were slaves before.

The " week-enders " become so happy, wandering and listening to the sounds of the friendly countryside, that when the time comes for them to return to work, for one instant they think of shirking :

> Week-end is very well on Saturday
> On Monday it's a different affair—
> A little episode, a trivial stay
> In some oblivious spot somehow, somewhere.

They find it very hard to tear themselves away from their Paradise :

> The lonely farm is wondering that we
> Can leave.   How every window seems to stare !

We leave the happy-unhappy pair

> Reading the morning paper in the sound
> Of the debilitating heavy Train.
> London again, again.   London again.

The whole poem is a gem of artistic description— light, airy, suggestive, and yet poignant.   In it Mr Monro has raised a commonplace idea into the realm of fancy and imagination.   Thousands of released workers will be eternally grateful to him for having expressed their thoughts and feelings so delightfully.

It is indeed a pleasure to find Mr Masefield returning to his earlier style of poetry. His period of long narrative verse is apparently over, and in the half-dozen Shakespearean sonnets here given us we gloat over the recovery of the author of *Poems and Ballads.* He sings again the hymn of Beauty simply and thoughtfully, seeking, as ever, for an answer to the riddle that so baffles us :

Here in the self is all that man can know
    Of Beauty, all the wonder, all the power,
All the unearthly colour, all the glow,
    Here in the self which withers like a flower ;
Here in the self, which fades as hours pass,
    And droops and dies and rots and is forgotten
Sooner, by ages, than the mirroring glass
    In which it sees its glory still unrotten.
Here in the flesh, within the flesh, behind,
    Swift in the blood and throbbing on the bone,
Beauty herself, the universal mind,
    Eternal April wandering alone ;
The God, the holy Ghost, the atoning Lord,
Here in the flesh, the never yet explored.

That is the unfathomable mystery to him, why the glory of the human face and form divine should contain all that there is of Beauty, and yet be allowed to decay like the rose. Like Rupert Brooke, he is infatuated with the glory of the material : he wants to get within and behind the " cells at their hidden marvels hard at work," and " attain to where the rulers lurk "—" Then, on man's earthly peak, I might behold The unearthly self beyond, unguessed, untold."

He proceeds to sing the praises of man's soul,

That takes its earth's contentment in the pen,
  Then sees the world's injustice and is wroth,
And flinging off youth's happy promise, flies
  Up to some breach, despising earthly things,
And, in contempt of hell and heaven, dies
  Rather than bear some yoke of priests or kings. . . .

As felicitous a description of the happy warrior of
to-day as one could wish.

There is nothing of Ralph Hodgson's this time to
compare in excellence of idea or execution with *The
Bull* or *The Song of Honour*, nor could we well expect
it ; but in the three short verses by which he is
represented there is enough music and sweetness to
send those who are still unacquainted with his work
back to his greater, more ambitious poetry.

In *The Gipsy Girl* he pictures with exquisite
economy and sureness of touch the " fair " girl at the
cocoanut-shy :

> A man came up, too loose of tongue,
>   And said no good to her ;
> She did not blush as Saxons do,
>   Or turn upon the cur :
> She fawned and whined, " Sweet gentleman,
>   A penny for three tries ! "
> But oh, the den of wild things in
>   The darkness of her eyes !

An equally happy note (which would please Mr
Galsworthy) is struck in *The Bells of Heaven* :

> 'Twould ring the bells of Heaven,
>   The wildest peal for years,
> If parson lost his senses
>   And people came to theirs,
> And he and they together
>   Knelt down with angry prayers

> For tamed and shabby tigers
> And dancing dogs and bears,
> And wretched, blind pit ponies,
> And little hunted hares.

With Robert Graves we return to the soldier-poets. In *It's a Queer Time* he takes four examples of the instantaneous change that comes over a man while he is fighting :

> One moment you'll be crouching at your gun
> Traversing, mowing heaps down half in fun :
> The next, you choke and clutch at your right breast—
> No time to think—leave all—and off you go . . .
> To Treasure Island where the spice winds blows,
> To lovely groves of mango, quince and lime—
> Breathe no good-bye, but ho, for the Red West !
> It's a queer time.

Or you may be charging madly, suddenly fall, and find yourself back in the Big Barn digging tunnels through the hay, clad in your old sailor suit ; or, again, you may be startled out of your doze in your dug-out by a cataclysmic shock, and then see Elsie (who died ten years ago) come tripping gaily down the trench, " hanky to nose," getting her pinafore all over grime :

> The trouble is, things happen much too quick ;
> Up jump the Bosches, rifles thump and click,
> You stagger, and the whole scene fades away :
> Even good Christians don't like passing straight
> From Tipperary or their Hymn of Hate
> To Alleluiah-chanting, and the chime
> Of golden harps . . . and . . . I'm not well to-
> day . . .
> It's a queer time.

In *Goliath and David,* an elegy on a friend, he reverses the Biblical story : " The historian of that fight had not the heart to tell it right." Here we

are shown the young boy foolishly flinging pebbles
which Goliath easily parries with his huge shield, and
then trying, with equal futility, to conquer the ogre
with his staff of Mamre oak. The inevitable happens,
and we are left looking at the sad picture of the spike-
helmeted, grey, dim Goliath straddling over the body
of the beautiful youth.

In another poem he paints a delicious picture of
a boy in church :

> I add the hymns up over and over
>   Until there's not the least mistake.
> Seven-seventy-one. (Look ! There's a plover !
>   It's gone !) . . .
> It's pleasant here for dreams and thinking,
>   Lolling and letting reason nod,
> With ugly, serious people linking
>   Prayer-chains for a forgiving God.

But his most beautiful piece of work is *Christ in the
Wilderness*, speaking soft words of grace unto lost
desert-folk :

> Basilisk, cockatrice,
> Flocked to his homilies . . .
> Great rats on leather wings
> And poor blind broken things, . .
> And ever with him went,
> Of all his wanderings
> Comrade, with ragged coat,
> Gaunt ribs—poor innocent—
> Bleeding foot, burning throat,
> The guileless old scapegoat.

Here, at any rate, we have a poet who thinks, who
has an original mind and a gift for weaving his
thoughts into a rhythmical, disciplined form.

Wilfrid Gibson gives us a glimpse of his musical
strength in *For G.* :

All night under the moon
        Plovers are flying
Over the dreaming meadows of silvery light,
Over the meadows of June,
        Flying and crying—
Wandering voices of love in the hush of the night.
All night under the moon,
        Love, though we're lying
Quietly under the thatch, in silvery light
Over the meadows of June
        Together we're flying—
Rapturous voices of love in the hush of the night.

That is a song which any poet might be proud to
have written, but he does not often reach this height.
He, too, touches on the war, for the most part with
no very marked success ; but *Lament*, at least, rings
true :

We who are left, how shall we look again
Happily on the sun, or feel the rain
Without remembering how they who went
Ungrudgingly and spent
Their lives for us loved, too, the sun and rain ?

A bird among the rain-wet lilac sings ;
But we, how shall we turn to little things,
And listen to the birds and winds and streams
Made holy by their dreams,
Nor feel the heart-break in the heart of things ?

John Freeman has already received some appreciation, for he has been writing poetry for several years—
poetry of a sort that made some of us wonder why
he was not included before.

Reparation has been amply made to him, for twelve
valuable pages are devoted to excerpts from his work.
In *Discovery* we get a clue to his attitude to life and
a glimpse of his gift.

It was my eyes, Beauty, that made thee bright ;
My ears that heard, the blood leaping in my veins,
The vehemence of transfiguring thought—
Not lights and shadows, birds, grasses and rains—
That made thy wonders wonderful.
For it has been, Beauty, that I have seen thee,
Tedious as a painted cloth at a bad play,
Empty of meaning and so of all delight.
Now thou hast blessed me with a great pure bliss,
Shaking thy rainy light all over the earth,
And I have paid thee with my thankfulness.

In his most ambitious poem, *The Pigeons,* he tells
most poignantly the story of two children dying of
starvation, " though food within the cupboard idle
lay beyond their thought, or but beyond their reach."

There is not pity enough in heaven or earth,
There is not love enough, if children die
Like famished birds—oh, less mercifully.
A great wrong's done when such as these go forth
Into the starless dark, broken and bruised,
With mind and sweet affection all confused,
And horror closing round them as they go.
There is not pity enough !

He, too, is driven by the war to write of the change
that has been wrought in us :

Whate'er was dear before is dearer now.
There's not a bird singing upon his bough
But sings the sweeter in our English ears :
There's not a nobleness of heart, hand, brain,
But shines the purer ; happiest is England now
In those that fight, and watch with pride and tears.

In many ways Mr Freeman seems to surpass the
other poets of his time : he is more severe, he is
harder to appreciate on a first reading, but he has the
power both to feel and to express what he feels,

whether it be the impression made on him by " these November skies " than which " is no sky lovelier," or by music when the brain's asleep, or by the " lovely moon that lovelike hovers over the wandering, tired earth, her bosom grey and dovelike, hovering beautiful as a dove, or the silver frost upon the window-pane, flowering and branching each starving night anew."

John Drinkwater sings again his eulogy of the Midlands and his Cotswold home :

> I see the valleys in their morning mist
> Wreathed under limpid hills in moving light
> Happy with many a yeoman melodist :
> I see the little roads of twinkling white
> Busy with fieldward teams and market gear
> Of rosy men, cloth-gaitered, who can tell
> The many-minded changes of the year,
> Who know why crops and kine fare ill or well ;
> I see the sun persuade the mist away,
> Till town and stead are shining to the day.
> I see the waggons move along the rows
> Of ripe and summer-breathing clover-flower,
> I see the lissom husbandman who knows
> Deep in his heart the beauty of his power.
> As, lithely pitched, the full-heaped fork bids on
> The harvest home. . . .
> I see the barns and comely manors planned
> By men who somehow moved in comely thought . . .
> I see the little cottages that keep
> Their beauty still where since Plantagenet
> Have come the shepherds happily to sleep. . . .

The beauty of the countryside so moves him that when night descends he turns to sleep, content that from his sires he draws the blood of England's midmost shires ; and, though he does not think that skies and meadows are moral, or that the fixity of a star comes of a quiet spirit, or that trees have wisdom, yet these things certainly exercise a moral effect on him, teaching him the virtues of constancy, peace, and fortitude.

Walter de la Mare is as musical as ever, but not so simple. He, too, is changed by the war :

> They're all at war !
>   Yes, yes, their bodies go
> 'Neath burning sun and icy star
>   To chaunted songs of woe,
> Dragging cold cannon through a mire
> Of rain and blood and spouting fire,
> The new moon glinting hard on eyes
>   Wide with insanities !

He is for the first time obscure, and we no longer feel the temptation to dwell on the magic lilt of his metre.

W. H. Davies continues to sing of simple country delights untouched by war's alarms, of larks and nightingales, and the thrush's five blue eggs, of cowslips and grass and storms on the Mendip hills. One singularly happy touch of his genius is to be found in *Easter* :

> A butterfly—from who knows where—
> Comes with a stagger through the air,
> And, lying down, doth ope and close
> His wings, as babies work their toes ;
> Perhaps he thinks of pressing tight
> Into his wings a little light !

It is good indeed for our peace of mind that some one should sing of Nature's charms with his eye on the object. Of all present-day singers Mr Davies comes nearest to Keats's definition of what a poet should be :

> And they shall be accounted poet kings
> Who simply tell the most heart-easing things.

Mr Gordon Bottomley, who follows next, gives us in *Atlantis* his view of poetry :

> Poetry is founded on the hearts of men :
> Though in Nirvana or the Heavenly courts
> The principle of beauty shall persist,
> Its body of poetry, as the body of man,
> Is but a terrene form, a terrene use,
> That swifter being will not loiter with ;
> And, when mankind is dead and the world cold,
> Poetry's immortality will pass.

Maurice Baring appears for the first time with a poem which is surer of immortality than any other in the book. It is great fun predicting lasting fame for contemporary poets, the more so because critics are nearly always wrong. One has only to turn back to the days of Keats and Shelley to see this ; but in Baring's long elegy, *In Memoriam, A. H.* (Auberon Herbert, Captain Lord Lucas, R.F.C.), we feel tempted to say that it will take its place among the great elegies, *Thyrsis, Lycidas, Adonaïs.* After all, great occasions bring out the great men, and of noble men it ought to be possible to write nobly. This Captain Baring has most certainly achieved, and we are grateful to him and to Mr Marsh for making accessible to the general public a poem about which every one had long been talking, but few had read. Unfortunately, it is one of those perfectly executed masterpieces out of which it is wellnigh impossible to extract adequate quotations. It must be read in its entirety before any judgment can be passed on it.

It opens with a description of the last meeting between " A. H." and the poet :

> The wind had blown away the rain
> That all day long had soaked the level plain . . .

> The streaming clouds, shot-riddled banners, wet
> With the flickering storm,
> Drifted and smouldered. . . .

The friends look at the orange sea, the flaming firmament, and wonder what they mean—the end of the world or the end of the war ?

> Alas ! it meant not this, it meant not that ;
> It meant that now the last time you and I
> Should look at the golden sky,
> And the dark fields large and flat,
> And smell the evening weather,
> And laugh and talk and wonder both together.

Then begins the keening of the friend for the departed :

> Something is broken which we cannot mend.
> God has done more than take away a friend
> In taking you ; for all that we have left
> Is bruised and irremediably bereft.

There follows a stanza calling up memories of " A. H.'s" early life :

> O liberal heart fast-rooted to the soil,
> O lover of ancient freedom and proud toil,
> Friend of the gipsies and all wandering song . . .
> We wondered could you tarry long,
> And brook for long the cramping street,
> Or would you one day sail for shores unknown ?

The poet thereupon returns to his lament :

> You shall not come again,
> You shall not come to taste the old spring weather,
> To gallop through the soft untrampled heather,
> To bathe and bake your body on the grass.

After which he refers to a dream he had that his

friend was missing, waking only to find it true : at
first he refused to believe it . . . but

> After days of watching, days of lead,
> There came the certain news that you were dead.

Then follows a passage which makes one's blood thrill
with pride to belong to such a race :

> You had died fighting, fighting against odds,
> Such as in war the gods
> Ethereal dared when all the world was young ;
> Such fighting as blind Homer never sung,
> Nor Hector nor Achilles never knew . . .

immediately succeeded by another that recalls the
end of *Samson Agonistes* :

> Here is no waste,
> No burning Might-have-been,
> No bitter after-taste,
> None to censure, none to screen,
> Nothing awry, nor anything misspent ;
> Only content, content beyond content,
> Which hath not any room for betterment.

From this point the poem rises higher and higher
in praise of the dead warrior now " passed a rightful
citizen of the bright commonwealth ablaze beyond
our ken." Surely he is now one with the Knights of
the Table Round, their long-expected guest, among
the chosen few welcomed to that companionship
which hath no end. Then the end comes quietly,
subdued, dwelling on us who are left :

> And then you know that somewhere in the world,
> That shines far off beneath you like a gem,
> They think of you . . .
> You know that they will wipe away their tears ; . . .

> That it is well with them because they know . . .
>   That it is well with you.
>   Among the chosen few,
>   Among the very brave, the very true.

For this poem alone the book would become one of our most treasured possessions. We have learnt to love Captain Baring as a humorist and as an authority on Russian literature : now he takes his place as one of the great poets of our time, and in taking leave of him we reluctantly close the book, only regretful that a long time must pass before we can hope to add another volume to our anthologies of contemporary poetry so good as this.

I cannot pass on to my detailed criticism without commenting on *The Dark Fire*, by W. J. Turner, which contains five exquisite sonnets on *The Pompadour in Art*, which I should like to quote *in extenso*, as they give such a splendid insight into what the younger generation is doing and thinking :

> Would'st thou go back to that white nakedness
> Among the dark trees glinting in the sun,
> Their feet white marble where the cool brooks run,
> Their frail, light fingers flushed with happiness ?
> A white dream in the hot day's breathlessness
> Would'st thou enfold in thy hot, lustful arms ?
> Or would'st thou have no traffic with these charms,
> Dost then indeed love primitive ugliness ?
> " To Nature " is thy cry, " abandon all
> Voluptuous ornament and toilet tricks ! "
> Back to the healthy days before the fall
> When mother Eve her food-foul fingers licks
> And recks not of her heavy shapelessness,
> Her dirty nails, her dark skin's hairiness ?
>
> As for myself, proudly I confess
> I love not matter lumped and unadorned,
> Five feet of flesh is but a cow unhorned

If the quick spirit show not in the dress ;
Blushes are roses in a wilderness,
And pencilled eyebrows are the soul's delight ;
The Moon is not more lovely in the night
Than are white shoulders in a shadowy dress :
And in silk stockings frailly gleam white limbs
Like candles drawing painted butterflies :
And dressed hair gives the soul an earthless flower
That shines into our eager, seeking eyes. . . .

His second sonnet on *Coquetry in Clothes*, and the fourth on *The Wife*, formed to stir clay, but only with the plough, I am perforce bound to omit.

But Beauty is more delicate than the wind,
Trackless and as intangible as light ;
It cannot be pinned down for common sight ;
Like violets in a wood it haunts us blind,
Though scentless trees are mirrored in our mind.
A girl's dress is a lovely wood, a night
Of flowing clouds and shattered, shaken light ;
An arabesque of dust to dust resigned,
With cloud and wood and star, and her bright love :
And in these rags, and in the dust of worlds,
Beauty departed lies as lies the dove
In a few feathers bleaching in the sun—
As the form crumbles so the spirit wanes
And we'll not find it more for all our pains.

It is worth noticing that the wheel has come full circle, and the poet of 1919 shakes hands with the mediæval pre-war age of Rupert Brooke, over the question of the value of material beauty. We may have lost our harsh note, the war has made us more unselfish and mellowed our thoughts, but we still hanker fiercely after material joys.

A word on Captain Paul Bewsher, D.S.C., and I have done. *The Bombing of Bruges* is an intensely

interesting book because it portrays in quite unforgettable verse the attitude of the airman towards life :

> The world looks barren from the air,
>   Its charms are lost—its soul is dead :
> None of a thrush's joy you share,
>   For, when you thunder overhead,
> Below you lies like some great plan
> A hundred miles in one brief span.
>
> You turn no corner with surprise
>   And wonder what your eyes will greet,
> And know not what before you lies,
>   Uncertainty is very sweet—
> To taste new pleasures with each mile
> And see new fields above each stile.
>
> There are no flowers in the sky
>   Which shyly lurk beneath the grass :
> You see no cowslip as you fly,
>   By no gay buttercup you pass :
> No waxen chestnut blossoms bloom
> To cast rich fragrance through the gloom.

And here is his confession of love :

> There are three things I love far more than all :
> The quiet hour of dusk, when all is blue,
> And trees and streets and roofs have one frail hue ;
> Sublime October, when the red leaves fall,
> And bronze chrysanthemums along the wall
> Burn bravely when the other flowers are few ;
> My grey and lovely London, where the view
> Is veiled in mist and crowned with spires tall. . . .

He gives us a vivid description of the thoughts that
pass through the mind of the airman as he bombs
unhappy innocents : he explains how " he who has
knelt high on the night " will lose his mind's perspective.

Every boast
Which man makes will seem so childish, vain,
That he himself will never boast again.
For men will seem so small, their work so frail
To him who has been often wont to sail
Where half a country lay before his eyes
As he gazed downwards from the midnight skies.

The air in Paul Bewsher has its interpreter, the Army its interpreter in Nichols, Sassoon, Ivor Gurney, and a host of other soldier-poets ; it is strange that we should still be waiting for an authentic voice to sing to us of war as visioned by the sailor, but the fact remains that the Navy has, as yet, produced no great, no authentic interpreter.

H

II

J. C. SQUIRE

I WANT to talk of J. C. Squire the poet, but two
things stand in the way, *Books in General*
and *Tricks of the Trade*, neither of which can
be classed as poetry. This most versatile of our
younger writers refuses to be classified as a mere
poet : whatever he touches he adorns, and therefore
it is necessary to notice briefly his achievement as a
critic and a parodist before we aspire to place him
in his proper category. Under the pseudonym of
" Solomon Eagle " he discourses glibly week by week
on " Books in General " in *The New Statesman*, and
under his own name on the same subject in *Land and
Water*. He is perpaps the ablest literary critic alive
and does for literature to-day much what Shaw did
for the theatre in *The Saturday Review* of several
years ago. All is equally good grist to his mill : his
object in *Books in General* (as he too modestly
puts it) " is to produce the sort of book that one
reads in, without tedium, for ten minutes before one
goes to sleep." He does far more than that ; he
makes such unlikely topics as " Who's Who " and
Political Songs matters of great and absorbing interest : he intrigues us afresh with the Baconian
theory and makes us rack our brains to remember a
worse line in poetry than " The beetle booms adown
the glooms and bumps among the clumps," or a more
futile stanza of verse than

Farewell, farewell, bonny St Ives,
May I live to see you again,
Your air preserves people's lives
And you have so little rain.

Occasionally he condescends to act the critic in
the conventional guise. " Mrs Barclay certainly has
skill. Nobody else can write a silly story half so
well as she. . . . The hero of this book [*The Rosary*]
is as generous as he is clever. He can conjure ; he
can make seagulls settle on his shoulder ; and he does
kind actions to widows." And again, " As I read
his [Mr Galsworthy's] books I feel as if I 'were in
some cheerless seaside lodging-house on a wet day."
He sees life as " meanly cruel and pallidly contemp-
tible." " At heart a humanitarian, he has got into a
dismal and costive kind of literary method which
makes him look like a fretful and dyspeptic man who
curls his discontented nostrils at life as though it
were an unpleasing smell. As Ibsen used so often to
remark, there is a great deal wrong with the drains ;
but after all there are other parts of the edifice."
He puts in a good word for Herrick as one of the
greatest small masters in the history of verse, and
in *The Muse in Liquor* quotes G. K. Chesterton's
wonderful drinking song, one stanza of which I hasten
to write out again for the sheer joy of so doing :

Old Noah he had an ostrich farm and fowls on the largest
scale,
He ate his eggs with a ladle in an eggcup big as a
pail,
And the soup he took was Elephant Soup, and the fish he
took was whale,
But they all were small to the cellar he took when he
set out to sail,

And Noah he often said to his wife when he sat down to
dine,
" I don't care where the water goes if it doesn't get into
the wine."

" Lives there," comments Squire, " a man with soul
so dead that when he comes across this . . . he does
not automatically improvise a tune to it and start,
according to his ability, singing it ? " It is splendid
to hear him say of Samuel Butler that " though the
worst of his books is good reading, the *Note-Books* is
as certainly his finest book as Boswell's *Johnson* is
the finest of Johnson's." He has an unerring instinct
for picking out the superlatively good among the
books he is called upon to review.

Sir Arthur Quiller-Couch's *On the Art of Writing*
he speaks of as " extraordinarily good. . . . Even
readers who do not desire to write at all will find
Sir Arthur's jokes very amusing and his criticisms,
general and particular, sound and (what is more un-
usual) new." He is not ashamed to say of Wordsworth, " And then one goes back to his poetry—
and his prose—and hears a voice of almost unsurpassed grandeur speaking the deepest of one's unex-
pressed thoughts, appealing to and drawing out all the
divinest powers in man's nature. . . . He speaks
direct to the labouring intellect and the sensitive
heart ; and the enjoyment of him, if great, is usually
enjoyment of the austerer kind, like mountain-climb-
ing." He defends Henry James : " In an age of sloppy
writing he stood for accuracy of craftsmanship." The
books that Mr Squire would choose for a long stay on
a desert island serve as an index to his character :
Shakespeare, Boswell, Rabelais, and *Morte d'Arthur*.
" There is a strong case for taking a selection of the
more morose and bewildered modern novels . . . or

a judicious selection from Artzybascheff, Mr Cannan, and Mr D. H. Lawrence. For these would do a great deal to reconcile one to one's lonely lot. One would find an everflowing spring of consolation in them. 'After all,' one would say, after each agued page, 'there is a good deal to be said for a desert island.'" On Lyly's *Euphues* he contributes a useful criticism : "What a really judicious critic would do would be to ridicule the style and admire the book." He is young enough to see genius in Mr James Joyce, though he laments that "he can never resist a dunghill. He is not, in fact, quite above the pleasure of being shocking," and he is poet enough to realise that Ralph Hodgson's *The Bull* is one of the finest poems of our generation. In fact, *Books in General* serves as an admirable prelude to a survey of his creative work : it shows us a young, sensitive, humorous genius, fully alive to the main tendencies of contemporary writers of prose and verse, in sympathy with his fellows, and a worshipper at the shrine of the established writers, and not without a love for the slaves of the craft.

Tricks of the Trade shows him as a consummate parodist.

The whole gospel of W. H. Davies becomes clear as one reads :

> I saw some sheep upon some grass,
>   The sheep were fat, the grass was green,
> The sheep were white as clouds that pass,
>   And greener grass was never seen :
> I thought, " Oh, how my bliss is deep,
> With such green grass and such fat sheep ! "

The secret of the source from which Sir Henry Newbolt derived his lilt is at once apparent when we read the following :

Blake and Drake and Nelson are listenin' where they lie,
Four and twenty blackbirds a-bakin' in a pie.

Chesterton's love of paradox and colour is flaunted once again in

With a rumour of ghostly things that pass
With a thunderous pennon of pain,
To a land where the sky is as red as the grass,
And the sun as green as the rain.

It is to be hoped that Canon Rawnsley will never again dare to attempt poetry after reading this merciless parody of his vein :

Britannia mourns for good grey heads that fall,
Survivors from our great Victoria's reign ;
For they were men : take them for all in all
We shall not look upon their like again.

Full justice is done to H. G. Wells' typographical idiosyncrasy, and to Shaw's dramatic qualities. The best part of the book is devoted to " How They Would Have Done It." Here we see Wordsworth rewriting *The Everlasting Mercy*, Swinburne at work on a modern edition of *The Lay of Horatius*, and Masefield out-Masefielding himself on the subject of *Casabianca*.

" You dirty hog," " You snouty snipe,"
" You lump of muck," " You bag of tripe,"
Such, as their latest breath they drew,
The objurgations of the crew.
—— —— —— they roared
As they went tumbling overboard,
Or frizzled like so many suppers
All along the halyard scuppers. . . .
Young Cassy cried again : " Oh, damn !
What an unhappy put I am !

Will nobody go out and search
For dad, who's left me in the lurch ?
For dad, who's left me on the poop,
For dad, who's left me in the soup. . . ."
And all the tender champaign fills
With hyacinths and daffodils,
And on God's azure uplands now
They plough the ploughed fields with a plough.

All the faults of the latter-day Masefield are to be found in this short extract. Gray writing his *Elegy* in the cemetery of Spoon River instead of in that of Stoke Poges gives Mr Squire another splendid chance :

Full many a vice is born to thrive unseen,
    Full many a crime the world does not discuss,
Full many a pervert lives to reach a green
    Replete old age, and so it was with us. . . .
There are two hundred only : yet of these
    Some thirty died of drowning in the river,
Sixteen went mad, ten others had D.T.'s
    And twenty-eight cirrhosis of the liver.

The Lotus Eaters, as written by a very new poet, strikes home :

Bring me six cushions
A yellow one, a green one, a purple one, an orange
    one, an ultramarine one, and a vermilion one,
Colours of which the combination
Pleases my eye.
Bring me
Also
Six lemon squashes
And
A straw. . . .
I have taken off my coat.
I shall now
Loosen
My braces.

Now I am
All right . . .
My God . . .
I do feel lazy !

The Church Catechism as rewritten by Henry James
is intensely funny, but too long to quote, and Lord
Byron's *Passing of Arthur* contains some rhymes that
would have made that poet extremely envious :

" Quite likely," answered Arthur, " and I'm sure
  That I have been so hammered by these swine
To-morrow's sun will find us yet one fewer.
  I prithee take me to yon lonely shrine
Where I may rest and die.   There is no cure
  For men with sixty-seven wounds like mine."
So Bedivere did very firmly grapple
His arm, and led him to the Baptist Chapel.

Again :

    . . . and Bedivere, who had
No nerve at all left now, exclaimed, " My Hat !
I'll never want another job like that ! "

And lastly :

        . . . and the disconsolate knight
In a harsh bitter voice replied, " Oh, damn it all,
I saw a mystic arm, clothed in white samite all."

Even from these disconnected excerpts it is easy
to see that Squire can challenge comparison in verse
with what Max Beerbohm has done in caricature and
A Christmas Garland : by slight exaggeration and
suggestion of the grotesque he can make us realise at
a lightning glance the essential weaknesses of great
masters of poetry.   It is all amazingly clever and
mirth-provoking.

But it is, I imagine, as a poet that Mr Squire would

have us finally pass judgment upon him. In March 1918
he issued a volume of poetry which, in his own words,
" contains all that I do not wish to destroy of the
contents of four volumes of verse."

> So I
> Here offer all I have found :
> A few bright stainless flowers
> And richer, earthlier blooms, and homely grain,
> And roots that grew distorted in the dark,
> And shapes of livid hue and sprawling form
> Dragged from the deepest waters I have searched.
> Most diverse gifts, yet all alike in this :
> They are all the natural products of my mind
> And heart and senses :
> And all with labour grown, or plucked, or caught.

The most obvious criticism to make on turning
over the pages is that there is, as we should have expected, always evidence of a sharpened intellect, but
by no means always a sense of beauty in these verses.
He tries all kinds of tricks with metres, and almost his
most ambitious poem *Rivers* relies very little on rhyme
for its success. This, of course, puts a large burden
on to the thought and vocabulary, and sometimes the
thought and the vocabulary are not strong enough to
stand the extra strain.

One of the reasons why one sees so quickly through
Wordsworth's poverty of thought (when it is poor) is
that he bravely discards all sensuousness of music
and inflated language by the use of which he might
have deceived even the elect. But surely such a man
is worthier of honour than a Swinburne, who so
seduces our senses that we are content to believe
that the juxtaposition of beautiful words really connotes beautiful ideas.

But our business is rather concerned with those

passages which exemplify the best of Squire and
explain the working of his mind :

> Even in peopled streets at times
> A metaphysic arm is thrust
> Through the partitioning fabric thin,
> And tears away the darkening pall
> Cast by the bright phenomenal . . .
> But rarely hold I converse thus
> Where shapes are bright and clamorous,
> More often comes the word divine
> In places motionless and far ;
> Beneath the white peculiar shine
> Of sunless summer afternoons ;
> At eventide on pale lagoons
> Where hangs reflected one pale star ;
> Or deep in the green solitudes
> Of still erect entrancèd woods.

His philosophy is best expressed in his own happiest
(but rather tricky) metre :

Fall the dice, not once or twice, but always, to make the
self-same sum ;
Chance what may, a life's a life and to a single goal must
come ;
Though a man search far and wide, never is hunger
satisfied ;
Nature brings her natural fetters, man is meshed and the
wise are dumb.
O vain all art to assuage a heart with accents of a mortal
tongue,
All earthly words are incomplete and only sweet are the
songs unsung,
Never yet was cause for regret, yet regret must afflict
us all,
Better it were to grasp the world, thwart which this world
is a curtain flung.

There is a *Song* of three verses which, better than
any other of his poems, shows his strange disregard
of more disciplined methods and yet succeeds in
achieving beauty :

There is a wood where the fairies dance
All night long in a ring of mushrooms daintily,
By each tree bole sits a squirrel or a mole,
And the moon through the branches darts.
Light on the grass their slim limbs glance,
Their shadows in the moonlight swing in quiet unison,
And the moon discovers that they all have lovers,
But they never break their hearts.
They never grieve at all for sands that run,
They never know regret for a deed that's done,
And they never think of going to a shed with a gun
At the rising of the sun.

In *The Mind of Man* he seems to be carrying on
a tradition started in the far-off Caroline days by
Donne, and carried on by Rupert Brooke among the
Georgians :

Beneath my skull-bone and my hair,
Covered like a poisonous well,
There is a land ; if you looked there
What you saw you'd quail to tell.
You that sit there smiling, you
Know that what I say is true.

In its clean groves and spacious halls
The quiet-eyed inhabitants
Hold innocent sunny festivals
And mingle in decorous dance ;
Things that destroy, distort, deface,
Come never to that lovely place.

Never could evil enter thither,
It could not live in that sweet air,

> The shadow of an ill deed must wither
> And fall away to nothing there.
> You would say as there you stand
> That all was beauty in the land.

But there are other compartments in the mind of man :

> Here in this reedy marsh of green
> And oily pools, swarm insects fat
> And birds of prey and beasts obscene,
> Things that the traveller shudders at,
> All cunning things that creep and fly
> To suck men's blood until they die.

And there are worse, more " purulent " places than these. *A Reasonable Protestation* again carries us a few steps further towards understanding his philosophic point of view :

> Thirsty as you, perhaps, I long
> For courtyards of eternal song, . . .
> But though I hope with strengthening faith
> To taste when I have traversed death
> The unimaginable sweetness
> Of certitude of such concreteness,
> How should I draw the hue and scope
> Of substances I only hope
> Or blaze upon a paper screen
> The evidence of things not seen ? . . .
> I see what I can, not what I will. . . .
> I see the symbols God hath drest. . . .
> Did I now glibly insolent
> Chart the ulterior firmament,
> Would you not know my words were lies,
> Where not my testimonial eyes
> Mortal or spiritual lodge,
> Mere uncorroborated fudge ?
> Praise me . . . that I what I see and feel I write,
> Read what I can in this dim light
> Granted to me in nether night. . . .

I have not lacked my certainties,
I have not haggard moaned the skies,
Nor waged unnecessary strife
Nor scorned nor overvalued life.
And though you say my attitude
Is questioning, concede my mood
Does never bring to tongue or pen
Accents of gloomy modern men. . . .

His *Ode : in a Restaurant* stands out from most
of the rest of the book, and will doubtless find its way
into future anthologies :

In this dense hall of green and gold,
Mirrors and lights and steam, there sit
Two hundred munching men ;
While several score of others flit
Like scurrying beetles over a fen,
With plates in fanlike spread . . .
Gobble, gobble, toil and trouble.
Soul !   This life is very strange,
And circumstances very foul
Attend the belly's stormy howl.

He compares the noise of the band to " keen-drawn
threads of ink dropped into a glass of water, which
curl and relax and soften and pass."   Disgusted with
the sight of people eating he yet calls upon his soul
to remember that

They also have hot blood, quick thought,
And try to do the things they ought,
They also have hearts that ache when strung,
And sigh for days when they were young . . .
Self, you can imagine nought
Of all the battles they have fought,
All the labours they have done,
All the journeys they have run.

Nay, more, the very food provides romance :

For this one meal
Ten thousand Indian hamlets stored their yields,
Manchurian peasants sweltered in their fields,
And Greeks drove carts to Patras . . .
To fabricate these things have been marchings and
    slaughters,
The sun has toiled and the moon has moved the waters . . .
    . . . paths have been hewn
Through forests where for uncounted years nor sun nor
    moon
Have penetrated . . . wrinkled sailors have shouted at
    shouting gales
In the huge Pacific, and battled around the Horn . . .
The mutton which these platters fills
Grazed upon a thousand hills ;
This bread so square and white and dry
Once was corn that sang to the sky ;
And all these spruce, obedient wines
Flowed from the vatted fruit of vines
That trailed, a bright maternal host,
The warm Mediterranean coast . . .
O wonderful procession fore-ordained by God !
Wonderful in unity, wonderful in diversity. . . .
    I was born for that reason,
        With muscles, heart and eyes,
    To watch each following season,
        To work and to be wise.

The whole poem is a wonderful attempt to grasp
at a problem which must have obsessed us all as we
have sat alone and aloof in some large restaurant,
letting our brain play on the reasons for all this
seeming orgy and waste.

On a Friend Recently Dead contains some good
lines, notably :

You are not here, but I am here alone.
And evening falls, fusing tree, water and stone
Into a violet cloth, and the frail ash-tree hisses

With a soft sharpness like a fall of mounded grain. . . .
And I, I see myself as one of a heap of stones
Wetted a moment to life as the flying wave goes over,
Onward and never returning, leaving no mark behind.

I suppose *The Lily of Malud* is the most famous
poem in the book, and certainly in this magic narrative
he justifies his use of his extraordinary metre :

The lily of Malud is born in secret mud.
It is breathed like a word in a little dark ravine
Where no bird was ever heard and no beast was ever seen,
And the leaves are never stirred by the panther's velvet
   sheen.

This lily blooms once a year and dies in a night :

And when that night has come, black small-breasted maids,
With ecstatic terror dumb, steal fawn-like through the
   shades . . .
                    From the doors the maidens creep,
Tiptoe over dreaming curs, soft, so soft, that not one stirs,
And stand curved and a-quiver, like bathers by a river,
Looking at the forest wall, groups of slender naked girls,
Whose black bodies shine like pearls where the moon-
   beams fall.

They move

Onwards on the scarce-felt path, with quick and desperate
   breath,
For their circling fingers dread to caress some slimy head,
Or to touch the icy shape of a hunched and hairy ape,
And at every step they fear in their very midst to hear
A lion's rending roar or a tiger's snore . . .
   And when things swish or fall, they shiver but dare not
   call.

Having beheld the vision they return home and are
as they ever were :

Save only for a rare shade of trouble in their eyes.
And the surly thick-lipped men, as they sit about their
    huts
Making drums out of guts, grunting gruffly now and then,
Carving sticks of ivory, stretching shields of wrinkled skin,
Smoothing sinister and thin squatting gods of ebony,
Chip and grunt and do not see.   But each mother, silently,
Longer than her wont stays shut in the dimness of her hut,

trying to remember

Something sorrowful and far, something sweet and vaguely
    seen
Like an early evening star when the sky is pale green . . .
Something holy in the past that came and did not last.
But she knows not what it was.

This poem as has much "atmosphere" in it as *The
Ancient Mariner*, and improves with every reading.

But for myself I prefer *To a Bulldog* to any other
poem that Mr Squire has written or is ever likely
to write.   It is by far the most effective war-poem
of its kind, its very simplicity adding a million-fold
to its poignancy.   It stands the test of being read
aloud without, as he himself says of some one else's
poetry, making you feel a fool at being let down in
any line :

We sha'n't see Willy any more, Mamie,
He won't be coming any more :
He came back once and again and again,
But he won't get leave any more.

We looked from the window and there was his cab,
And we ran downstairs like a streak,
And he said "Hullo, you bad dog," and you crouched to
    the floor,
Paralysed to hear him speak,
And then let fly at his face and his chest
Till I had to hold you down,

While he took off his cap and his gloves and his coat,
And his bag and his thonged Sam Browne. . . .

Then follows a picture of the dog's master on leave fondling all the drawings he had left behind, and opening the cupboard to look at his belongings every time he came :

But now I know what a dog doesn't know . . .
And all your life you will never know
What I wouldn't tell you even if I could,
That the last time we waved him away
Willy went for good. . . .

He ruminates over the good days that are now over for ever :

When summer comes again,
And the long sunsets fade,
We shall have to go on playing the feeble game for two
That since the war we've played.

And though you run expectant as you always do
To the uniforms we meet,
You'll never find Willy among all the soldiers
In even the longest street. . . .
I must sit, not speaking, on the sofa,
While you lie asleep on the floor ;
For he's suffered a thing that dogs couldn't dream of,
And he won't be coming here any more.

I pass over *Under*, which is an unintelligible nightmare, and the long poem on *Rivers*, which almost succeeds in being great in spite of its lack of rhyme, and he finishes with a sonnet which many people place at the head of his achievement :

I shall make beauty out of many things :
Lights, colours, motions, sky and earth and sea,
The soft unbosoming of all the springs
Which that inscrutable hand allows to me,

I

Odours of flowers, sounds of smitten strings,
   The voice of many a wind in many a tree,
Fields, rivers, moors, swift feet and floating wings,
   Rocks, caves, and hills that stand and clouds that flee.
Men also and women, beautiful and dear,
   Shall come and pass and leave a fragrant breath ;
And my own heart, laughter and pain and fear,
   The majesties of evil and of death ;
But never, never shall my verses trace
The loveliness of your most lovely face.

A poem which taken together with *Envoi* may well be said to place Mr Squire high among contemporary poets :

Beloved, when my heart's awake to God
And all the world becomes his testimony,
In you I most do see, in your brave spirit,
Erect and certain, flashing deeds of light,
A pure jet from the fountain of all being,
A scripture clearer than all else to read.
And when belief was dead and God a myth,
And the world seemed a wandering mote of evil,
Endurable only by its impermanence,
And all the planets perishable urns
Of perished ashes, to you alone I clung
Amid the unspeakable loneliness of the universe.

III

SIEGFRIED SASSOON

IT seems a far cry from the old days of the Bullingdon, the Rousers, and the Loder, when whips were cracked in " Peck," and young men rejoiced in the hunt of the fox with the Bicester and the " Drag," to the war-poetry of 1917, but Mr Sassoon has effectually bridged the distance.

In *The Old Huntsman and Other Poems* he has collected some seventy-odd poems, which mark him out as one of the little group of young warriors who felt impelled to put their impressions of war into verse, one with them in his appreciation of the beautiful and his curiosity about the dead, but not in the least like any other of them in his manner of writing or the conclusions at which he arrives about the effect which fighting has upon him.

In the first place he is colloquial, pellucidly clear, simple, terse, and straightforward. He dwells rather on the ironic side of it all ; as a satirist in verse he excels. He, least of all the younger poets, can find glamour and nobility in the war. He paints ruthlessly what he sees, and what he sees is no thin red line or charge of heavy or light brigade. For the most part he regards war as an intolerable waste of good material.

To any Dead Officer who left School for the Army in 1914, he writes :

Good-bye, old lad ! Remember me to God,
And tell Him that our Politicians swear

They won't give in till Prussian Rule's been trod
Under the heel of England. . . . Are you there ? . . .
Yes . . . and the War won't end for at least two years ;
But we've got stacks of men . . . I'm blind with tears,
Staring into the dark.   Cheero !
1 wish they'd killed you in a decent show.

This reads amazingly like prose, but the white heat
of his indignation raises the simple theme of his
thought up out of the ruck of ordinary commonplace, and the very ordinariness of it takes on the
guise of something that is unforgettable ; it may not
be poetry, according to the critic's canon, but it
strikes home and we feel, with the writer, " blind
with tears " at the purposelessness of such wanton
destruction.

In the poem which gives the title to the book we
are shown an old huntsman living over again by his
cottage fireside great days of old with the hounds.
He ponders on his probable future when he is dead :

Hell was the coldest scenting land I've known,
And both my whips were always lost, and hounds
Would never get their heads down ; and a man
On a great yawing chestnut trying to cast 'em
While I was in a corner pounded by
The ugliest hog-backed stile you've clapped your eyes on.
There was an iron-spiked fence round all the coverts,
And civil-spoken keepers I couldn't trust,
And the main earth unstopped.

There will be many lovers of the chase who will sympathise with that picture and turn with a thrill of
further appreciation to this :

I've come to think of God as something like
The figure of a man the old Duke was
When I was turning hounds to Nimrod King,
Before his Grace was took so bad with gout,

And had to quit the saddle. Tall and spare,
Clean-shaved and grey, with shrewd, kind eyes that
   twinkled
And easy walk . . . Lord God might be like that,
Sitting alone in a great room of books
Some evening after hunting.

Already we can see why Mr Sassoon dedicated his
book to Thomas Hardy.   There is the same passionate
love of the countryside, the same sympathetic vision
of the rustic, the same keen irony and Swift-like
detestation of frippery and unreality.

Mr Sassoon, like many other subalterns taking a
hand in the " great game," is filled with loathing at
war under modern conditions, and he is too courageous
to pretend that it is otherwise with him.   He can
even dare to sympathise with and openly print the
sentiments of the one-legged man, which would certainly be censored or else howled down by nine-tenths
of the fire-eating civilian population :

Propped on a stick he viewed the August weald ;
Squat orchard trees and oasts with painted cowls ;
A homely, tangled hedge, a corn-stooked field,
With sound of barking dogs and farmyard fowls.
And he'd come home again to find it more
Desirable than ever it was before.
How right it seemed that he should reach the span
Of comfortable years allowed to man !
Splendid to eat and sleep and choose a wife,
Safe with his wound, a citizen of life.
He hobbled blithely through the garden gate,
And thought : " Thank God they had to amputate ! "

It is just as well that when future generations find
themselves forgetting, amid the calm, slack waters of
peace, the horrors that belong to war, they should

have the testimony and warning before them of some
one who knew, having seen and felt and suffered, and
in his suffering told what he endured in no uncertain
voice.

Mr Sassoon is at one again with all the other poets
of his time when he comes to write about his dead
comrades. The unanimity with which the modern
soldier-poets sing of the mingling of their lost companions with the glories of nature is worth the
psychic's earnest attention : it is a phenomenon not
the least marvellous in an age of amazing discoveries :

> Their faces are the fair, unshrouded night,
> And planets are their eyes, their ageless dreams.
> Tenderly stooping earthward from their height,
> They wander in the dusk with chanting streams :
> And they are dawn-lit trees, with arms up-flung,
> To hail the burning heavens they left unsung.

His anger at the war itself is as nothing compared
with the fury into which he lashes himself when he
writes of the way that the war is treated at home, in
the music-halls for example. Perhaps the supreme
example of this is to be found in *Blighters* :

> The House is crammed : tier beyond tier they grin
> And cackle at the Show, while prancing ranks
> Of harlots shrill the chorus, drunk with din ;
> " We're sure the Kaiser loves the dear old Tanks ! "
> I'd like to see a Tank come down the stalls,
> Lurching to rag-time tunes, or " Home, Sweet Home,"
> And there'd be no more jokes in music-halls
> To mock the riddled corpses round Bapaume.

In a poem, entitled *Stretcher Case*, " dedicated to
Edward Marsh," he depicts the impression which
England makes on the returned casualty in a quite
new light :

But was he back in Blighty ?   Slow he turned,
Till in his heart thanksgiving leapt and burned.
There shone the blue serene, the prosperous land,
Trees, cows, and hedges ; skipping these, he scanned
Large, friendly names that change not with the year,
Lung Tonic, Mustard, Liver Pills, and Beer.

But it is not only upon the war that Mr Sassoon
dwells : he has that deep passion for beauty without
which no poet can hope for a permanent place in our
hearts, beauty whether expressed in the petals of a
rose or a sky at dawn or any other natural glory :
this on rain is typical :

Rain ; he could hear it rustling through the dark ;
Fragrance and passionless music woven as one ;
Warm rain on drooping roses ; pattering showers
That soak the woods ; not the harsh rain that sweeps
Behind the thunder, but a trickling peace
Gently and slowly washing life away.

This is not only beautiful, but true. Mr Sassoon
fulfils Wordsworth's conditions of keeping his eye on
the object, and he heightens his effect by the strict
accuracy of each stroke.

Many poets have (of late) tried to describe in poetry
the romance of the train, but in *Morning Express*
Mr Sassoon has, I think, eclipsed the others, partly
because of his literal precision, his selection, and his
simplicity, partly also because of his economy in the
use of words : it is a severely reticent picture, austere,
exact, and withal beautiful. There is something of
the Pre-Raphaelite in his work here :

Along the wind-swept platform, pinched and white
The travellers stand in pools of wintry light,
Offering themselves to morn's long, slanting arrows.
The train's due ; porters trundle laden barrows.

The train steams in, volleying resplendent clouds
Of sun-blown vapour. . . .
Boys, indolent-eyed, from baskets leaning back,
Question each face ; a man with a hammer steals
Stooping from coach to coach ; with clang and clack,
Touches and tests and listens to the wheels . . .
       . . . the monster grunts : " Enough ! "
Tightening his load of links with pant and puff.
Under the arch, then forth into blue day,
Glide the processional windows on their way,
And glimpse the stately folk who sit at ease
To view the world like kings taking the seas
In prosperous weather : drifting banners tell
Their progress to the counties : with them goes
The clamour of their journeying. . . .

But by far the most precious quality about Mr Sassoon is that in spite of his righteous anger there is behind all this an indomitable courage and a splendid optimism :

I keep such music in my brain
No din this side of death can quell,—
Glory exulting over pain,
And beauty, garlanded in hell.

Like his own old huntsman and Rupert Brooke he shows very clearly that he is a real lover of life, and furthermore that he is a devout lover of life.   For

Where's the use of life and being glad
If God's not in your gladness ?

he asks not once nor twice but many times in these poems ; " Jesus keep me joyful when I pray."   There is an ever-present hopefulness and joy in his work which charms us and rings all the truer because we feel so certain that this hopefulness and this joy are not an insecure refuge, built upon insincerity and lies, but found after many searchings of heart and much striving to winnow the chaff from the wheat in the harvest of life.

Poets of his calibre are rare indeed : so many of those who showed promise of great things, like Francis Ledwidge and Rupert Brooke, are now silent.   It will be the fervent wish of all those who read Mr Sassoon's work that he may be spared to fulfil the prophecies which the critics have ventured upon with regard to his powers, and continue to sing even more sweetly, more surely now that peace has returned.

Even now, above the tumult and the din of the aftermath of war, his voice rings out, irrepressible, strangely elated and clear :

> The world's my field, and I'm the lark,
> Alone with upward song, alone with light.

Are we not justified in hoping for even more haunting melodies, even grander poems when quietude descends upon the land ?

IV

ROBERT NICHOLS

IN any discussion or criticism of modern art it is impossible to avoid imagining what the artist would have achieved had he not been swept into the swirl and eddy of war. In the Napoleonic era it seemed possible to pursue one's craft as though no world-shaking conflict were taking place. Not so to-day. Far too many of our most promising young writers have been killed, cut off in the middle of their song.

No man can pretend to view life as he saw it a few years ago : whether we like it or not our very souls are altogether changed, in many instances not for the better. It is, however, a truism that the poet thrives best when he is suffering most ; consequently not a few whose names were unknown in 1914 found themselves on the battlefield and leapt into fame as poets.

High among these I would place Robert Nichols. So new a poet is he that you will search in vain for his name in any anthology published before Mr Edward Marsh included some of his work in the third volume of *Georgian Poetry* (1915–1917).

But in the volume of poems called *Ardours and Endurances* there is sufficient warrant for my assertion that he is one of the major poets of the day.

At the end of the most ambitious poem of the book (it occupies nearly seventy pages), *A Faun's Holiday,* he writes :

> There is something in me divine,
> And it must out. For this was I
> Born, and I know I cannot die
> Until, perfected pipe, thou send
> My utmost : God, which is the end.

In other words, like so many other poets, he recognises that he is one of those rare beings chosen to voice the delight of life, and that he is bound to fulfil his mission before death can claim him.

" Beauty, be thou my star ! " he sings in another poem. Not that he need have said so in so many words, for dull must he be of vision who cannot realise from the very first pages of this book that he pursues his one aim with a persistent zeal and a wealth of diction that will ensure his reaching heights undreamt of by most other poets of our time. But he warns us that

> Those whose love but shines a hint
> Fainter than the far sea's glint
> To the inland gazer's sight—
> These alone, and but in part
> Guess of what my songs are spun,
> And Who holds communion
> Subtly with my troubled heart . . .
> One Day, or maybe one Night —
> Living ? Dying ?—I shall see
> The Rose open gloriously
> On its heart of living light.
> Know what any bird may mean,
> Meteor in my heart shall rest,
> Spelled on my brain blaze th' unguessed
> Words of the rainbow's dazzling sheen.

The volume is divided up into three books : the first dealing entirely with the war. In Part I he tells of the summons :

Honour it is that calls : canst thou forget
 Once thou wert strong ?   Listen ; the solemn call
Sounds but this once again.   Put by regret
 For summons missed, or thou hast missed them all.

Then comes the approach, the distant boom of the guns :

Nearer and ever nearer . . .
My body, tired but tense,
Hovers 'twixt vague pleasure
And tremulous confidence.
Arms to have and to use them,
And a soul to be made
Worthy if not worthy ;
If afraid, unafraid.

These last four lines sum up the gospel of the soldier before his initiation into war more aptly and perfectly than many volumes of so-called battle psychology have been able to.

When the soul has been made worthy there appears to the proved soldier a vision : he becomes articulate. He discovers what war really means, which is not at all what he expected or the civilian would believe. All these young men have given utterance to what they have seen, and in each case it is the same.   We have, for instance, the testimony of Hugh Walpole (perhaps the most brilliant novelist of our time), who says :

" War is made up of a million million past thoughts, past scenes, streets of little country towns, lonely hills, dark sheltered valleys, the wide space of the sea, the crowded traffic of New York, London, Berlin, yes, and of smaller things than that, of little quarrels, of dances at Christmas time, of walks at night, of dressing for dinner, of walking in the morning, of meeting old friends, of sicknesses, theatres, Church services, slums, cricket-matches, children, rides on a tram, baths on a hot morning, sudden unpleasant truth from a friend, momentary consciousness of God. . . ."

That is the vision vouchsafed to the prose-writer, but the poet goes even deeper. Robert Nichols only voices the general feeling of all the war-poets when he writes :

> Now that I am ta'en away,
> And may not see another day,
> What is it to my eye appears ?
> What sound rings in my stricken ears ?
> Not even the voice of any friend
> Or eyes beloved-world-without-end,
> But scenes and sounds of the countryside
> In far England across the tide . . .
> The gorse upon the twilit down,
> The English loam so sunset brown,
> The bowed pines and the sheep-bells' clamour.
> The wet, lit lane and the yellow-hammer,
> The orchard and the chaffinch song,
> Only to the Brave belong.
> And he shall lose their joy for aye
> If their price he cannot pay,
> Who shall find them dearer far
> Enriched by blood after long war.

But in *Fulfilment* he has penetrated even deeper than the rest of his school, and left an imperishable memorial of the effect of war upon one great soul :

> Was there love once ?   I have forgotten her.
>   Was there grief once ? grief yet is mine.
> Other loves I have, men rough, but men who stir
>   More grief, more joy, than love of thee and thine.

Faces cheerful, full of whimsical mirth,
  Lined by the wind, burned by the sun ;
Bodies enraptured by the abounding earth,
  As whose children we are brethren ; one.
Was there love once ?   I have forgotten her.
  Was there grief once ? grief yet is mine.
O loved, living, dying, heroic soldier,
  All, all, my joy, my grief, my love are thine !

In the description of the actual fighting itself Mr Nichols is not so happy. Nothing, not even the greatness of the occasion can make poetry out of this staccato realism :

Deafness.   Numbness.   The loudening tornado.
Bullets.   Mud.   Stumbling and skating.
My voice's strangled shout :
" Steady pace, boys ! "
The still light.   Gladness.
" Look, sir.   Look out ! "
Ha, ha !   Bunched figures waiting,
Revolver levelled quick !
Flick !   Flick !
Red as blood.
Germans, Germans.
Good !   O good !
Cool madness.

It is pleasant to turn from this to his Sonnet on the Dead, where he again joins hands with Rupert Brooke and all the other poets of the war who have seen their friends die before their faces, times without number :

They have not gone from us.   O no ! they are
  The inmost essence of each thing that is
Perfect for us ; they flame in every star ;
  The trees are emerald with their presences.

They are not gone from us ; they do not roam
  The flow and turmoil of the lower deep,
But have now made the whole wide world their home,
  And in its loveliness themselves they steep.
They fail not ever ; theirs is the diurn
  Splendour of sunny hill and forest grave ;
In every rainbow's glittering drop they burn ;
  They dazzle in the massed clouds' architecture ;
They chant on every wind, and they return
  In the long roll of any deep blue wave.

It must not be supposed, however, that Mr Nichols is a war-poet only. Long before the war, in Oxford days, he was already haunted by the spell of beauty, and had answered the call.

In his short introduction he quotes Mark Liddell on the nature of the poet, and of what English poetry consists, to defend his attitude, which is that the poet is after all only one of us : he speaks our language better than we do merely because he is more skilful with it than we are : " Given a little more sensitiveness to external stimuli, a little more power of associating ideas . . . a sense of rhythm somewhat keener than the average—given these things we should be poets too. . . ." He warns us that English poetry is not a rhythm of sound, but a rhythm of ideas : he who would think of it as a pleasing arrangement of vocal sounds has missed all chance of ever understanding its meaning. There awaits him only the barren generalities of a foreign prosody, tedious, pedantic, fruitless.

In other words, it is the firm ground of truth we have to search for in his work, not a magic manipulation of iambuses, spondees, dactyls, and tribrachs.

In spite of his warning, however, we find ourselves again and again delighted at the lilt and lovely melody of his songs :

Kingcups flare beside the stream,
  That not glides now, but runs brawling ;
That wet roses are asteam
  In the sun and will be falling,
Say the chestnut sheds his bloom ;
  Honey from straw hivings oozes ;
There's a nightjar in the coombe ;
  Venus nightly burns, and chooses
Most to blaze above my room ;
  That the laggard 'tis that loses.

His philosophy is akin to that of Wordsworth :

First must the spirit cast aside
This world's and next his own poor pride
And learn the universe to scan
More as a flower, less as a man.

Occasionally he almost captures an Elizabethan
lightness and limpidity in his lyrics, as in

Our fast-flickering feet shall twinkle,
And our golden anklets tinkle,
While fair arms in aery sleeves
Shiver as the poplar's leaves.

Frequently he shows traces of a careful training in
the school of Milton. We should be inclined to place
that poet as far the most prominent among those
who have influenced Mr Nichols. He has inherited
a splendid vision and developed an intense emotional
realisation of the meaning of beauty. In his war
poems he has sounded depths that no other war-
poet has touched. He can be realistic and grim when
occasion calls for it : he understands the mind of the
soldier completely, and brings a sympathetic humour
to the study of the warrior temperament. But it is
in his passion for natural scenery that we learn to
love him best and see him most clearly :

So when my dying eyes have loved the trees
Till with huge tears turned blind,
When the vague ears for the last time have hearkened
To the cool stir of the long evening breeze,
The blackbird's tireless call,
Having drunk deep of earth-scent strong and kind,
Come then, O Death, and let my day be darkened.
I shall have had my all.

V

DORA SIGERSON

MRS CLEMENT SHORTER was killed by
the war.

Summer with her pretty ways now is taking leave of me,
Slow the ling'ring roses fall, softly sings the honey-bee,
How can I go back again to the horrors of the town,
Where the husky voice of war fiercely echoes up and down ?

Other women have had to suffer, but most of them
came through : Dora Sigerson not only did not come
through, but she gave vent to piteous cries of anguish
which rise through their pathos to heights of real
poetry :

But, God ! to dream, to wake, and dream again,
Where screams red war in harvesting dead men.
Ah ! dream of home, of love, of joy, all thrilling,
To wake once more to killing, killing, killing.

She was obsessed by the horror of the whole thing :
naturally fragile she could not withstand the avalanche
of blood : she had not the capacity that so many of
us had of becoming more and more hardened by the
holocaust : first there came the inevitable breakdown
and illness which she has interpreted for us in unforgettable verse in *The Hours of Illness* :

How slow creeps time ! I hear the midnight chime,
And now late revellers prepare for sleep ;
A last gay voice rings in a passing rhyme,
And past my door the anxious footsteps creep.

146

The little clocks from hidden places call
'Tis one o'clock ; downstairs the big clock's bell
Tolls deep, and then comes forth the merry chime,
Like laughing children calling, " All is well ! "

'Tis two o'clock !   Why in the lonesome room
This creak and crack, if there be no one here ?
Whose feet disturb the loose board of the floor ?
Whose secret presence fills the dark with fear ?

'Tis three o'clock !   O God, when comes sweet rest ?
To sleep, to sleep, within this sleeping house,
Where all could wake with less fatigue than I,
Where no one stirs save some adventurous mouse !

'Tis four o'clock !   Death stands at my bed-head
In meditation deep, with hidden face,
And I alone—a coward alone, afraid,
Lest he from his dread brow his shroud displace.

'Tis five o'clock !   Within the empty room,
Threading their way, the happy dead appear,
More living than the quick in this still night—
All whom I loved or ever held me dear.

'Tis six o'clock !   Death moves from my bed-head.
Flings high the shroud from off his hidden face.
" O gentle Death !   O fair and lovely shade,
Lift this sad spirit from its dwelling-place ! "

The clock at seven !   Hear the milkman come.
Loud clangs the gate ; the room is chill and dark.
The maid, reluctant rising, frees the door ;
A dog runs forth with shrill, offensive bark.

The clock strikes eight !   The curtains pulled aside
Let in the light, so cold, so bleak, so grey.
From their dark hiding come familiar things,
And through my window looks another day.

There will be few (how lucky they) who will not
at once respond to the feelings herein expressed : the
sweet simplicity of it is reminiscent of Cowper in his
truest vein. That really is her secret : she had a
purity of mind like one of Shakespeare's later heroines :
she sings as one would expect Perdita or Miranda to
sing had they been gifted with tongues :

> If by my tomb some day you careless pass,
>   A moment grieved by coming on my name,
> Ah ! kneel awhile upon the tender grass
>   In some short prayer acquitting me of blame.
>
> If I reached not your pinnacle of right,
>   Or fell below your standard of desire,
> If to my heart alone my hopes were white,
>   And my soul built its own celestial fire,
>
> Then let your grief, be it a single tear,
>   Upon your cheek in tender sorrow fall,
> Forget where I did fail ; keep only dear
>   The deeds for which you loved me over all.

There are two famous dirges in our language written
to be sung over Fidele's tomb, but if Imogen could
have phrased it thus, in such a manner would she
have sung her swan-song. Christina Rossetti approaches most nearly among the moderns to this
spirit : and what is the spirit ? Simplicity and
sincerity perfectly commingled in a haunting musical
refrain :

> I want to talk to thee of many things
> Or sit in silence when the robin sings
> His little song, when comes the winter bleak
> I want to sit beside thee, cheek by cheek.

I want to hear thy voice my name repeat,
To fill my heart with echoes ever sweet ;
I want to hear thy love come calling me,
I want to seek and find but thee, but thee.

I want to talk to thee of little things
So fond, so frail, so foolish that one clings
To keep them ours—who could but understand
A joy in speaking them, thus hand in hand

Beside the fire ; our joys, our hopes, our fears,
Our secret laughter, or unchidden tears ;
Each day old dreams come back with beating wings,
I want to speak of these forgotten things.

I want to feel thy arms around me pressed,
To hide my weeping eyes upon thy breast ;
I want thy strength to hold and comfort me
For all the grief I had in losing thee.

Such a poem as this really does defy analysis. It
would be in some degree comparable with applying
the cold knife of scientific criticism to a passionate
love-letter. These poignant heart-cries are either real,
in which case all criticism is absurd, or they are false,
in which case they are beneath criticism : one's only
object after reading *I Want to Talk to Thee* is to give
it to as many friends as possible that they may derive
from it the same æsthetic thrill that we experienced
when we first chanced upon it.

No wonder Meredith, Swinburne, Francis Thompson, Theodore Watts-Dunton, Masefield, Katharine
Tynan, Lascelles Abercrombie, and most of the other
poets of our own and the last generation unite in hailing
her as one of themselves. For gentleness and delicacy
she o'ertops them all.

Bring to me white roses, roses, pinks, and lavender,
Sweet stock and gillyflowers, poppies mauve and red,
Bee-flowers and mignonette, with blue forget-me-not—
I would make a coverlet for my narrow bed.

Bring me no silken cloth, velvet sheen or satin shine,
Gossamer of woven lace, gold and silver thread,
Purple deep and dove, and grey, through my idle fingers
    fall,
Bidding me in patient hours make a patchwork spread.

Since I must go forth alone, far beyond the roof-tree's
    shade,
Out into the open soon lonely there to lie,
What want I of silken cloth woven by the hands of men ?
Time would soon despoil me there as he passed me by.

Bring to me white roses then, roses, pinks, and lavender,
Sweet stock and gillyflowers, poppies gold and red,
Bee-flowers and mignonette and blue forget-me-not,
So I have a coverlet for my narrow bed.

Are not these the very accents of the innocent
Ophelia ? It is almost uncanny how often Dora
Sigerson merges herself into a Shakespearean heroine.
But the figure I conjure up when I think of her is
not Shakespearean : I see a lonely, tragic figure,
unable to find consolation even among those who
loved her most dearly, broken in pieces by the
savagery of war and the wreck of her ambitions for
her own country. To me *The Comforters* is her finest
achievement because it is her cry from the cross ;
so surcharged is it with emotion, that it is difficult to
read it dry-eyed. It is the hymn for all time for the
sorrowful and the broken-hearted :

When I crept over the hill, broken with tears,
    When I crouched down on the grass, dumb in despair,

I heard the soft croon of the wind bend to my ears,
   I felt the light kiss of the wind touching my hair.

When I stood lone on the height my sorrow did speak,
   As I went down the hill, I cried and I cried,
The soft little hands of the rain stroking my cheek,
   The kind little feet of the rain ran by my side.

When I went to thy grave, broken with tears,
   When I crouched down in the grass, dumb in despair,
I heard the sweet croon of the wind soft in my ears,
   I felt the kind lips of the wind touching my hair.

When I stood lone by thy cross, sorrow did speak.
   When I went down the long hill, I cried and I cried.
The soft little hands of the rain stroked my pale cheek,
   The kind little feet of the rain ran by my side.

No anthology of English poetry in the future will be complete without this priceless, flawless gem. Whatever else of hers is imperfect, this at any rate is as nearly perfect as any poem can be. There can be but few written in the last twenty years worthy to be ranged with it. *On the Other Side* is scarcely less memorable.

What will you do through the waiting days,
   What will my darling do ?
Will you sleep, or wander in those strange ways
   Until I can come to you ?

Do you cry at the door as I cry here,
   Death's door that lies between ?
Do you plead in vain for my love, my dear,
   As you stand by my side unseen ?

Who will comfort your difficult ways
   That were hard to understand,
When I who knew you through all your days,
   Can give you no helping hand ?

When I who loved you no word can speak,
  Though your ghost should cry to me,
Can give no help, though my heart should break
  At the thought of your agony.

You were shy of strangers—and who will come
  As you stand there lone and new,
Through the long years when my lips are dumb
  What will my darling do ?

But it is the war that takes her and breaks her,
and it is on a note of war that one is forced to take
one's leave of her :

God, the earth shakes with it !
Down in the hellish pit,
Where the red river ran,
Hatred of man to man ;
Maddened they rush to kill,
That but their single will ;
Strangle or bayonet him !
Trample him life and limb
Into the awful mire ;
Break him with knife or fire !
So that we know he lie
Dead to the smiling sky.
And in a thousand years
It will be all the same.
Which of us was to blame ?
What will it matter then ?
Over the sleeping men
Grass will so softly grow
No one would ever know
Of the dark crimson stain,
Of all the hate and pain
That once had fearful birth
In the black secret earth.
Ah ! in a thousand years
Time will forget our tears.

Babes in their golden hour
Seeking some hidden flower
Will, in those years afar,
Play on the fields of war;
And as they laughing roam
Mothers will call them home;
Laden with fruit or flower
Run they at twilight hour . . .
Over the meadow grass
Slow the moon's shadows pass.
Only the chirp of bird
· From the deep hedge is heard.
This in a thousand years
Payment of blood and tears,
Horrors we dare not name,
It will be all the same.
What is the value then
To all those sleeping men?
It will be all the same,
Passion and grief and blame.
This in the years to be,
My God, the tragedy!

Here we see Rachel weeping for her children,
refusing to be comforted in very truth: forgotten or
dismissed is the glamour: only the gnawing horror
of pain and separation remains behind: if it is the
test of genius that it feels more acutely than the
rest of us, Dora Sigerson must stand at the head of
the geniuses of our time.

A HUNDRED AND SEVENTY CHINESE POEMS

TO read Mr Arthur Waley's translation of ancient Chinese poetry after seeing some such ridiculous presentation of the East as we get in *Mr Wu* and *The Chinese Puzzle* is to escape from inept, ludicrous falsities into the clear light of day.

" Those who wish to assure themselves that they will lose nothing by ignoring Chinese literature, often ask the question : ' Have the Chinese a Homer, an Æschylus, a Shakespeare or Tolstoy ? ' The answer must be that China has no epic and no dramatic literature of importance. The novel exists and has merits, but never became the instrument of great writers. . . . In mind, as in body, the Chinese were for the most part torpid mainlanders. Their thoughts set out on no strange quests and adventures, just as their ships discovered no new continents. To most Europeans the momentary flash of Athenian questioning will seem worth more than all the centuries of Chinese assent. Yet we must recognise that for thousands of years the Chinese maintained a level of rationality and tolerance that the West might well envy. . . . In the poems of Po Chü-i no close reasoning or philosophic subtlety will be discovered ; but a power of candid reflection and self-analysis which has not been rivalled in the West.

" Turning from thought to emotion, the most conspicuous feature of European poetry is its preoccupa-

tion with love. . . . The Chinese poet has a tendency
different, but analogous. He recommends himself not
as a lover, but as a friend. He poses as a person of
infinite leisure and free from worldly ambitions. He
would have us think of him as a boon companion,
a great drinker of wine, who will not disgrace a social
gathering by quitting it sober. To the European
poet the relation between man and woman is a thing
of supreme importance and mystery. To the Chinese
it is something commonplace, obvious—a need of the
body, not a satisfaction of the *emotions*. . . . We idealise
love at the expense of friendship, and so place too
heavy a burden on the relation of man and woman.
The Chinese erred in the opposite direction, regarding
their wives and concubines simply as instruments of
procreation. For sympathy and intellectual companionship they looked only to their friends . . . half
the poems in the Chinese language are poems of
parting or separation. . . . The poet usually passed
through three stages of existence. In the first we find
him with his friends at the capital, drinking, writing,
and discussing : . . . next, having failed to curry
favour with the Court, he is exiled : . . . finally, having
scraped together enough money to buy husbands for
his daughters, he retires to a small estate. . . .

" In the first four centuries of our era the poetess
flourished : her theme varies little : she is almost
always a ' rejected wife ' . . . there was no place for
unmarried women in the Chinese social system : so
the moment which produced such poems was one of
supreme tragedy in a woman's life."

Thus far Mr Waley in a preface which is a most
masterly précis of the salient features of a literature
which has hitherto been a sealed book to most of us.
To turn for a moment to technique. The expedients

used by the Chinese before the sixth century were
rhyme and length of line. A third element was
" tone." The rhyme was a vowel assonance : words
in different consonants rhymed so long as the vowel-
sound was exactly the same. Mr Waley aims at
literal translation, which is bound to be to some
extent rhythmical, for the rhythm of the original
always obtrudes itself. On the other hand, he does
not attempt rhyme because of the impossibility of
rendering adequately any notion of Chinese rhyming :
nor does he employ " blank verse " because that
would demand variation of pause, whereas in Chinese
the stop always comes at the end of the couplet.

We English might well desire to take a leaf out of
their book if the following is typical of Chinese prose :

" The girl next door would be too tall if an inch
were added to her height, and too short if an inch
were taken away. Another grain of powder would
make her too pale ; another touch of rouge would
make her too red. Her eyebrows are like the plumage
of the kingfisher, her flesh is like snow. Her waist
is like a roll of new silk, her teeth are like little shells.
A single one of her smiles would perturb the whole
city of Yang and derange the suburb of Hsia-ts'ai."

That was written in the third century before Christ.
General Su Wu's poem *To his Wife* might have been
written during the Great War instead of two thousand
years :

Since our hair was plaited and we became man and wife
The love between us was never broken by doubt.
So let us be merry this night together,
Feasting and playing while the good time lasts.

I suddenly remember the distance that I must travel
I spring from bed and look out to see the time.

The stars and planets are all grown dim in the sky ;
Long, long is the road ; I cannot stay.
I am going on service, away to the battle-ground,
And I do not know when I shall come back.
I hold your hand with only a deep sigh ;
Afterwards, tears—in the days when we are parted.
With all your might enjoy the spring flowers,
But do not forget the time of our love and pride.
Know that if I live, I will come back again,
And if I die, we will go on thinking of each other.

The perfect simplicity both of the diction and the
emotion here is a delicious change from the euphuistic
epigrams that we are led to believe from *The Chinese
Puzzle* are the staple diet of the Chinese in their most
ordinary conversation.

The wife's reply is on the same high level :

The good time will never come back again :
In a moment,—our parting will be over.
Anxiously—we halt at the roadside,
Hesitating—we embrace where the fields begin. . . .
From now onwards—long must be our parting,
So let us stop again for a little while.
I wish I could ride on the wings of the morning wind
And go with you right to your journey's end.

Another husband, Ch'in Chia, writes to his absent
wife in these terms :

When I think of all the things you have done for me,
How ashamed I am to have done so little for you !
Although I know that it is a poor return,
All I can give you is this description of my feelings.

It is obvious that lucidity of this sort is a happy
medium for satire. In the year A.D. 250 we find
Ch'ēng Hsiao writing on the horror of paying calls
in August :

The conversation does not end quickly :
Prattling and babbling, what a lot he says !
Only when one is almost dead with fatigue
He asks at last if one isn't finding him tiring.
(One's arm is almost in half with continual fanning :
The sweat is pouring down one's neck in streams.)
Do not say that this is a small matter :
I consider the practice a blot on our social life.
I therefore caution all wise men
That August visitors should not be admitted.

Occasionally there is an attempt to formulate some
ethical point as in T'ao Ch'ien's :

That when the body decays Fame should also go
Is a thought unendurable, burning the heart.
Let us strive and labour while yet we may
To do some deed that men will praise.
Wine may in truth dispel our sorrow,
But how compare it with lasting Fame ?

Or again :

God can only set in motion :
He cannot control the things he has made. . . .
You had better go where Fate leads—
Drift on the stream of Infinite Flux,
Without joy, without fear :
When you must go—then go,
And make as little fuss as you can.

As an example of how the Chinese spend their
time T'ao Ch'ien may again be quoted :

In the month of June the grass grows high
And round my cottage thick-leaved branches sway.
There is not a bird but delights in the place where it rests :
And I too—love my thatched cottage.
I have done my ploughing :
I have sown my seed.

Again I have time to sit and read my books.
In the narrow lane there are no deep ruts :
Often my friends' carriages turn back.
In high spirits I pour out my spring wine
And pluck the lettuce growing in my garden.
A gentle rain comes stealing up from the east
And a sweet wind bears it company.
My thoughts float idly over the story of King Chou ;
My eyes wander over the pictures of Hills and Seas.
At a single glance I survey the whole Universe.
He will never be happy, whom such pleasures fail to please !

It seems queer that such a race, the embodiment of quiet content, should have found it necessary to have recourse to opium : the pleasures of lotus-eating would seem to come naturally without artificial narcotic.

The loneliness that is so often accentuated in Chinese poetry finds excellent expression in *Winter Night* :

My bed is so empty that I keep on waking up :
As the cold increases, the night-wind begins to blow.
It rustles the curtains, making a noise like the sea :
Oh that those were waves which could carry me back to
    you !

And in *People Hide their Love* Wu-Ti hits a note that will awaken a sympathetic echo in many a modern breast :

Who says
That it's by my desire,
This separation, this living so far from you ?
My dress still smells of the lavender you gave :
My hand still holds the letter that you sent.
Round my waist I wear a double sash :
I dream that it binds us both with a same-heart knot.
Did not you know that people hide their love,
Like a flower that seems too precious to be picked ?

Su Tung-p'o (A.D. 1036–1101), *On the Birth of His Son*, comes into line with the ultra-moderns in his irony :

Families, when a child is born
Want it to be intelligent.
I, through intelligence,
Having wrecked my whole life,
Only hope the baby will prove
Ignorant and stupid.
Then he will crown a tranquil life
By becoming a Cabinet Minister.

For the pleasure of unearthing so rare a gem as this it would be worth while wading through ten thousand uninteresting verses.

But the great poet of China is Po Chü-i (A.D. 772–846) : he held many official posts from time to time, including that of assistant secretary to the Princes' tutor, but he was banished and recalled to become a second-class assistant secretary and ultimately Governor of Soochow. The most striking feature of his work is its verbal simplicity : he followed Confucius in regarding art solely as a method of conveying instruction : his satires are just moral tales in verse and have none of the wit we should expect, but much true poetry. He enjoyed a very wide contemporary popularity which lasted for some considerable time after his death.

One of his most pleasing traits is his love of children :

When I was almost forty
I had a daughter whose name was Golden Bells.
Now it is just a year since she was born ;
She is learning to sit and cannot yet talk.
Ashamed,—to find that I have not a sage's heart :
I cannot resist vulgar thoughts and feelings.

Henceforward I am tied to things outside myself :
My only reward,—the pleasure I am getting now.
If I am spared the grief of her dying young,
Then I shall have the trouble of getting her married.
My plan for retiring and going back to the hills
Must now be postponed for fifteen years !

Unfortunately for him " Golden Bells " did die young :

Ruined and ill,—a man of two score ;
Pretty and guileless,—a girl of three.
Not a boy,—but still better than nothing :
To soothe one's feeling,—from time to time a kiss !
There came a day,—they suddenly took her from me ;
Her soul's shadow wandered I know not where.
And when I remember how just at the time she died
She lisped strange sounds, beginning to learn to talk,
Then I know that the ties of flesh and blood

Only bind us to a load of grief and sorrow.
At last, by thinking of the time before she was born,
By thought and reason I drove the pain away.
Since my heart forgot her, many days have passed
And three times winter has changed to spring.
This morning, for a little, the old grief came back,
Because, on the road, I met her foster-nurse.

How much more poignantly effective the man's sorrow stands out because of its lack of ornament and all the trappings of conventional elegiac poetry. It is a cry wrung straight from the heart, naked and pure.

The story of *The Old Man with the Broken Arm* presents a naïve attitude to warfare which is singularly foreign to our own :

In the depth of the night not daring to let any one know
I secretly took a huge stone and dashed it against my arm.
For drawing the bow and waving the banner now wholly
  unfit ;

L

I knew henceforward I should not be sent to fight in
Yün-nan. . . .
My arm—broken ever since ; it was sixty years ago.
One limb, although destroyed,—whole body safe !
But even now on winter nights when the wind and rain
blow
From evening on till day's dawn I cannot sleep for pain.
Not sleeping for pain
Is a small thing to bear,
Compared with the joy of being alive when all the rest
are dead.

There is a ring in *Madly Singing in the Mountains*
which would have endeared Po-Chü-i to Hazlitt :

There is no one among men that has not a special failing :
And my failing consists in writing verses.
I have broken away from the thousand ties of life :
But this infirmity still remains behind.
Each time that I look at a fine landscape,
Each time that I meet a loved friend,
I raise my voice and recite a stanza of poetry
And am glad as though a God had crossed my path.

He is candidly sceptical about a philosophical point
that has bothered many men before and since the
days of Job :

I have heard a saying " He that has an upright heart
Shall walk scatheless through the lands of Man and Mo."
How can I believe that since the world began
In every shipwreck none have drowned but rogues ?

Again he comes very near the spirit of the author
of Ecclesiastes in this poem :

Ever since the time when I was a lusty boy
Down till now when I am ill and old,
The things I have cared for have been different at different
times,
But my being *busy, that* has never changed.

Then on the shore,—building sand-pagodas ;
Now, at Court, covered with tinkling jade.
This and that,—equally childish games,
Things whose substance pass in a moment of time !
While the hands are busy, the heart cannot understand ;
When there are no Scriptures, then Doctrine is sound.
Even should one zealously strive to learn the Way,
That very striving will make one's error more.

It would be hard to name any poem in our own language which contains more food for thought in less space, or one more compactly, neatly, and rhythmically expressed.

This succinctness is one of his most excellent charms. *On Being Sixty* is a variant on the Seven Ages of Man :

Between thirty and forty, one is distracted by the Five
    Lusts ;
Between seventy and eighty, one is a prey to a hundred
    diseases.
But from fifty to sixty one is free from all ills ;
Calm and still—the heart enjoys rest.
I have put behind me Love and Greed ; I have done with
    Profit and Fame ;
I am still short of illness and decay and far from decrepit
    age.
Strength of limb I still possess to seek the rivers and hills ;
Still my heart has spirit enough to listen to flutes and
    strings.
At leisure I open new wine and taste several cups ;
Drunken I recall old poems and sing a whole volume.

The candour of this is as refreshing as the point of view is novel. And to an Englishman it is amazing to find the Oriental so forthright and positive in his statements. He writes, to our astonishment, not vaguely and slackly, but with his eye on the object, meticulously accurate over details : listen to his last poem :

They have put my bed beside the unpainted screen ;
They have shifted my stove in front of the blue curtain.
I listen to my grandchildren, reading me a book ;
I watch the servants, heating up my soup.
With rapid pencil I answer the poems of friends ;
I feel in my pockets and pull out medicine-money.
When this superintendence of trifling affairs is done,
I lie back on my pillows and sleep with my face to the
  South.

I have, I think, quoted enough to prove that Chinese poetry cannot be neglected by any lovers of the simple, the true, the clear-cut elementary principles of life. These poets are all essentially modern in their outlook in spite of the fact that many of them lived thousands of years ago, and that all of them belong to a civilization as remote from ours as it is possible to imagine. But love, friendship, solitude, and grief are not of any one time ; their expression is of eternal interest, and it is because these Chinese poets elected to write of the things that lie always nearest to the human heart that they are never likely to lose their charm. Mr Waley has made England permanently his debtor for introducing them to us in our own language.

PART III
BOOKS IN GENERAL

I

EMINENT VICTORIANS

LYTTON STRACHEY, the author of *Eminent Victorians*, is not to be confused with St Loe Strachey, the editor of *The Spectator* : he is as much like him as liqueur brandy is like tea, as the reader will discover from the short foreword with which he prefaces his first essay in biography.

"The history of the Victorian Age," he begins, "will never be written : we know too much about it. For ignorance is the first requisite of the historian— ignorance, which simplifies and clarifies, which selects and omits, with a placid perfection unattainable by the highest art. . . . It is not by the direct method of a scrupulous narration that the explorer of the past can hope to depict that singular epoch. . . . It has been my purpose to illustrate rather than to explain. . . . In the lives of an ecclesiastic, an educational authority, a woman of action, and a man of adventure, I have sought to examine and elucidate certain fragments of the truth which took my fancy and lay to my hand. . . . The art of biography seems to have fallen on evil times in England : . . . we do not reflect that it is perhaps as difficult to write a good life as to live one. Those two fat volumes, with which it is our custom to commemorate the dead—who does not know them, with their ill-digested masses of material, their slip-shod style, their tone of tedious panegyric, their lamentable lack of selection, of detachment, of design ? . . . What I have aimed at in this book is to lay bare the facts of some cases, as I understand them, dispassionately, impartially, and without ulterior intentions.   To quote the words of a master—' Je n'impose rien ; je ne propose rien : j'expose.' "

There is a " bite " about these remarks which prepares us for a very definite ulterior intention : whatever else Mr Strachey does not do he certainly means to lacerate an age on which, one would have thought, enough scorn had been heaped since the nineties.   Bitterly ironical, he portrays the lives of Cardinal Manning, Florence Nightingale, Dr Arnold, and General Gordon from a most peculiar and highly individual angle for his own very definite purposes. It is as an amusing example of what perverted cleverness can do that I would recommend this book.   In the initial essay (which is also the longest) on Manning I was not at first interested : it is said to be the best. For the late R. H. Benson and the living R. A. Knox it would provide very great attraction, but most of us are not deeply concerned in the struggles which take place in the minds of men who begin life as members of the Established Church and ultimately veer round to Rome.   It is like reading of sportsmen who played " Soccer " at school, and later found " Rugger " the better game.   So long as a man is enthusiastically a lover of games, or is possessed of a deeply religious sense, that is all that the majority of us worry our heads about.   Sectarianism or partisanship of this sort seems a rather stupid splitting of hairs, and long arguments about it " much ado about nothing."

On the other hand, it is entertaining to read of young men who are impelled with the sort of ardour which drives normal youths to haunt music-halls and fall in love with actresses to form a romantic attachment with the Deity and find an intense interest in the states of their own souls.

It is refreshing to view the lives of Froude, Newman, and Manning through the eyes of a sceptic : it is better than reading Gibbon on Christianity : the way in which Manning made his spiritual side toe the line to forward his temporal ambitions is inimitably suggested in this most typical passage :

" In such a situation the voice of self-abnegation must needs grow still and small indeed. Yet it spoke on, for it was one of the paradoxes in Manning's soul that that voice was never silent. Whatever else he was, he was not unscrupulous. Rather, his scruples deepened with his desires : and he could satisfy his most exorbitant ambitions in a profundity of self-abasement. And so now he vowed to Heaven that he would *seek* nothing—no, not by the lifting of a finger or the speaking of a word. But, if something came to him—? He had vowed not to seek ; he had not vowed not to take. Might it not be his plain duty to take ? Might it not be the will of God ? "

Equally deft are the strokes with which Newman's characteristics are limned :

" When he had left the Church of England he was its most distinguished, its most revered member, whose words, however strange, were listened to with a profound attention, and whose opinions, however dubious, were followed in all their fluctuations with an eager and indeed a trembling respect. He entered the Church of Rome, and found himself forthwith an unimportant man. He was received at the Papal Court with a politeness which only faintly concealed a total lack of interest and understanding. His deli-

cate mind, with its refinements, its hesitations, its
complexities—his soft, spectacled, Oxford manner,
with its half-effeminate diffidence—such things were
ill-calculated to impress a throng of busy Cardinals
and Bishops, whose days were spent amid the practical
details of ecclesiastical organisation, the long-drawn
involutions of papal diplomacy, and the delicious
bickerings of personal intrigue. And when, at last,
he did succeed in making some impression upon these
surroundings, it was no better ; it was worse. An
uneasy suspicion gradually arose ; it began to dawn
upon the Roman authorities that Dr Newman was
a man of ideas. Was it possible that Dr. Newman
did not understand that ideas in Rome were, to say
the least of it, out of place ? "

Mr Strachey's opinion of the Church of Rome, as
may be guessed, is not high. But his ironic attacks
are far more effective than the bludgeon hatred of
George Borrow. He is, at any rate, logical in his
disdain. We are shown Newman as a thoroughbred
harnessed to a four-wheeled cab and being used as
a pawn in a political game. Not only was he a thorn
in Manning's path to be plucked and destroyed, but
Charles Kingsley attacked his good faith and drew
from him the world-famous *Apologia pro Vita Sua*,
of which Mr Strachey writes :

" The success of the book, with its transparent
candour, its controversial brilliance, the sweep and
passion of its rhetoric, the depth of its personal feeling, was immediate and overwhelming," and brought
him a triumph which Manning had to exert all his
powers to defeat. " It is remarkably interesting,"
he observed of the book, " it is like listening to the
voice of one from the dead." Luckily for Manning

the contest was unequal owing to the dove-like nature of Newman and his own eagle qualities.

Some very shrewd hits are levelled by Mr Strachey at the subject of a controversy which then perplexed the Roman Church—namely, the Infallibility of the Pope. " It is not," he writes, " because he satisfies the reason, but because he astounds it, that men abase themselves before the Vicar of Christ."

Lord Acton, who in Mr Strachey's words " swallowed the camel of the Roman Catholic Faith," had also "strained at the gnat of Infallibility," but then " there are some who know how to wear their Rome with a difference ; and Lord Acton was one of these." It was of Acton that Manning said, " such men are all vanity : they have the inflation of German professors, and the ruthless talk of undergraduates."

As a result of the controversy several canons were laid down, of one of which the biographer caustically writes : " In other words, it became an article of Faith that Faith was not necessary for a true knowledge of God."

To return to the subject of the biography. We are shown in picturesque phrase the old Manning as the ordinary Englishman knows him.

" The spare and stately form, the head, massive, emaciated, terrible, with the great nose, the glittering eyes, and the mouth drawn back and compressed into the grim rigidities of age, self-mortification, and authority—such is the vision that still lingers in the public mind—the vision which, actual and palpable like some embodied memory of the Middle Ages, used to pass and repass through the streets of London."

We see him sitting on Royal Commissions, lecturing on temperance, writing books, quelling strikes, haunt-

ing the Athenæum, an active member of the Metaphysical Society, indefatigably active while Newman
languished in Birmingham : but in spite of an amazingly shady action on Manning's part Newman
eventually rose to be a Cardinal and enjoyed his
glory for ten years.

At last after eighty-five years of strenuous living,
marked by a fervour of terrestial ambition, the
Archbishop-Cardinal himself died in 1892, having
won by art what he would never have won by force,
a leader of the procession less through merit than
through a superior faculty for gliding adroitly to the
front rank : in him the Middle Ages seemed to have
lived again, and the imagination of all England was
touched by the mysterious glamour of his personality.
It has been left for Mr Strachey to destroy our
illusions, and by so doing to turn our allegiance from
the eagle to the dove, from the autocratic despot to
the author of the *Apologia*.

In his second Life, that of Florence Nightingale,
Mr Strachey again sets out to destroy an idol : the
popular conception of the saintly, self-sacrificing
woman, he would have us believe, is the wrong one.
There was more, he suggests, that was interesting,
less that was agreeable.

In very able language he depicts for us the aristocratic, well-to-do young girl who at the age of twenty-
five came near to desperation because she was pre-
vented from going to Salisbury Hospital as a nurse.
Mr Strachey draws a lurid picture of the " nurse "
of the time : " a coarse old woman, always ignorant,
usually dirty, often brutal, a Mrs Gamp, tippling at
the brandy-bottle, or indulging in worse irregularities.
The nurses in the hospitals were especially notorious
for immoral conduct ; sobriety was almost unknown

among them ; and they could hardly be trusted to carry out the simplest medical duties. . . . That things have changed is due, far more than to any other human being, to Miss Nightingale."

For eight years after her rebuff over Salisbury Hospital she struggled and worked and planned. She devoured reports of medical commissions, pamphlets of sanitary authorities, and the histories of hospitals : when she went abroad she visited all the great hospitals in Europe, and while her mother and sister were at Carlsbad she slipped off to a nursing institution at Kaiserswerth for three months and gained there the experience which formed the foundation of all her future action. For a moment, it is true, she nearly gave up her ambitions in order to marry.

" I have an intellectual nature which requires satisfaction," she wrote, " and that would find it in him. I have a passional nature which requires satisfaction, and that would find it in him. I have a moral, an active nature which requires satisfaction, and that would not find it in his life. Sometimes I think that I will satisfy my passional nature at all events . . ." but she had the strength of mind to stamp this craving underfoot. " The first thought I can remember, and the last, was nursing work ; and in the absence of this, education work, but more the education of the bad than of the young. . . . Everything has been tried. . . . My God ! what is to become of me ? . . . In my thirty-first year I see nothing desirable but death." After three more years her family relented and she became the superintendent of a charitable nursing home in Harley Street. After she had spent one year there the Crimean War broke out, and the terrible condition of our military hospitals at Scutari began to be known in England. Florence Nightingale was now thirty-four, experienced, free, mature, yet still young, desirous to serve, accustomed to command : she had, moreover, in Sidney Herbert, a devoted friend in the War Office : with thirty-eight nurses, amid a great burst of popular enthusiasm, she left for Constantinople : she arrived in Scutari ten days after the Battle of Balaclava and the day before the Battle of Inkerman, on November 4, 1854. The conditions were appalling. The wounded men were being shipped in batches of two hundred across the Black Sea without any comforts at all. There were no beds, no blankets, and no medical stores. The average death-rate on these voyages was seventy-four in the thousand . . . and when the men eventually reached the hospital they were scarcely better off. " Huge sewers underlay it, and cess-pools loaded with filth wafted their poison into the upper rooms. The floors were in so rotten a condition that they could not be scrubbed ; the walls were thick with dirt; vermin swarmed everywhere. . . . There were four miles of beds, crushed together so close that there was but just room to pass between them . . . there was no ventilation, not enough bed-steads, no bedroom furniture, empty beer bottles being used for candlesticks, no basins, no towels, no soap, no brooms, no mops, no trays, no plates : neither slippers nor scissors, no forks, knives, or spoons ; the cooking was preposterously inadequate, the laundry a farce." And yet Miss Nightingale had been assured on leaving England that nothing was needed. Luckily she had come, in spite of that assurance, well provided with money and provisions : her difficulty was to obtain leave to utilise either : the head doctor regarded her with suspicion : stores were held up for an incredible time before being unpacked.

But by dint of continued agitation she at length reorganised the kitchens and laundries : she procured socks, boots, and shirts in enormous quantities, and, as she herself phrased it, " clothed the entire British Army." She also enlarged the buildings and supplied all utensils for an extra five hundred men.

" It was not by gentle sweetness and womanly self-abnegation . . . but by strict method, by stern discipline, by rigid attention to detail, by ceaseless labour, by the fixed determination of an indomitable will that she achieved all this. Beneath her cool and calm demeanour lurked fierce and passionate fires : . . . she struck the casual observer simply as the pattern of a perfect lady : but the keener eye perceived something more than that—the serenity of high deliberation in the capacious brow, the sign of power in the dominating curve of the thin nose, and the traces of a harsh and dangerous temper . . . in the small and delicate mouth." Late at night she would write hundreds of letters for the soldiers, and compose long confidential reports to Sidney Herbert full of recommendations, criticisms, statistics, and denunciations. After six months she had had so far provided for the physical needs of the men that the death-rate fell from 42 per cent. to twenty-two per thousand. She now set to work to look after mental and spiritual needs. She set up and furnished reading-rooms and recreation rooms, and started classes and lectures. The private soldier began to drink less and save his pay. In six months £71,000 was sent home : she personally inspected all the hospitals in the Crimea, and nearly killed herself with the fatigue of travel. Dr Hall, who had bungled everything, meanwhile was rewarded with a K.C.B., " Knight of the Crimean Burial-grounds," in Miss Nightingale's bitter language, and in July 1856 she, who had done everything, came home to receive in her turn a letter of thanks from Queen Victoria and a brooch !

Hereafter the conception of Florence Nightingale fades into a quite different embodiment from that which we were brought up to believe. So far as her legendary reputation is concerned she might well have died then : in point of fact she lived for more than fifty years longer, insatiably energetic. The Crimean War was no more than an incident to her ; a fulcrum with which she hoped to move the world. Her real life only began when, in the popular imagination, it had ended.

Shattered in health as she was by reason of her superhuman energy she was now ordered to rest : for months at a time she never left her bed, but as she lay there, gasping, she devoured Blue Books and evolved more and more schemes. She was perpetually haunted by the ghost of Scutari ; the whole system of the Army Medical Department needed reform : even in peace and at home the mortality in barracks was double that in civil life. " You might as well take 1100 men every year out on Salisbury Plain and shoot them," she said.

Her business now was to gather round her satellites to help her in her mission. Sidney Herbert was her right-hand man ; him she taught, shaped, dominated, and swept along in the path she had chosen for him. Arthur Hugh Clough, to whom Mr Strachey is a trifle unkind, was used to buy railway-tickets, do up and carry parcels, and correct proof-sheets ; there was also " Aunt Mai," and Dr Sutherland, the sanitary expert, who acted as her private secretary.

The first great measure was the appointment of a Royal Commission to report on the health of the

Army. Not relying on this she decided to draw up her own report, and after six months' incredible industry she produced *Notes Affecting the Health, Efficiency, and Hospital Administration of the British Army*, a book of 800 closely printed pages, laying down vast principles of far-reaching reform, containing an enormous mass of information of the most varied kinds, a book which still remains as the leading authority on medical administration.

But there was an obstruction in her path in the person of Lord Panmure, who triumphed over Miss Nightingale in making the chief military hospital in England (Netley) completely insanitary, with unventilated rooms, and with all the patients' windows facing north-east.

But when Sidney Herbert became Secretary for War Miss Nightingale got her chance, and between 1859 and 1861 she introduced the whole system of reforms for which she had struggled so fiercely. Barracks and hospitals were remodelled : they were properly ventilated and warmed and lighted for the first time ; there was water, there were kitchens. By 1861 the mortality had decreased by a half since the Crimea : the Army Medical Department had been completely reorganised : it only remained to reform the War Office itself, and her mission would be accomplished. While Sidney Herbert was pledging himself to do even this, she turned her attention to the army in India, and with the opening of the Nightingale Training School for Nurses at St Thomas's Hospital in 1860 she became the founder of modern nursing. But Sidney Herbert's health gave way under the struggle of pitting himself against such a doughty opponent as Mr Gladstone, and failed. A beaten man he reported himself to his chief. " Beaten ! " exclaimed

M

Florence Nightingale. "Can't you see that you've simply thrown away the game ? And with all the winning cards in your hands ! It is a worse disgrace . . . a worse disgrace than the hospitals at Scutari."

He crawled away to die, followed by Clough : Aunt Mai deserted her niece, and the embittered reformer was left alone.

For ten years more she remained a potent influence at the War Office and then turned from the world of action to that of thought. Her *Suggestions for Thought to the Searchers after Truth among the Artisans of England* unravels religious difficulties for the working classes. As might be expected she is, however, scarcely orthodox. As Mr Strachey says : " She felt towards God as she might have felt towards a glorified sanitary engineer : she seems hardly to distinguish between the Deity and the drains." In the middle of this religious disquisition she bursts out into biting invective on the falsities of family life, the ineptitudes of marriage, and the emptiness of convention. As Jowett said : " Your work might be carried on, not with less energy, but in a calmer spirit."

And then came old age, and the sarcastic years brought the proud woman her punishment. The terrible commander who had killed Sidney Herbert, to whom Jowett had applied the Homeric words " raging insatiably," began to indulge in sentimental friendships with young girls, and to smile all day long.

Three years before her death (1907) she was offered the Order of Merit, and her legendary reputation revived. But Mr Strachey has lifted the veil, and no one who reads this essay will ever again be able to regard this amazing Victorian giantess with the same vague, sloppy, sentimental affection that he indulged in before. She is certainly, as he says, "more in-teresting . . . and far less agreeable."

The sketch of Dr Arnold is the shortest in the book, but a most illuminating record of how the Public School system has come to be what it is to-day. Here we have the picture of a young man who early in life put his religious difficulties behind him, who at the age of thirty-three became Headmaster of Rugby and changed the whole face of education in one or two aspects by the vigour of his personality. The Public Schools of his day were virgin forests : at Eton under Keate we read of a life of freedom and terror, prosody and rebellion, interminable floggings, and appalling practical jokes. Every Sunday after-noon Keate attempted to read sermons to the whole school : every Sunday afternoon the whole school shouted him down. Rats would be let loose . . . but next morning discipline would be reasserted by means of the whipping block. "The Public Schools," said Mr Bowdler, "are the very seats and nurseries of vice."

Arnold set out to change all this. His mission was to make of Rugby "a place of really Christian education " : "first, religious and moral principles ; secondly, gentlemanly conduct ; thirdly, intellectual ability." The order is significant. To do this he decided to treat the boys as Jehovah treated the Chosen People : he would found a theocracy : and there should be Judges in Israel. He converted the Præposter into an organ of government. The school, like the human race, should work out its own salva-tion. To the Sixth Form the severe formality of his demeanour was to some degree relaxed : to the rest of the school never. The Sixth Form alone were excused from chastisement : it was privileged to chastise.

So far as teaching went his reforms were few. To
the teaching of history he allotted one hour a week :
he took it for granted (like H. G. Wells) " that boys
at a Public School will never learn to speak or pro-
nounce French well, in any circumstances." So
modern languages were to be learnt grammatically
as dead ones ! Mathematics fared very little better.
The classics were left to form the basis of all teaching.
Latin verses and Greek prepositions divided between
them the labours of the week. The reading of the
school was devoted exclusively to selected passages
from the prose writers of antiquity. " Boys do not
like poetry " was one of his more ingenuous dicta.
Science was not taught at all. To be a Christian and
a gentleman was the aim. Consequently the fundamental lesson could only be taught in the school
chapel, and it was there that the centre of his system
was fixed. As might be expected he acted on the
theory that the spirit of Elijah must precede the
spirit of Christ. Consequently his tolerance did not
extend itself to modern movements. " You have
heard, I doubt not, of the Trades Unions," he wrote,
" a fearful engine of mischief, ready to riot or to
assassinate."

In addition to his labours as a Headmaster, with
" unhasting, unresting diligence " he wrote many
books and reared a family of ten children. He died
at the age of forty-six and left behind him a name
which in educational circles is ever fresh. Yet so far as
the machinery of education is concerned he changed
nothing. Under him the Public Schools remained
devoted to the teaching of Latin and Greek. The
moment was ripe for educational reform, and he
deliberately threw the whole weight of his influence
into the reactionary scale : consequently the ancient

system became more firmly established than ever. On the other hand, by introducing morals and religion he altered the whole atmosphere. No longer could the schools of this country ignore the virtues of respectability. By the introduction of the prefectorial system he produced effects which would have startled and perplexed him beyond measure. In his day when school was over the boys were free to enjoy themselves as they liked : " the taste of the boys of this period leaned strongly towards flowers." When they played games they did so for pleasure. The system of handing over the government to an oligarchy, to a dozen youths of seventeen, had not yet borne its fruit. Dr Arnold would be surprised to find that he has proved to be the founder of the worship of athletics and the worship of good form. It was not so before his day : it remains to be seen if it will be so always after him. The schoolboy of to-day is beginning to chafe. The general unrest pervades even the sacrosanct study of the præposter. A schoolboy has written a novel : a whole school has dared to be interested in politics. Is the tyranny of athletics already being broken, is the tyranny of the " Bloods " coming to an end ? It will be an interesting world if the tyranny of the Intellect and the tyranny of Æsthetics supersede these Spartan gods.

And so we come to the last and perhaps most interesting of the Eminent Victorians, General Gordon. He was born in 1833, educated at Woolwich, and given a commission in the Royal Engineers : when he was twenty-one the Crimean War claimed him, and he fought there with conspicuous gallantry. In 1860 he was sent to China and had his first great adventure.

A village schoolmaster (Hong-siu-tsuen) began to

see visions after an illness and proclaimed himself as Tien Wang, the Celestial King : having conceived a grudge against the Government because he had failed in an examination he decided to head a rebellion : his band captured Nankin and afterwards Shanghai. The Empire's forces under the title of " The Ever-Victorious Army " met with slight success, but were unable to make any real headway until Gordon, at the age of thirty, was put in command of them. His difficulties were very great : the rebels were in possession of 14,000 square miles of territory containing twenty million people. Its complicated geographical system of interlacing roads and waterways, canals, lakes, and rivers was turned by Gordon into a means of offensive warfare. He had a passion for map-making and was thus able to execute a series of swift manœuvres which took the enemy always by surprise : armed steamboats wrought great havoc in the rear while he cut them off piecemeal in the field. The " Ever-Victorious Army " was changed by his genius from an ill-disciplined body of 3000 men, constantly on the verge of mutiny, and at the slightest provocation melting into thin air, into a real army. There were terrible scenes in which Gordon faced the whole furious army alone and quelled it. Finally, he attained an almost magical prestige. He used to walk at the head of his troops with a light cane in his hand and completely overawed even his enemies. He could not, however, keep on good terms with the Chinese authorities : when he captured Soo-chow he agreed to spare the lives of the leaders, who were immediately assassinated by order of Li Hung Chang. As a result of this he resigned his command, and it was only with the utmost reluctance that he agreed to resume it in order to finish the war. Tien Wang,

" judging that the time had come for the conclusion
of his mission, swallowed gold leaf until he ascended
to Heaven," and, the rebellion at an end, Gordon was
free to return to England, having refused an enormous
sum of money and accepted the Companionship of
the Bath, " a reward usually reserved for industrious
clerks." He was then sent for six years to Gravesend
to supervise the erection of forts : he spent his time
in giving away all his food, money, and affection to
the poor people of the place, and reading the Bible
in lonely poverty. By an accident he was then
offered the Governorship of Equatoria, and spent six
more years in fighting against an appalling climate,
loathsome diseases, indifference of superiors and sub-
ordinates, the savagery of slave-traders, and the hatred
of the inhabitants. He reduced his own salary from
£10,000 to £2000 a year, and consoled himself with
reading the Bible, drinking, and giving vent to fits
of explosive wrath.

Succeeding to the Governor-Generalship of the
Sudan he fixed his headquarters at Khartoum and
quashed a native rebellion by riding a camel alone
in the blazing heat across eighty-five miles of desert
to Suleiman's camp, and signifying that the rebels
would have two days in which to disperse. At his own
request he was sent on a diplomatic mission to the
Negus of Abyssinia and failed owing to his refusal
of a bribe : he was arrested and reached Cairo after
incredible hardships and dangers only to find the
whole official world up in arms against his honesty.
He arrived in England in 1880 ill and exhausted, but
instead of resting accepted the private secretaryship
to the Viceroy of India and stayed with him three
days. He was asked to state that an address had
been read with interest when it had not been read

at all. He refused, and two days later set out for
Pekin, spent two and a half days there, and returned to
England. He then offered his services to the Government of the Cape of Good Hope in their war with the
Basutos : receiving no answer to his telegram he
took over the command of the Royal Engineers in
Mauritius for a year : the Cape authorities then urged
him to come to their aid, and after a violent quarrel
with them he returned home. Meanwhile in the
Sudan Mohammed Ahmad, the " Mahdi," had started
on his adventurous career. Like Tien Wang he began
as a religious reformer and ended as a rebel king.
He, too, fell into trances, and saw visions, prophesied
and performed miracles. A holy war was proclaimed
against the Egyptian misbelievers : Khartoum fell into
their hands, together with great quantities of guns
and ammunition and £100,000 in specie. The Mahdi
now began to have visions of a universal empire and
drew up rules of living and codes of punishment for
his followers. Blasphemers were to be hanged, thieves
to have their right hand and left foot hacked off in
the market-place ; the rhinoceros whip was the
favourite instrument of chastisement : men were
flogged for drinking a glass of wine, they were flogged
for smoking : if they swore, they received eighty
lashes for each expletive. The Mahdi himself is
excellently described by Mr Strachey : " Fascination
dwelt in every movement, every glance. The eyes,
painted with antimony, flashed extraordinary fires ;
the exquisite smile revealed, beneath the vigorous
lips, white upper teeth with a V-shaped space between
them—the certain sign of fortune. His turban was
folded with faultless art, his *jibbeh*, speckless, was
perfumed with sandal-wood, musk, and attar of roses.
. . . Thousands prostrated themselves before him. . . .

Then all at once the elephant's-tusk trumpet would give out its enormous sound. The brazen war-drums would summon, with their weird rolling, the whole host to arms. The green flag and the red flag and the black flag would rise over the multitude. The great army would move forward, coloured, glistening, dark, violent, proud, beautiful. The drunkenness, the madness, of religion would blaze on every face. . . ."

It is like a page out of Macaulay. Mr Strachey has an inimitable gift for conjuring up a picture as he has for précising documents : all these essays are models in the art of condensation : it is really a pity that he should at times descend to take such pains to be merely clever or ironical.

To combat this and other movements the English Government intervened : an English fleet bombarded Alexandria, an English army under Lord Wolseley won a big battle at Tel-el-Kebir. We had become the masters of Egypt and restored the rule of the Pashas, who now decided to destroy the Mahdi. For this purpose they sent Colonel Hicks with 10,000 men to suppress him. This force was ambushed by 40,000 and annihilated : the gravity of this disaster was recognised even in England : a minority of the Liberal party was in favour of withdrawing from Egypt altogether and at once. Another section was in favour of a more active intervention, but the great bulk preferred a middle course.

The Pall Mall Gazette pressed that Gordon should be sent out to Egypt, Lord Cromer rejecting the idea with all his might at first, but accepting him on the understanding that he would facilitate the evacuation in the quickest possible time. It is easy to see that Gordon's last thought was evacuation : he favoured

vigorous military action.   It is less easy to see why he
was sent if the Government really wished to evacuate.
On his arrival at Cairo he was proclaimed Governor-
General of the Sudan.   He made a triumphal entry into
Khartoum, where he was hailed as a deliverer : taxes
were remitted, even slavery was sanctioned, the Egyptian troops attended morning and evening prayers.

" The glare and the heat of that southern atmosphere, the movement of the crowded city, the dark-
faced populace, the soldiers and the suppliants, the
reawakened consciousness of power, the glamour and
the mystery of the whole strange scene—these things
seized upon him, engulfed him, and worked a new
transformation in his intoxicated heart. . . . He was
Gordon Pasha, he was the Governor-General, he was
the ruler of the Sudan. . . . The distant Governments
might mutter something about ' evacuation ' : his
thoughts were elsewhere."

Meanwhile England had been stirred to a warlike
feeling by the defeat of General Baker by the Mahdi's
troops, and had sent out Sir Gerald Graham, who
avenged him at El Teb and Tamai.   Gordon then
made the fatal mistake of advocating the appointment
of Zobeir (the notorious slave-hunter) as the ruler of
the Sudan : the Anti-Slavery Society set on foot a
violent agitation, and Sir Gerald Graham and his
army were withdrawn.   Gordon's position at once
changed, the whole scheme of his mission had failed,
and so far from having effected the evacuation of the
Sudan he was himself surrounded and cut off.   He
had six months' supplies, much ammunition, 8000
men, and nine small paddle-wheel steamers : the
home Government did nothing owing to the intervention of Gladstone, of whom Mr Strachey has many
interesting things to say.   " Speech was the fibre of

his being ; and, when he spoke, the ambiguity of ambiguity was revealed. The long, winding, intricate sentences, with their vast burden of subtle and complicated qualifications, befogged the mind like clouds, and like clouds, too, dropped thunderbolts . . . his views upon religion were uncritical to crudeness : he had no sense of humour. Compared with Disraeli's, his attitude towards life strikes one as that of an ingenuous child."

Gladstone, at any rate, refused to move a finger to save Gordon, who all this time overlooked Gladstone and vented his wrath on Lord Cromer, of whom we read that " he had a steely colourlessness, and a steely pliability and a steely strength. . . . His views were long, and his patience was even longer : . . . he passed his life entirely in the East ; and the East meant very little to him ; he took no interest in it. . . . He kept up his classics : his ambition was to become an institution, and he achieved it." To this man, his very antithesis in every way, Gordon would send twenty or thirty telegrams every day divulging his whole character, its incoherence, its eccentricity, its impulsiveness, its romance, its frenzied enthusiasm. When Gordon found that nothing in the shape of help was forthcoming he set to work to outwit the Mahdi's force as best he might. Whatever the emergency, he was ready with devices and expedients. When the earthworks were still uncompleted he procured hundreds of yards of cotton, which he dyed the colour of earth, and spread out in long sloping lines, so as to deceive the Arabs, while the real works were being prepared further back. He printed and circulated a paper currency : he instituted a system of orders and medals : the Mahdi sent him the uniform of his new religion in the hope that he would come out and join him.

And now Lord Hartington enters upon the scene,
Lord Hartington who was never self-seeking, never
excited, and who had no imagination at all, the man
who confessed to two ambitions, to be Prime Minister
and to win the Derby, who said that the proudest
moment of his life was when his pig won the prize
at Skipton Fair, a duke who might have passed for
a farm hand.

" The fate of General Gordon, so intricately inter-
woven with such a mass of complicated circumstance—
with the policies of England and of Egypt, with the
fanaticism of the Mahdi, with the irreproachability
of Lord Cromer, with Mr Gladstone's mysterious
passions—was finally determined by the fact that
Lord Hartington was slow."

First, he discovered that he was responsible for
Gordon's appointment ; then, that his conscience
would not allow him to remain inactive ; thirdly, he
made an attempt to induce the Cabinet to take action ;
fourthly, he realised that the Cabinet had decided
to postpone relief ; fifthly, he realised that he must
put pressure on Gladstone ; sixthly, he attempted to
exert this pressure and failed ; seventhly, he succeeded, and the relief expedition was ordered. All
this took a considerable time, and it was only because
he threatened to resign that action was ultimately
taken. A grant of £300,000 was made ; Lord
Wolseley was placed in command of the relief.

Gordon in the meantime was now without any
European to talk to or communicate with, and so
wrote untiringly on his telegraph forms to put his
case clearly before posterity : with bitterness he
caricatured his enemies at home. Of his 40,000 inhabitants he trusted none : the soldiers were cowards :
his admiration was reserved for the foe.

Owing to the fact that the Nile was exceptionally low the flotillas, upon which Wolseley's force relied, were unable to surmount the cataracts. A swift dash across the desert was the only alternative, but weeks elapsed before sufficient camels could be collected. Sir Herbert Stewart at the head of 1100 British troops eventually left Korti on a 170-mile trek across the desert, his advance being disputed at every step. He himself was killed, and there were over 250 casualties before they reached Metemmah. Sir Charles Wilson, succeeding to the command, started up the river for Khartoum, and his ship struck on a rock and further delayed the force. . . . On January 28 he arrived within sight of Khartoum and saw that the Egyptian flag was not flying . . . the relief was two days too late. Fragments of evidence give us some idea of the final stages of the catastrophe : Gordon's hair had turned suddenly white. The famine was so acute that dogs, donkeys, skins, gum, and palm fibre were devoured by the people. Hundreds died of hunger daily. By rumours, letters, and printed papers Gordon endeavoured to inspire the garrison with courage to hold out. When the Mahdi actually attacked resistance was futile and scarcely offered. Gordon was transfixed by Dervish spears and then hacked to death. His head was taken to the Mahdi and then fixed between the branches of a tree in the public highway, and all who passed threw stones at it. The Mahdi remained supreme lord of the Sudan. Not until thirteen years after was Gordon's death avenged by Lord Kitchener in the slaughter of Omdurman . . . and in Mr Strachey's trenchant phrase, " it all ended very happily—in a glorious slaughter of 20,000 Arabs, a vast addition to the British Empire, and a step in the Peerage for Sir Evelyn Baring " (Lord Cromer).

Such is Mr Strachey's contribution to the history
of a period which we have for some time been pleased
to malign. If it is his purpose to add another nail
to the coffin he will be disappointed, for the general
impression given by reading these lives of Manning,
Miss Nightingale, Dr Arnold, and General Gordon is
that the quartette have a more vigorous personality,
more tenacity of purpose, more British pluck and
heroism than we have ever accredited them with
before. Mr Strachey has been savagely attacked for
wanton perversion of the truth, for drawing totally
inaccurate pictures of famous men, for casting ridicule
on respected institutions and persons. His asperity
is to some of us his chief charm : like Newman we
imagine him to be a great hater, and what is the use
of a historian who is not avowedly a partisan ? The
difficulty is rather to see what were the " certain
fragments of the truth " about the Victorian age that
Mr Strachey found in delving through the masses of
compilations written round his four representatives. If
he merely wanted to cast aspersions on the Established
Church or religion in general, as we find him doing so
frequently, he might have done so more directly : he
certainly makes no point of convention or " groovi-
ness " which is our usual charge against our grand-
fathers : Gordon was the least of a " groovy " man
imaginable. We are shown the dilatoriness of politicians, the shocking and culpable inefficiency of
departments, it is true, but these things are not
peculiar to the Victorians.

No—it is better to search for no underlying policy,
but merely to revel in a well-told tale. There can
be no doubt in the mind of any reader that here is a
book which will take deeper and deeper hold on the
public mind as time goes on. It is a fresh method of

biography, brief, biased, and ruthless ; it is in some ways reminiscent of Macaulay, but the touch of wickedness in it is all Mr Strachey's own. Whatever else it does not do, it sends us back to study very carefully all the contemporary documents written about the four subjects of his study, if only to have the joy of proving him wrong.

Furthermore, it destroys at a blow all the nebulous but deeply cherished visions and legends which we had conjured up from our nursery tales and at the hands of uneducated pastors and masters. Most of us have a theory that English history ceased with the fourth George : at any rate we know nothing of the last hundred years beyond a few facts which are mainly wrong. Mr Strachey does give us a picture of life : it is interesting to know that in that molluscous age there were found people of energy, people of ambition, crafty, mean, spiteful, petty, passionate men and women.

II

TRIVIA

HAVING read Mr Logan Pearsall Smith's most respectable and informative book on the English Language in The Home University Library you will be totally unprepared for *Trivia*, but the first note in this amazingly frank book will key you up to the proper atmosphere required for appreciation of his philosophy.

"These pieces of moral prose," he writes, "have been written, dear Reader, by a large Carnivorous Mammal, belonging to that sub-order of the Animal Kingdom which includes also the Orang-outang, the tusked Gorilla, the Baboon with his bright blue and scarlet bottom, and the gentle Chimpanzee." And what is it that we are to learn from this large carnivorous mammal ? Like a true son of the twentieth century he shows us the futility of the Eastern proverb which suggests that we should " go to the ant, thou sluggard."

" I have sought instruction from the Bees, and tried to appropriate to myself the old industrious lesson. And yet, hang it all, who by rights should be the teacher and who the learners ? For those peevish, over-toiled, utilitarian insects, was there no lesson to be derived from the spectacle of Me ? Gazing out at me with myriad eyes from their joyless factories, might they not learn at last—might I not finally teach them—a wise and more generous-hearted way to improve the shining hours ? "

In other words, doesn't our Western civilisation need to be taught to seek a point of rest, not to be for ever patting itself on the back on account of its feverish energy ? There are lessons to be learnt from the lilies of the field, which toil not, neither do they spin.

For instance, Mr Pearsall Smith in slack, reflective mood can absorb beauty without wishing to put it to a utilitarian use. " I had not remembered the glory of the wheat, nor imagined in my reading that . . . there could be anything so rich, so prodigal, so reckless, as this opulence of ruddy gold."

It is not to be expected that such an attitude could win approval from his elders.

" They sit there for ever on the dim horizon of my mind, that Stonehenge circle of elderly, disapproving Faces—Faces of the Uncles and Schoolmasters and Tutors who frowned on my youth. In the bright centre and sunlight I leap, I caper, I dance my dance ; but when I look up, I see they are not deceived. For nothing ever placates them, nothing ever moves to a look of approval that ring of bleak, old, contemptuous faces."

His hatred of all that these Stonehenge Faces stand for can be judged by his note *In Church.* " ' For the pen,' said the Vicar ; and in the sententious pause that followed, I felt that I would offer any gifts of gold to avert or postpone the solemn, inevitable, and yet, as it seemed to me, perfectly appalling statement that ' The pen is mightier than the sword.' " And again :

" ' Yes,' said Sir Thomas, speaking of a modern novel, ' it certainly does seem strange ; but the novelist was right. Such things do happen.'

" ' But, my dear sir," I burst out, in my rudest manner, ' think what life is—just think what really

N

happens ! Why, people suddenly swell up and turn
dark purple ; they hang themselves on meat-hooks :
they are drowned in horse-ponds, are run over by
butchers' carts, and are burnt alive and cooked like
mutton chops.' "

"When," he writes later, " in modern books . . . I
read about the Needs of the Age, its Dismays, Doubts,
and Spiritual Agonies, I feel an impulse to go out and
comfort it, wipe away its tears, still its cries, and
speak earnest words of Consolation to it . . . but
how can one toil at the great task with this hurry and
tumult of birds just outside the open window ? I
hear the Thrush, and the Blackbird, that romantic
liar ; then the delicate cadence, the wiry descending
scale of the Willow-wren, or the Blackcap's stave of
mellow music. . . . Why should all the birds of the air
conspire against me ? My concern is with the sad
Human Species, with lapsed and erroneous Humanity,
not with that inconsiderate, wandering, feather-
headed race." But he is at his best in such a note
as *Vertigo* : " No, I don't like it ; I can't approve of
it ; I have always thought it most regrettable that
serious and ethical Thinkers like ourselves should go
scuttling through space in this undignified manner.
Is it seemly that I, at my age, should be hurled with
my books and dictionaries and bedclothes and hot-
water bottle, across the sky at the unthinkable rate
of nineteen miles a second ? As I say, I don't at all
like it. This universe of Copernican whirligigs makes
me a little giddy. That God should spend His
eternity—which might be so much better employed—
in spinning endless Solar Systems, and skylarking, like
a great child, with tops and teetotums—is not this
a serious scandal ? I wonder what all our circum-
gyrating Monotheists really do think of it ? "

It is pleasant, now and again, to come across a man
who is not so encrusted with tradition that he must
needs take everything for granted, a man, too, of no
little wit and humour, who can see clearly and face
every issue without flinching, a philosopher who is so
much at the mercy of ludicrous images that he can
see nothing in front seats, episcopal, judicial, parliamentary benches, but things for serious, middle-aged
ambition to sit on. It is his whimsical sense of the
incongruous that so endears him to us, his catching
and nailing down those sweet fleeting impressions
which seize upon us when our senses for a moment
are alive. " I who move and breathe and place one
foot before the other, who watch the moon wax and
wane, and put off answering letters, where shall I
find the bliss which dreams and blackbirds' voices
promise, of which the waves whisper, and hand-
organs in streets near Paddington faintly ring ? "

Though he frequently imagines himself an immense
thought-bubble, a floating, diaphanous, opal-tinted
dream, he is human enough to peer in through
windows left open on hot nights and look in at dinner-
parties, through lace curtains and window-flowers,
at the silver, the women's shoulders, the shimmer of
their jewels, and the divine attitudes of their heads
as they lean and listen, imagining extraordinary intrigues and unheard-of wines and passions. He is
human enough to hate social success. " The servant
gave me my coat and hat, and in a glow of self-
satisfaction I walked out into the night. ' A delightful evening,' I reflected, ' the nicest kind of people.
What I said about finance and French philosophy
impressed them ; and how they laughed when I imitated a pig squeaking.' " But soon after : " God,
it's awful," I muttered, " I wish I were dead."

Though that particular feeling must be common to all of us who feel or think at all, I can remember no occasion when any one has expressed it before either in writing or in speech. That is one of the reasons why *Trivia* is the kind of book one will neither forget nor part with. ·It is just us at our freshest, most child-like, most individual, most human self-prattling, se-curing to all eternity the thoughts that matter, which are so precious and yet so evanescent that we never actually formulate them in speech or on paper.

It is a grand thing to be able to project oneself from one's wretched surroundings, as Mr. Pearsall Smith always seems able to do : " As I sat inside that crowded 'bus, so sad, so incredible and sordid seemed the fat face of the woman opposite me, that I thought of Kilimanjaro . . . the grassy slopes and green Arcadian realms of negro kings from which its great cone rises, the immense, dim, elephant-haunted forests which clothe its flanks, and above, the white dome of snow. . . ." Here we have the secret of him : the author of these inconsequent notes is a poet in disguise : he could sit all day by a waterfall reading *The Faerie Queene*, or listen all day to the rain on the roof : instead of liberty, fraternity, and equality he preaches the golden gospel of Dignity, Stateliness, and Leisure, and the greatest of these is Leisure. He is one of those lucky men who " can hardly post a letter without marvelling at the excel-lence and accuracy of the postal system " : like Dorothy Richardson he is definitely and literally in love with life, and is never able to cease from bursting into shouts of applause at things which most men regard with the utmost complacence. As a frame of mind the following has much to commend it : " I am sometimes afraid of finding that there is a moral for everything : . . . it would be a kind of Hell, surely, a world in which everything could be at once explained, shown to be obvious and useful. I am sated with Lesson and Allegory, weary of monitory ants, industrious bees, and preaching animals. . . . I hate Ibsen and problem plays and the Supernatural and Switzerland and Adultery."

It is not that he is blind to realities. " Too often, among the thoughts in the loveliest heads, we come on nests of woolly caterpillars."

In spite of being able to assume an Asiatic detachment in Oxford Street the sight of a neatly fitted suit-case in a shop window is enough to chain him once more to the wheel of existence and envelope him again in the mists of illusion.

" And what are you doing now ? " his school contemporaries ask. . . . And the answer is important.

" It somehow seemed enough, just to be alive in the Spring, with the young green of the trees, the smell of smoke in the sunshine ; I loved the old shops and books, the uproar darkening and brightening in the shabby daylight. Just a run of good-looking faces—and I was always looking for faces—would keep me amused . . . and anyhow, soon, so soon (in only seven million years or thereabouts, the Encyclopædia said), this Earth would grow cold, all human activities end, and the last wretched mortals freeze to death in the dim rays of the dying Sun." It is this happy knack of linking up the trivial with the colossal, the transient with the eternal, that causes us to readjust our values after reading Pearsall Smith. His criticism of Anglican Church Services is shrewd and to the point : " We had gathered together to pay our duty to a highly respected Anglican First Cause—undemonstrative, gentlemanly, and conscientious—whom, without loss of self-respect, we could decorously praise."

A ruthless critic of others he is not blind to the possibility that others may find in him faults which he cannot see.

" 'But there are certain people I simply cannot stand. A dreariness and sense of death comes over me when I meet them—I really find it difficult to breathe when they are in the room, as if they had pumped all the air out of it. Wouldn't it be dreadful to produce that effect on people ! But they never seem to be aware of it. I remember once meeting a famous Bore ; I really must tell you about it, it shows the unbelievable obtuseness of such people.' I told this and another story or two with great gusto, and talked on of my experiences and sensations, till suddenly I noticed, in the appearance of my charming neighbour, something—a slightly glazed look in her eyes, a just perceptible irregularity in her breathing— which turned that occasion for me into a kind of Nightmare."

A man who is as human as that is worth his weight in rubies. He has found out many secrets worth knowing, not the least important of which is contained in *Inconstancy*.

" The rose that one wears and throws away, the friend one forgets, the music that passes—out of the well-known transitoriness of mortal things I have made myself a maxim or precept to the effect that it is foolish to look for one face, or to listen long for one voice, in a world that is, after all, as I know, full of enchanting voices. But all the same, I can never quite forget the enthusiasm with which, as a boy, I read the praises of Constancy and True Love, and the unchanged Northern Star."

When all else fails, wine, friendship, eating, making love, the consciousness of virtue, and we find ourselves lamenting our lost youth, we may turn to *Trivia* and find the true consolation of life. . . . " Reading, the nice and subtle happiness of reading. This was enough, this joy not dulled by Age, this polite and unpunished vice, this selfish, serene, lifelong intoxication."

That is the whole secret of *Trivia's* success : it is full of intoxications.

" I should be all right . . ." he writes. " If it weren't for these sudden visitations of Happiness, these downpourings of Heaven's blue, little invasions of Paradise, or waftings to the Happy Islands, or whatever you may call these disconcerting Moments, I should be like everybody else, and as blameless a ratepayer as any in our Row."

That is just the point : he might be all right, but we should have had no *Trivia* : it is just because he has had the sense to realise the importance of the fleeting vision and refused to be " bluffed " into believing in the ordinary man's sense of values that he has been able to scatter his pearls of wisdom over these all too brief pages.

Trivia not only deserves prominence, it deserves permanence. The few who care most passionately for its clear-sightedness, its warm, rich humour, its profound truth, its wholesale destruction of shams, and its touches of gorgeous colour and subtle music, will not lightly allow it to pass unrecognised. There is no book quite like it.

III

"Q" AS CRITIC

I

SIR ARTHUR QUILLER-COUCH'S reputation
as a literary critic rests on three books, *Studies
in Literature, Shakespeare's Workmanship,* and
On the Art of Writing. In all these he has brought something quite fresh into the academic world to which he
now belongs, an atmosphere that one associates with
Hazlitt and Frank Harris, and certainly not with University Dons ; in other words, he approaches literature
as a man of the world who realises how near it all is
to actual life, and how far removed from codified
formulæ or the rarefied atmosphere of the study.

In *Studies in Literature,* which is a collection of
familiar discourses, and only a prelude to sterner work,
he leads off with an essay on *The Commerce of Thought*
which serves as an excellent index of the richness of
his imagination. Why does not some one, he asks,
write a History of Trade-Routes ?

" By what caravan tracks, through what depots,
did the great slave traffic wind up out of Africa and
reach the mart at Constantinople ? What sort of men
worked goods down the Rhone valley ; and, if by water,
by what contrivances ? . . . How did the Crusaders
handle transport and commissariat ? . . . Who planted
the vineyards of Bordeaux, Madeira, the Rhine-land,
and from what stocks ? . . . Why and how did England
and Flanders come to supply Europe, the one with
wool, the other with fine linen and naperies ? . . .

These and like questions are of the first importance,
if you would understand history, if you would take
hold, in imagination, of the human motives which make
history. . . ." Roughly, he says, it is love and hunger
that drive man to make wars and to migrate, though
hundreds of thousands of men have left home and
country for the sake of learning. Trade disputes,
money—these are the causes of wars. Let your
imagination play on these old trade-routes and you
will wonderfully seize the romance of history. " You
will see . . . dotted ships on wide seas, crawling trains
of emigrant wagons, pioneers, tribes on the trek, . . .
families loading their camels with figs and dates for
Smyrna, . . . olive-gatherers, long trains of African
porters, desert caravans, dahabeeyahs pushing up the
Nile, puffs of smoke where the expresses run across
Siberia, Canada, or northward from Cape Town,
Greenland whalers, trappers around Hudson's Bay."

It is easy to see, in the light of this extract, the
spirit of the romantic novelist, the passionate enthu-
siast of far-off days, the devotee of an ever-living
history hard at work to rouse his pupils to a like
interest. His fancy plays lightning-like on all sorts
of obscure corners, revealing through the dust the
underlying glory. From the dissemination of plants
(" take some seed that has lodged on his long tramp
northward in the boot-sole of a common soldier in
Vespasian's legion. The boot reaches Dover, plods
on, wears out, is cast by the way, rots in a ditch.
From it, next spring, Britain has gained a new flower ")
he passes to the wanderings, alightings, and fertilising
of man's thought.

" Some one copies down a little poem on reed paper,
on the back of a washing bill : the paper goes to wrap
a mummy ; long centuries pass ; a tomb is laid bare

of the covering sand, and from its dead ribs they un-
wind a passionate lyric of Sappho's."   Again : " How
do you account for the folk-stories ?   Take *Cinderella*,
or *Red Riding Hood*, or *Hop-o'-my-Thumb*.   How can
you explain that these are common not only to widely
scattered nations of the race we call Aryan, from Asia
to Iceland, but common also to savages in Borneo
and Zululand, the South Sea Islander, the American
Indian ?   The missionaries found them there. . . . The
story of Jason and Medea we find in Japan, among the
Eskimo, among the Bushmen, the Samoyeds and the
Zulus, as well as in Hungarian, Magyar, Celtic, and
other European household tales."

It is the Roads.   " I see the Roads glimmer up
out of the morning twilight with the many men, like
ants, coming and going upon them ; meeting, passing,
overtaking ;   knights, merchants, carriers, justiciars,
King's   messengers ;   friars,   pardoners,   minstrels,
beggar-men ; it is noticeable how many of the great
books of the world—the *Odyssey*, the *Æneid*, the
Canterbury Tales, Don Quixote, The Pilgrim's Progress,
Gil Blas, Pickwick, and *The Cloister and the Hearth*—
are books of wayfaring."   He might have added
*Lavengro, Romany Rye, The Path to Rome, Travels on a
Donkey in the Cevennes, An Inland Voyage*, and half
a hundred more.   The recipe of a good book would
seem to be, plenty of food, plenty of travel.

" In the commerce of thought the true carrier is
neither the linotype machine, nor the telegraph at the
nearest post office, nor the telephone at your elbow,
nor any such invented convenience : but even such
a wind as carries the seed ; the old, subtle, winding,
caressing, omnipresent wind of man's aspiration.   For
the secret—which is also the reward—of all learning
lies in the passion for the search."

On the much vexed question of ballads " Q " has much that is interesting to say : he ridicules the idea of communal authorship thus : " If you think a ballad can be composed by public meeting, call a public meeting, and try ! In human experience poetry doesn't get written in that way : it requires an author. These ballads, though overlaid by improvements, are things of genius, individual." On the other hand, he realises that " the really important point about ballads has nothing to do with ' who wrote them ? ' even if that could be discovered at this time of day. It matters very little to us, at any rate, if they were written by the people. What gives them their singularity of nature is that, whoever wrote them, wrote them for the people."

As to what a ballad is Professor Ker says that " a ballad is an idea, a poetical form, which can take up any matter and does not leave that matter as it was before : a ballad is *Sir Patrick Spens, The Douglas Tragedy, Childe Maurice,* and things of that sort."

> Janet has kilted her green kirtle
>   A little abune her knee ;
> And she has snooded her yellow hair
>   A little abune her bree,
>   And she is on to Miles Cross
> As fast as she can hie.
>
> About the dead hour o' the night
>   She heard the bridles ring ;
> And Janet was as glad at that
>   As any earthly thing.
>
> And first gaed by the black, black steed,
>   And syne gaed by the brown ;
> But fast she gript the milk-white steed
>   And pu'd the rider down.

> They shaped him in her arms at last
> A mother-naked man ;
> She cast her mantle over him,
> And sae her love she wan.

That is what a ballad is, also :

> Then up bespake the bride's mother—
> She never was known to speak so free—
> " Ye'll not forsake my only daughter
> Though Susie Pye has crossed the sea."

And :

> Half-owre, half-owre to Aberdour
> 'Tis fifty fathom deep ;
> And there lies gude Sir Patrick Spens
> Wi' the Scots lords at his feet.

It is quite clear, quite unmistakable, but absolutely defiant of analysis. That is why it is impossible to imitate it : that is why Scott's, Coleridge's, Kipling's, Rossetti's, and Morris's ballads are not ballads at all. It must be remembered that they were never " litera-ture " until Bishop Percy in 1765 started apologetically to make them so.

The extraordinary rapidity of movement that is so marked a characteristic of ballads is well noted by " Q " : " Almost always you will find the intervals hurried over."

There then comes the question of geographical limits : it is significant that most of the ballads we now know are Border ballads, songs of fights between Douglases and Percies : " We do our scientific sense some help by fixing the best of this form of our litera-ture upon a certain folk inhabiting a certain limited region, which we find to lie between the Forth and the Tyne." Chronologically, too, it is possible to draw certain definite lines : almost all the evidence shows that the ballad with the impress we know upon it, rose, flourished, and declined within the period 1350 and 1550. The ballad never philosophised its emotion. In spite of the fact that " Q " recognises that ballads are " genuine poetry, peculiar poetry, sincere poetry," he does not adore them idolatrously.

" They appealed in their day to something young in the national mind. They have all the winning grace of innocence : but they cannot scale the great poetical heights any more than mere innocence can scale the great spiritual heights."

The Horatian Model in English Verse is an attempt to show how often English writers have caught the very trick of the Latin master : it succeeds more in driving us back to re-read our original than in breaking fresh ground with his imitators and translators. " Q " has, as usual, some trenchant comments to make on satire in general. " Satire has come to connote something of savagery, of castigation : to be indignant is better than to be cynical : to rage is manlier than to sneer. Yet to be constitutionally an angry man—to commence satirist and set up in business as a professionally angry man—has always seemed to me more than a trifle absurd. . . . But the satires of Horace were not satires in this sense at all. With a man of Horace's temperament such *sermones* could not miss to be urbane, gossipy, sententious a little, wise a great deal, smooth in address, pointed in wit . . . and these qualities have been achieved by his English and French descendants." Horace invented a style, and to invent a style is in itself a triumph of genius : as Newman said, " it is like crossing a country before roads are made between place and place." But the truly magical secret of Horace lies in his *Odes*. *"There* haunts that witchery of style which, the moment you lose grasp of it, is dissipated into thin air and eludes your concentrated pursuit : . . . its clarity, its nicety, its felicity of phrase, its instinct for the appropriate, its delicate blend of the scholar and the gentleman all give his verses such a diuturnity of charm that ' men so wide apart in temperament and spirit as Newman and Gibbon, Bossuet and Voltaire, Pope and Wordsworth, Thackeray and Gladstone, Rabelais and Charles Lamb, seem all to have felt in Horace a like attraction, and to have made of him an intimate friend.' The magnetic attraction to which such names as these collectively testify is a phenomenon of sufficient rarity to invite some attempt to explain it."

Of all the English poets the one who, but for a stroke of madness, would have become our English Horace, in " Q's " mind, was Cowper. " He had the wit, with the underlying moral seriousness. You will find almost everywhere in his poetry hints of the Horatian touch. Moreover he had originality along with the Horatian sense of the appropriate."

But " the Horatian phrase is everywhere in our best literature—even in the Book of Common Prayer. See how it leaps out in the *Te Deum*, ' When thou hadst *overcome the sharpness of death.*' "

" Q " finds the metrical secret of Horace in the fact that " he chose the most tantalisingly difficult foreign metres, and with consummate skill tamed them to the Latin tongue."

If any one feels that he has the Horatian *genius* he commends to him the experiment of rendering it in delicate metres divorced from rhyme, and quotes as a supreme example Collins's *Ode to Evening*. There, if anywhere in English poetry, he will find the secret of Horace's " falling close."

In his lecture *On the Terms " Classical " and " Romantic,"* he bids us dismiss the words out of our vocabulary for a while, together with all such phrases as " tendencies," " influences," " revivals," and " revolts." He selects Dr Georg Brandes as the arch-offender among critics in this respect, as a man who ascribes all works of genius to tendencies rather than to individual writers. In everything classical we find a romantic strain, and in the most romantic writers we see the classical touch.

The whole trouble amounts to this : " Some men have naturally a sense of form stronger than their sense of colour : some men have a sense of colour stronger than their sense of form. In proportion as they indulge their proclivities or neglect to discipline them, one man will be a classical, the other a romantic, writer."

It is significant to notice that " Q " comes into line with all the moderns in praising that long-neglected genius of the seventeenth century, John Donne : "Truly he was a great man : one of the greatest figures in English literature, albeit perhaps the worst understood : he wrote some of the most magnificent and astounding pages in our literature, if we know where to look for them." His poems tell us autobiographically of wild living and licentiousness : they exhibit him as insatiable alike in carnal and intellectual curiosity : mad to possess and violent in reaction, cruelly, cynically cold in analysing the ashes of disgust :

> Th' expense of spirit in a waste of shame
> Is lust in action ; and, till action, lust
> Is perjured, murderous, bloody, full of blame,
> Savage, extreme, rude, cruel, not to trust ;
> Enjoy'd no sooner but despiséd straight ;
> Past reason hunted ; and, no sooner had,
> Past reason hated . . .

" Nowhere lives a woman true, and faire " is his
verdict on the other sex : he shared the triumph of
the Cadiz exploit and visited Italy and Spain, and
on his return contracted a clandestine marriage with
the sixteen-year-old daughter of Sir George More.
" The wandering bark of his love had found a pole-
star in his most adored wife, and he burnt up past
sins on the altar of a single devotion." At the persuasion of King James he took Orders in 1615 : two
years later his wife died : and in 1621 he was made
Dean of St Paul's at forty-eight, the most solitary,
melancholy man of his age. . . . And " Q " would
have us believe that it is here that we shall find the
great Donne, the real Donne, not in his verse, but
in his sermons, " which contain the most magnificent
prose ever uttered from an English pulpit, if not the
most magnificent prose ever spoken in our tongue."
He had no architectonic gift in poetry : in poetry the
skill that articulated, knit, compacted his sermons,
and marched his arguments as warriors in battalion,
completely forsook him. But his verse did smash up
an effete tradition. It smashed up Petrarch-in-
English : it did so influence English verse for at
least half a century, that, like a glove of civet, it
scents every garment you take out of the wardrobe.

Donne was an imperfect poet because (1) he had
no constant vision of beauty ; (2) he had too busy
an intellect, which ever tempted him to be breaking
his shins on his own wit : in lines, and short passages,
he could be exquisite :

> I long to talke with some old lover's ghost
> Who dyed before the God of Love was borne

is a case in point, but more than half the time we
see the man sweating and straining at his forge and

bellows : later in life his mind played more and more
constantly upon death and its physical horrors ; he even
slept for years with a full-length portrait of himself
(for which he stood on an urn, naked, clad in a winding-
sheet) laid alongside his bed : " reflex action of car-
nality *in exitu*," comments " Q."

In his second lecture on *Seventeenth-Century Poets*
(Herbert and Vaughan) " Q " attempts to give a
true meaning to mysticism. "The function of all true
art is to harmonise the soul of man with the immense Universe surrounding him : the universe is not
a chaos, but a harmony, which cannot be appre-
hended at all except as it is focussed upon the eye,
intellect, and soul of man : the poet aspires to appre-
hend : the central tenet of the mystics lies in getting
to be like God : they wait, receptacles of the divine
passing breath : the poet merely by waiting and
trusting arrives *per saltum* at truths to which the
philosopher, pack-laden and varicose upon the military
road of logic, can never reach : all mystics have been
curiously gracious and yet more curiously happy men :
they have a propensity to deal in symbols, to catch
at illustrations which to them seem natural enough,
but to us far-fetched, conceited. Donne is too restless
to be a perfect mystic : he has no ' wise passiveness.' "

Quite otherwise is it with George Herbert, the
priest of Bemerton, who studied to be quiet, of
whom the critic wrote : " Nature intended him for
a knight-errant, but disappointed ambition made him
a saint " : but even he spoils many of his best
lyrics by conceits. In Henry Vaughan we find traces
of Herbert's influence everywhere, traces which at
times sink to downright pilfering. And yet this most
imitative of poets " is actually more original, and
certainly of deeper insight, as well as of ampler, more

o

celestial range, than the man he copied." The truth
may lie in the fact that some men want starting :
" They have the soluble genius within them, but it
will not crystallise of itself : it must have a shape,
a mould . . . and such men take the mould supplied
by their age."

In his third lecture he treats of Thomas Traherne, who
confessed " I chose rather to live upon ten pounds a
year, and to go in leather clothes, and feed upon bread
and water, so that I might have all my time clearly to
myself," who died at the age of thirty-eight, and
whose writings were lost for 250 years, and only discovered by the loving energy of Bertram Dobell.
" Of Traherne, the first and last word is that he
carries into a sustained ecstasy this adoration of the
wisdom of childhood," as this extract will show :

" The streets were mine, the temple was mine, the
people were mine, their clothes and gold and silver
were mine, as much as their sparkling eyes, fair skins,
and ruddy faces. The skies were mine, and so were
the sun and moon and stars, and all the World was
mine ; and I the only spectator and enjoyer of it . . .
so that with much ado I was corrupted, and made
to learn the dirty devices of this world. Which now I
unlearn, and become, as it were, a little child again
that I may enter into the Kingdom of God."

Centuries of Meditations is the kind of book that
one had been looking for all one's life, certain that
it must exist, but ever doomed to failure in the search.
If you still haven't read it, get it to-day and thank
Heaven for Thomas Traherne. It is not without significance that Donne, Herbert, Vaughan, and Traherne all came from the Welsh Marches. There must
be something in " the Celtic spirit " after all. In like
manner most of us owe an unpayable debt to " Q "

for introducing us to lyrics of unsurpassed loveliness,
and ballads of ineffable charm : as an anthologist we
have reverenced him all our lives . . . it was only to
be expected that he would find something for us in
this lecture which once read can never be forgotten.
Henry King's *Exequy on his Wife* cannot be quoted
here, but it would be worth buying *Studies in Literature* for the sake of this one quotation, even if the
rest of the volume were dull, which it is very far from
being.

In discussing Quarles, " Q " points out how the
idea of a Christ bruising His feet endlessly over stony
places, insatiate in search of lost Man, His brother,
or the lost Soul, His desired bride, haunts all our
mystical poetry from the fifteenth century down to
Francis Thompson. He dismisses the quaint metrical
and typographical devices, the artificialities and affec-
tations of the mystics (on which we are inclined to
dwell far too much) in a paragraph : " You may see
as good sights, many times, in Tarts," he shrewdly
says, quoting Bacon. Every one is ready to quote
Crashaw's lapses : fewer are ready to probe beneath
until they reach such a flawless stanza as this :

> The dew no more will weep
>   The primrose's pale cheek to deck,
> The dew no more will sleep
>   Nuzzled in the lily's neck :
> Much rather would it tremble here
> And leave them both to be thy tear.

But " Q," with that sterling honesty which makes
him so companionable a critic, confesses that he finds
the atmosphere of the metaphysical poets too rare,
too nebulous, their manna too ambrosial, for human
nature's daily food. " I want Daphnis at the spring,
Rebecca at the well, Ruth stretched at Boaz's feet,

silent in the sleeping granary. So from symposia of
these mystics, rapturous but jejune, as from the vege-
tarian feasts of Eugenists and of other men made
perfect, I return to knock in at the old tavern with
the cosy red blinds, where I may meet Don Quixote,
Sancho Panza, Douglas and Percy, Mr. Pickwick and
Sam Weller, Romeo and the Three Musketeers—above
all, Falstaff, with Mistress Quickly to serve me. I
want the personal—Shakespeare, Johnson, Goldsmith,
Lamb, among men ; of women I need to worship no
Saint Teresa, but Miranda the maid, Imogen the wife.
· . . For we come out of earth and fall back to earth ;
and the spring of our craving soars—though it reach
to God—on the homely jet of our geniture." That
is fine criticism, finely said, but it is only half the
truth. Remember Po-Chü-i :

> Ever since the time when I was a lusty boy
> Down till now when I am ill and old,
> The things I have cared for have been different at
>   different times.

There are times when we all tire of the earthly and
the full-blooded, when we soar ecstatically in the very
heavens themselves : at such times the mystics are
the only people who can satisfy our craving : Falstaff
with his grossness must be curtly dismissed : we are
now crowned King, Henry V, not " Hal, sweet Hal,"
the buffoon and cheap jester : mystic sweet communion with the saints is our need, not a stoup of
sack in an Eastcheap tavern. Such moods are not
common, but " Q " ought to have allowed for them.

He opens his lecture *On George Meredith's Poetry*
with a well-deserved rebuke : " We have so far ignored
academic tradition, and dared the rage of schoolmasters as to open the study of English down to our

own times, declining to allow that any past date could
be settled as the one upon which English literature
took to its bed, and expired, and was beatified." It
is surely time that it was recognised that history did
not cease with the Reform Bill, or literature with
Wordsworth. Quite half the enjoyment to be got
from the study of both these entrancing subjects lies
in linking up the present with the past and searching
for the " continuity." In order that the average
educated Englishman may learn to write English as
deftly, as scrupulously as the average educated
Frenchman writes French, to have at least an equal
respect for his language, it is necessary that he should
study how good writers to-day are adapting the language to express what men and women think and do in
our time. " Q " does not attempt to defend Meredith's
obscurity, but he does ask us to differentiate between
obscurity and ugliness, which is valuable advice.
On the other hand, he does point out that Meredith
left many poems unchallengeably beautiful which are
not in the least obscure. He quotes *Phœbus with
Admetus* in full, and asks us to go on from *Melampus*,
and *The Day of the Daughter of Hades* to the real
heart of Meredith's muse in *The Woods of Westermain*,
Earth and Man, *A Faith on Trial*, *The Empty Purse*,
Night of Frost in May, and the like. " The juvenile
poems will but poorly reward you, the later odes
reflecting French history should be deferred. It is
rather in the poems named above, and *A Reading of
Earth* and *A Reading of Life*," that you will find the
essential Meredith . . . the teacher, the expositor.
The philosophy of Meredith is strong, arresting, ath-
letic, lean, hard, wiry, Stoical, uncomfortable : it is
reared on the two pillars of Faith and Love. But
the Faith differs utterly from the Faith which sup-

ports most religions : he finds there is no true promise
in religious promises of a compensating life beyond
this one : he is not appalled by the prospect of sinking
back and dissolving into the earth of which we are
all created :

> Into the breast that gave the rose
> Shall I with shuddering fall ?

" We do not get to any heaven by renouncing the
mother we spring from." To be true sons of earth,
our mother : to learn of our dependence on her, her
lesson : to be frugal of self-consciousness and of all
other forms of selfishness : to live near the bare
ground, and finally to return to it without whining :
that is the first article of his creed. To set up your
hope on a world beyond this one is but ' a bloodthirsty
clinging to life '—demanding a passport beyond our
natural term : transience, to be gratefully accepted,
like human love, for transience : earth will not
coddle :

> He may entreat, aspire,
> He may despair, and she has never heed ;
> She, drinking his warm sweat, will soothe his need,
> Not his desire.

Meredith promises nothing—nothing beyond the
grave, nothing on this side of it but love sweetening
hard fare.

The lecture concludes with *Love in the Valley,*
quoted in full, " The greatest song of human love in
our language, a veritable Song of Songs."

In *The Poetry of Thomas Hardy* he calls attention
to the rule that each new generation turns iconoclast
on its father's poetic gods : " To dream of these
things [snatches of Morris, Tennyson, and Browning]

and to awake and find oneself an uncle—that is the common lot." So as a corollary it follows that " young poets write not for antiquity, nor for middle age : all that *we* (fathers and uncles) can do is to keep our hearts as fresh as we may."

The point now to be discussed is what Thomas Hardy has to say to us, the youth of to-day : " That his Muse is predominantly melancholy I brush aside as no bar at all : it is as proper to youth to know melancholy as it is to have raptures : only to middle age is it granted to be properly cheerful. . . . As for Hardy's pessimism, that does not consort well with youth, but it always challenges it : in his depths the man is always thinking, and his perplexities, being all-important and yet unsolved, are by you to be faced." Hardy's first poems were stiff and awkward : they were architectural draughts : the words were hard and precise. At fifty his metrical muscles were stiff, at seventy he has worked them supple. As a countryman it was necessary for him to dig vertically down through strata. He knows the woods so intimately that his ear detects and separates the notes of the wind as it soughs in oak, hornbeam, or pine. He knows that under one innocent-looking thorn such-and-such a parish tragedy was enacted : his countryman's heart is strangely tender : above all, his pity is for women ; his soul grows to abhor the duel of sex : " poor wounded name ! my bosom as a bed shall lodge thee." His indignation is noble and chivalrous. It is ironical that women should distrust Hardy's irony : he would break down their servility, and they eye him with suspicion ; but his creed differs from that of Meredith in that it is childless, without hope : incidentally Hardy is obsessed with irony : we begin to say to ourselves, " These things happen : but in any such crowd they never, and in no life, happen."

It is good to listen to " Q's " praise of *The Dynasts*, " the grandest poetic structure planned and raised in England in our time," even though he condemns much of the verse as too prosy.

On Coleridge he is not so helpful : lightly skimming over the main incidents of the poet's life he cannot help wondering what Dorothy Wordsworth might have made of him as his wife, but it is pleasing to read his rhapsodies on *The Ancient Mariner* : " Not in the whole range of English poetry—not in Shakespeare himself— has the lyrical genius of our language spoken with such a note : its music is as effortless as its imagery : we forget almost, listening to the voice, that there are such things as words, and we should call that voice seraphic."

Again, of *Christabel*, " where it rings true, we ask, was there ever such pure romantic music ? " Of *Kubla Khan* : " It abides the most entrancing musical fragment in English poetry."

Returning to the story of the poet's life he asks us to remember that even in the lowest depths he still fought, and in the end he *did* emerge with the victory. Also let us note how the essential goodness of the man shines through and through the petty quarrels and misunderstandings that dogged his steps : how, in almost any given quarrel, as the years go on, we see that after all Coleridge was right. In justice, and in decency, we should strive to imagine Coleridge as he impressed those who loved him :

> You will see Coleridge—he who sits obscure
> In the exceeding lustre and the pure
> Intense irradiation of a mind
> Which, with its own internal lightning blind,

Flags wearily through darkness and despair—
A cloud-encircled meteor of the air,
A hooded eagle among blinking owls.

Of Matthew Arnold he has much to say which is
shrewd and informing : " He was never popular, and
never will be : yet no one can say that his poetry
missed its mark. He was a serious man who saw
life as a serious business, and chiefly relied on a serene
common sense. The man and the style were one.
Alike in his writings and his life he observed and
preached the golden mean. It is important to remember that he gained the world's ear, not as a poet, but
as a critic, by treating criticism as a deliberate, disinterested art, with laws and methods of its own, and
certain standards of right taste by which the quality
of any writing, as literature, might be tested. When
he wrote poetry he elaborately assumed the singing-
robe, but always had something of the worldling
mingled with the bard about him. Through all his
work there runs a strain of serious, elevated thought,
and preserved the precepts of his own criticism in
observing two conditions : that the theme must be
worth saying, and that it must be worthily written.
" Nature is always behind his poetry as a living
background . . . and this sense of atmosphere and
of background gives his teaching a wonderful comprehension, within its range. ' This,' we say, ' is
poetry we can trust, not to flatter us, but to sustain,
console,' but if the reader mistakes it for the last
word on life his trust in it will be illusory."

His essay on Swinburne is one of the best in the
book. It is a joy to find a modern who has the
honesty to write of him in such glowing terms as
these : " The real marvel of *Poems and Ballads* lay
in its *poetry*, as in that lay the real innovation. Here

was a man who had suddenly discovered a new door and thrust it open upon what seemed endless vistas of beauty. Here was a man who could take the language and convert it to music as absolutely fresh and original, as it was patently the music of a peer . . . he was a tremendous force in poetry : the force died : the man outlived it : he has left an indelible mark on English verse : but he who had inspired parodists innumerable, and many pale imitators, has left us no school of poets : upon the literature of Victorian England he made an amazing irruption, and passed. His genius was elfish : and like an elf he never grew up." " Q " runs over the main incidents of his life with subtle skill, stopping to marvel at the elfin mystery of his birth—the child of a British admiral and the daughter of an earl—asking us to note that all his literary convictions were formed while he was at school, that Lamb's *Specimens of the English Dramatic Poets* and the Bible were his great formative influences, that his lack of curiosity in younger men may explain why he founded no school ; that his physical courage was always beyond question, that he hated Oxford, that he fell easily into the Pre-Raphaelite circle, that Richard Burton was bad for him, that Watts-Dunton saved his life, but committed the unpardonable fault of encouraging him to substitute rhetoric for poetry, and rhetoric for prose, that the irregularity of his life helped towards that ossification which overtook his genius . . . and many other things which materially help us to form a complete picture of the great poet that he was, and the great prose writer that he might have been.

" I don't see any internal centre from which springs anything that he does," writes Meredith. " He will make a great name, but whether he is to distinguish

himself solidly as an artist I would not willingly
prognosticate."

" Set apart *Hertha*, that glorious poem," comments
" Q," " Swinburne's own best beloved, and all the
blazing rhetoric of *Songs before Sunrise* falls short of
convincing us that Swinburne ever understood that
greatest of all maxims, ' Look into thine own heart,
and write,' or even that he had a real heart to look
into. It fails to persuade, having neither sap nor
growth nor any fecundity : it neither kindles us,
where it is right, to passionate assent, nor moves us
to forgive where it is wrong. Over it all lies the
coming shadow of pedantry. So it is with almost all
his verse after *Poems and Ballads, Second Series.*
Pegasus seems to be at a gallop all the while, but his
hoofs are for ever coming down in the same place : and
while monotony can be pleasant enough, nothing in
the world is more tedious than a monotony of *strain*."

" Q's " paper on Charles Reade was a centenary
article for *The Times' Literary Supplement,* and nicely
apportions praise and blame :

" When he ' got going ' upon high, straight, epic
narrative no one of his contemporaries could touch
him ; but he had a fatal talent for murdering his own
reputation, for capping every triumph with an instant
folly, and these follies were none the less disastrous
for being prompted by a nature at once large, manly,
generous, tender, incapable of self-control, constitutionally passionate, and in passion as blind as a bat."
He was privately educated, and after Oxford met
with many adventures, the most important of which,
from the point of view of his art, was his meeting
with the actress Mrs Seymour : he forthwith *saw* all
his novels first as plays. When he saw men and
women with her help he saw them as dolls making

their exits and their entrances behind footlights. The pity is the greater because he took enormous trouble to be true to fact, and above everything prided himself upon being *therefore* true to nature ! " He did, indeed, distort men, women, things, but he always saw them as tangible, and detested all writing that was nebulous, high-faluting, gushing. His style is ever lively and nervous : it abounds in errors of taste : but it is always vigorous, compelling—the style of a man." The amount of positive good he did, not only towards reforming social abuses by such works as *It Is Never Too Late To Mend* and *Hard Cash*, but by pamphlets and letters, would amount to a fine total. . . . " If there is a first place among ' historical ' novels, *The Cloister and the Hearth* and *Esmond* are the great challengers for it. . . . Reade, vain and apt to write himself down in the act of writing himself up, was all but consistently the worst foe of his own reputation. It will probably survive all the worst he did, because he was great in a way, and entirely sincere."

II

Having now examined at length some of " Q's " suggestive criticisms on divers writers of repute it is time to turn our attention to his theories on *Shakespeare's Workmanship*, and try to find out under his tutelage exactly what Shakespeare was trying to do *as a playwright.* He begins with an examination of *Macbeth*, and an excellently told account of the conditions under which Shakespeare built his plays. From the material out of which he built *Macbeth*, " Q " professes to find Shakespeare's secret. " I mean the element of the supernatural : it is the element which

almost every commentator, almost every critic, has
done his best to belittle. . . . Without the supernatural
we simply have a sordid story of a disloyal general
murdering his king : and it is worth noticing that
instead of extenuating Macbeth's criminality Shakespeare doubles and redoubles it. . . . Deliberately this
magnificent artist locks every door on condonation,
plunges the guilt deep as hell, and then—tucks up
his sleeves. . . . How of such a criminal to make a hero.
There is only one way—to make him proceed to his
big crime *under some fatal hallucination,* the hallucination in this case of exchanging moral order for something directly opposed to it. . . . ' Evil, be thou my
good.' Hence the importance of the witches in which
the mass of Elizabethan audiences would devoutly
believe. Furthermore, Shakespeare conceived the
whole play in darkness, and in darkness—in a horror
of darkness only—can one mistake and purchase evil
for good. ' Fair is foul and foul is fair.' "

After commenting on the relevance of the knocking
on the gate " Q " passes on to discuss the *punctum
indifferens,* the Point of Rest, Banquo the ordinary
man as a foil to Macbeth, and thence to the oft-
discussed irony which prevails throughout. It is an
ingenious essay, and in bringing into prominence the
supernatural element certainly sheds a fresh light on
one of Shakespeare's most perfectly conceived dramas.

In the chapter on *A Midsummer Night's Dream* he
runs through Shakespeare's pet devices, that of the
woman disguised in man's apparel, of working the
plot upon a shipwreck, of the jealous husband or
lover, and the woman foully misjudged, of the trick
of the potion which arrests life without slaying it,
and so on.

" Shakespeare having once employed a stage device

with some degree of success had never the smallest scruple about using it again. I see him as a magnificently indolent man, not agonising to invent new plots, taking old ones as clay to his hands ; anon unmaking, remoulding, reinspiring it. We know for a fact that he worked upon old plays, old chronicles, other men's romances. . . . Imagine, then, a young playwright commissioned to write a wedding play : his mind works somewhat as follows :

" A wedding calls for poetry—I long to fill a play with poetry . . . mistaken identity is a trick I know . . . in which I am known to shine . . . if I could only make it poetical I . . . a pair of lovers ? For mistaken identity that means two pairs of lovers . . . I like, too, that situation of the scorned lady following her sweetheart. . . . I must use that again—lovers mistaking one another . . . scorned lady following the scorner . . . wandering through a wood . . . yes— and by night : this play has to be written for a bridal eve—a night for lovers—a summer's night— a midsummer's night—the moon—er—and—oh—of course—fairies—fairies full of mischief and for a wedding, too—Interlude—we must have an Interlude —suppose we make a set of clowns perform the Interlude and get them chased by the fairies . . . gross flesh and gossamer.

" I suggest that we can immensely increase our delight in Shakespeare and strengthen our understanding of him if, as we read him, we keep asking ourselves *how the thing was done*."

Even if " Q " has not discovered Shakespeare's secret, he has divulged his own : we feel that we have been allowed to pry behind the scenes and see, at any rate, how one artist sets to work, even though we do not concede that Shakespeare worked thus.

" Barring the merchant himself," says " Q," in his
lecture on *The Merchant of Venice,* " a merely static
figure, and Shylock, who is meant to be cruel, every
one of the dramatis personæ is either a ' waster ' or a
' rotter ' or both, and cold-hearted at that . . . it is
interesting to think, that while character reigns in
drama, if one thing be more certain than another it is
that a predatory young gentleman such as Bassanio
would *not* have chosen the leaden casket. . . . This
flaw in characterisation goes right down through the
workmanship of the play. . . . Shakespeare's first
task as an artist was to distract attention from the
monstrosities and absurdities in the plot. Get the
Trial Scene (for which there ought to be a close season)
back into focus and note how absolutely real and
likely is the opening of the play : there is nothing
about any pound of flesh in it, there is not a word
about a casket : by the time that the incredibilities
are introduced Shakespeare has us at his mercy : all
the characters are so real to us that we have no choice
but to accept all the incredibilities to come."

There is much wisdom in his contention that
Shakespeare was in such a hurry to get to the " Forest
of Arden " that he made his opening scenes of *As You
Like It* dull and heavy, and wrote them carelessly,
as there is in his qualified approval of the play as a
whole. " Full though it is of life and gaiety and
exquisite merriment it does not quite reach perfection." In the creation of Falstaff we read :
" Shakespeare set up a permanent artistic principle
in the treatment of history by fiction, the principle
that your best protagonists are invented men and
women—pawns in the game—upon whose actions
and destinies you can make the great events play at
will."

In the sombre tetralogy then of stately wooden personages following high selfish ambitions Shakespeare thrusts the jollity of common folk by taking a leaf out of the interludes : Gluttony becomes Falstaff, and Drunkenness Bardolph : the whole Elizabethan drama is in ferment, yeasting up from type to individual. Prince Hal has to be converted from scapegrace to ideal warrior-king. Into Falstaff is packed all that is sensual, all that would drag the Prince down, but it must be remembered that no true artist develops or fashions a real character, once brought to birth, any more than a mother thenceforth develops or fashions a child : he was possessed by him far more than he possessed him. As for Henry V . . . we feel as Hazlitt said, that by the time he has finished with him, Shakespeare has made Falstaff the better man.

Some sixty pages are devoted to an analysis of *Hamlet*, which contain, in spite of the mass of literature that has been written on the subject, much that is new and helpful.

" To understand *Hamlet*, the best way is to see it acted on the stage ; a second best way is to read it by ourselves, surrendering ourselves to it as a new thing, as childishly as any one pleases. Take *Hamlet* as a new thing." Again : " It can be counted on, above any other play, to fill the house. . . . Whenever any actor comes to it he always plays *Hamlet* successfully. I suggest that all actors have made a success in *Hamlet* simply because it was there all the time, simply because there never was any mystery, and consequently no secret heart to pluck out. One reason for this opinion is that it has never been a test of the highest art to be unintelligible. It is rather the last triumph of a masterpiece that all men

in their degree can understand and enjoy it. Does the
man in the street pay to see something he cannot
understand ? He goes to *Hamlet* because it is an
amazingly fine play. The very first scene is an
astounding achievement, preparing the mind for the
unfolding of some crime : an abyss of horror is half
opened to us, and then comes the subtlest of comedy
in the pratings of the worldly-wise Polonius and
Laertes to Ophelia, comedy on the very edge of deep
tragedy."

Coming to the question of Hamlet's " madness,"
" Q " calls attention to two points : (i) the Elizabethan audiences would not be sympathetic to an
exhibition of real madness ; (ii) no doctor could
possibly grant a certificate of insanity to such a man
as Hamlet. His mother and Horatio know better.
It is true that he was beside himself—ridden by
furious disgust of the lechery that can inhabit
woman, much as Shakespeare himself must have been
to write as he did in *Troilus*, *Othello*, and *Lear*.

Hamlet loves Ophelia, but the discovery of his
mother's lust drives him into a loathing perversion of
mind against *all* women, and especially towards this
single maid of his choice.

" Q " metes out but short shrift to those commenta-
tors who want to know why Hamlet did not hurry to
his revenge at once.

" One meets these men going to the University
Sermon or shuffling along upon some other blameless
errand, and . . . any one of these Harry Hotspurs
will have killed him some six or seven dozen Scots at a
breakfast, washed his hands, and said to his wife :
' Fie upon this quiet life ! I want work.' . . . Why
should a man like Hamlet, noble, gentle, thoughtful,
scrupulous, *not* shrink from the deed ? "

P

It will be news to many to learn that in the original Belleforest made Ophelia a courtesan and specially used her as a decoy to entrap Hamlet into betraying his design, but both Horatio and she gave the game away. " Being an indolent man Shakespeare failed to remove or to recast some sentences which, cruel enough even when spoken to a woman of easy virtue, are intolerable when cast at Ophelia."

The lecture concludes with a brilliant defence of the pliant capacity of blank verse as the ideal vehicle for dramatic usage.

In *Shakespeare's Later Workmanship* he brings out many features which have escaped other critics : but he does well to call attention to the outstanding fact about the later plays, that the hard shadows have all melted, all the passion, cynicism, and fierce judgment fade into a benign, permeating, charitable sunset . . . every critic has noted this mellowly romantic atmosphere, that every one of these plays ends happily, that they all show a common disobedience to what is called " Unity of Time," as is inevitable when the process of cooling, of appeasement, of repentance, and of forgiveness has to be shown. It may be that having triumphed in the possible, this magnificent workman grew discontented and started out to conquer the impossible : so he set out to show human forgiveness, such forgiveness as Imogen's, which has something nobler in it than any revenge, even than God's revenge against murder.

" Do we not *feel*, that though we may talk of God's being injured, insulted, wounded by our sins, He cannot be injured by Posthumus's cruel wrong as Imogen is injured ? It costs Him so much less. It cost Imogen all she had in the world."

The Shakespeare of the later plays who deals with

atonement and reconciliation was not necessarily a
weaker workman than the Shakespeare who triumphed
in *Macbeth* and *Othello.*

" Q " asks us to notice that every artist of the first
class tires of repeating his successes, but never of
repeating his experiments. Your inventive master
never cares for a success but as a step to something
further. What he achieves may be unworthy of his
powers, but he is still trying : he has the divinest of
discontent, discontent with achievement.

In point of fact, the workmanship of *Cymbeline* is
masterly, and the final scene almost the last word in
dramatic skill ; nine-tenths of the weakness of
Pericles is most likely not chargeable to Shakespeare
at all. It must be remembered, too, that while
Shakespeare was writing, the scenic resources of the
stage were being steadily developed ; moreover, the
masque was coming more and more into fashion, both
items to be reckoned with when we come to sum up
his latest achievements.

The critic makes a valiant effort to vindicate
Cymbeline from the heaped-up charges brought
against it by Doctor Johnson ; as " Q " says :
" There is a truth of imagination, a truth of emotion,
and a truth of fact." The fact that stands out about
Cymbeline is the complete perfection of Imogen, " the
most adorable woman ever created by God or man."
When we start picking *Cymbeline* to pieces we find
ourselves disheartened ; Cymbeline is an inferior
Lear, Iachimo an inferior Iago, Posthumus an
inferior Othello ; *Cymbeline* is constructed out of
fragments, but what about the total effect ? " Why
on earth should it be a reproach against *Cymbeline*
that in *Lear* Shakespeare did something better than
this, in *Othello* something better than *that,* when out of

the inferior *this* and *that* he has built the incomparable Imogen ? " Johnson made too much of the incongruities ; " Q's " complaint lies against the complexity of the plot.

In *The Winter's Tale* he asks us to believe that Shakespeare was attempting to work into one drama two different stories in two separate categories of Art ; in a world where Nature mixes comedy with tragedy, Art must always be impatient of hard definitions; the fault lay not in Shakespeare's attempt to do this, but in the astounding carelessness which he showed. Why did he take no trouble to make Leontes' jealousy credible ? Why bring in the naughty superfluity of the bear to polish off Antigonus, unless the Bear-pit at Southwark had a tame animal to let which the Globe used as a bait to draw the public ? What possible difference could Autolycus make to the action ? Why was the Recognition scene scamped ? The truth is we never think of the total play, but ever of separate scene after separate scene, particularly the unapproachable one in which Florizel and Perdita find themselves the centre, being young and innocent and in love.

" Q's " first lecture on *The Tempest* is an admirable résumé of the controversy which has raged so long over the date of the play, reviving the strange story of the forger, J. P. Collier, and the misjudged Peter Conningham, and incidentally upsets the theory that *The Tempest* was written to celebrate the wedding of that wonderful woman, Elizabeth of Bohemia. " Q " then asks us, as usual, to test the play by its workmanship ; first there is the identity between *The Winter's Tale* and *The Tempest* in stage devices, about a dozen of which are cited, but with how much greater skill Shakespeare works in *The Tempest* is evident everywhere : in Antigonus's counterpart, Gonzalo, for instance, for whom the critic has a very warm place in his heart, praising even his Utopian visions ; in Ferdinand, who is an improvement on Florizel in every way, in the spirit of his wooing and his courage, and so on. Having convinced us that *The Tempest* resembles *The Winter's Tale* in dozens of ways, and improves on each one of them, he proceeds to prove that *The Tempest* came after it in point of time by repeating his phrase that every artist tires of repeating his successes, but never of renewing his experiments.

The theme which Shakespeare seeks to engraft upon his old ones is that of Reconciliation ; the difficulty of presenting a complete story dwelling on this in two or three hours was almost heartbreaking ; again and again it beats him. Suddenly, in *The Tempest,* he brings off the trick by marvellous stage-craft ; is it likely that having succeeded he would turn back in *The Winter's Tale* to imitate old failures ? Such an argument seems to me to clinch the matter, so far as it is important at all that we like to feel that Shakespeare left off on a top note. That it was written for the Court, and for a wedding, " Q " seeks to prove in his final lecture, by its resemblance to *A Midsummer Night's Dream,* the " notion " of the play, and its position in the First Folio (a most ingenious theory !) ; he passes on to conjure up a vision of the first night most ably visualised, dwelling again on one of his favourite first principles to help us appreciate the storm and shipwreck : " *If you are an artist and are setting out to tell the incredible, nothing will serve you so well as to open with absolute realism,*" quoting in happy illustration the opening sentence of *Robinson Crusoe.* Of the wonderful

Miranda he refuses to say more than that Coleridge
has expressed what we all feel of her, and that it is
just in Shakespeare's creation of such a peerless girl
that his genius vanishes and leaves us hopelessly
foundered ; " he invented Lady Macbeth and Miranda,
both to be acted by boys." The thought is in
itself stupefying, and proves, if proof were needed,
that it is folly to think of Shakespeare as limited by
the conditions of his craft. Of Caliban he can find
it in his heart to say : " If he were to come fawning
into the room, our impulse would be to pat him on
the head—' Good old doggie ! Good monster,' that
would be the feeling," which is in itself a lightning
flash of criticism, revealing exactly what excellent
qualities " Q " brings to his art as a critic.

He notes as a curious point of similarity between
The Tempest and *A Midsummer Night's Dream* that
these two *require* to be acted by amateurs ; " the
professional never made any hand with either play."
He asks us to believe that Prospero was no photograph
of an individual, neither James I nor Shakespeare.
" For in truth that is not the way of the imaginative
artist ; and if the reader will not take it from me he
may take it from Aristotle." " Q " concludes his thesis
by boldly declaiming that were the choice offered
him " which of all the books ever written I would
select—not the *Odyssey*, not the *Aeneid*, nor the
Divine Comedy, nor *Paradise Lost*, nor *Othello*, nor
Hamlet, nor *Lear*, but *The Tempest* should be mine.
The Tempest forces diviner tears, tears for sheer
beauty ; we *feel* that we are greater than we know.
So on the surge of our emotion is blown a spray, a
mist—and its colours are wisdom and charity, with
forgiveness, tender ruth for all men and women
growing older, and perennial trust in young love."

IV

ALICE MEYNELL AS CRITIC

" WE must study other men's inventions in
our closet, but need we now print our
comments on them ? Exposition, interpretation, by themselves are not necessary. But for
controversy there is cause." So does Alice Meynell,
herself one of the most polished of our prose writers
and most mystically gifted of our poets, excuse herself
for writing *Hearts of Controversy*. Whatever the excuse, whatever the cause, we cannot but feel thankful
that she felt impelled to be controversial about
Tennyson, Dickens, Swinburne, and the Brontës,
for she sheds a clear light on each of these in her
criticisms.

Her essay on Tennyson, for instance, is a precious
gem, clear-cut, crystalline for all its poetic cadences ;
for Alice Meynell writes prose as a poet writes it, as her
own beloved Francis Thompson wrote it.

" If there ever was a poet who needed to be ' parted,'
it is he who wrote both narrowly for his time and
liberally for all time, and who had both a style and a
manner ; a masterly style, a magical style, a too dainty
manner ; a noble landscape and in it figures something
ready-made. . . . We have the style and the manner
locked together at times in a single stanza, locked and
yet not mingled . . . but the little nation of lovers of
poetry . . . cannot remain finally insensible to what is
at once majestic and magical in Tennyson. . . . How,
valuing singleness of heart in the sixteenth century,

splendour in the seventeenth, composure in the eighteenth, how shall we long disregard these virtues in the nineteenth-century master for the insignificant reasons of his bygone taste, his insipid courtliness, his prettiness . . . or what not ? " Who would disparage a poet who can write :

> On one side lay the ocean, and on one
> Lay a great water, and the moon was full ?

" His blank verse is often too easy; it slips by, without the friction of the movement of vitality ; . . . he shows us that of all merits ease is the most dangerous, but ease in him does not mean that he has any unhandsome, slovenly ways. . . . In the first place, the poet with the welcome style and the little unwelcome manner, he is, in the second place, the modern poet who withstood France." Not the Elizabethans were more insular. We are apt to judge a poet too exclusively by his imagery. " Tennyson has more imagination than imagery. His homely unscenic scenery makes his vision fresh ; but he is equally fresh with the things that others have outworn ; mountains, desert islands, castles, elves . . . in his ' horns of elfland ' there is the remoteness and light delirium of rapturous and delicate health. . . . There is never a passage of manner but a great passage of style rebukes our dislike and recalls our heart again. . . .

" Tennyson is an eminently all-intelligible poet. . . . Where he hesitates his is the sincere pause of process and uncertainty. It has been said that midway between the student of material science and the mystic, Tennyson wrote and thought according to an age that wavered between the two minds, and that men have now taken one way or the other. Is this true ? The religious question that arises upon experience of death has never been asked with more sincerity than by him. If *In Memoriam* represents the mind of yesterday, it represents no less the mind of to-morrow. . . . In so far as the poem attempts, weighs, falters, and confides, it is true to the experience of human anguish and intellect ; I say intellect advisedly ; he doesn't slip into the errors of a Coleridge, whose senses were certainly infinitely and transcendently spiritual, but who told a silly story in *The Ancient Mariner* (the wedding guest might rise a sadder, but he assuredly did not rise a wiser man), or those of Wordsworth, who imagined that grass would not grow where a stag had died. Nowhere in the whole of Tennyson's thought is there such an attack on our reason and our heart as this. . . . But he is, before all, the poet of landscape ; the sense of hearing, as well as the sense of sight, has never been more greatly exalted than by Tennyson ; his own especially is the March month —his ' roaring moon.' His is the spirit of the dawning month of flowers and storms ; his was a new apprehension of Nature, an increase in the number of our national apprehensions in Nature.

" Tennyson, the clearest-headed of poets, is our wild poet ; wild, notwithstanding that little foppery we know of in him, that walking delicately, like Agag ; wild, notwithstanding the work, the ease, the neatness, the finish ; notwithstanding the assertion of manliness which, in asserting, somewhat misses the mark ; a wilder poet than the rough, than the sensual, than the defiant, than the accuser, than the denouncer. Wild flowers are his—wild winds, wild hearts, wild lights, wild eyes ! "

We may not agree with Mrs Meynell's estimate of Tennyson any more than we agree with her on the subject of Dickens, but we can scarcely withhold

admiration for her courage, or love for the delicacy of
her feeling. She is too prone to cast aspersions on
our parts of speech ; that she has no great love for
the Georgians is evident from this : " Nothing
places Dickens so entirely out of date as his trust in
human sanctity, his love of it, his hope for it, his leap
at it." This is a gross misstatement of fact, due to a
misconception in Mrs Meynell's mind of the word
" sentiment." Where she scores in her criticism here
is in combating the superstition that " caricature "
means something derogatory. " Caricature, when it
has the grotesque inspiration, makes for laughter,
and when it has the celestial, makes for admiration ;
it is quite different from exaggeration, the worst form
of violence. Exaggeration takes for granted some
degree of imbecility in the reader, whereas caricature
takes for granted a high degree of intelligence. ' Caricature,' which is used a thousand times to reproach
Dickens, is the word that does him singular honour."

Mrs Meynell's devotion to Dickens is based on admiration of his humour, his dramatic tragedy, and his
watchfulness over inanimate things and landscape ;
" he is master of wit and derision." She defends his
diction and grammar, though she laments that he has
" no *body* of style," and comments on his joy in mis-
shapen and grotesque things, his whimsically ugly
names, and the fact that all his people, suddenly surprised, lose their presence of mind. One feels that a
" fuller-blooded " critic would have made a better
case. It is part of our case against Dickens that he
would not have appreciated Mrs Meynell's art at all.

She is far more fitted by temperament to apportion
blame and praise to Swinburne, her next subject.
She is, at any rate, sufficiently concise and direct here,
in spite of her sometimes exotic style of writing

(what does "rachitic" mean ?).[1]   "We predicate of a
poet a great sincerity, a great imagination, a great
passion, a great intellect ; these are the master
qualities, and yet we are compelled to see in Swinburne
a poet, yes, a true poet, with a perfervid fancy rather
than an imagination, a poet with puny passions, a
poet with no more than the momentary and impulsive
sincerity of an infirm soul, a poet with small intellect
—and thrice a poet. . . . A vivid writer of English was
he, and would have been one of the recurring renewers
of our oft-renewed and incomparable language, had his
words not become habitual to himself, so that they
quickly lose the light, the breeze, the breath ; . . .
his recklessness of appreciation is less than manly, it
is ideally feminine ; but no woman has yet been
capable of so entire an emotional impulse and impetus ;
his failure of intellect was a national disaster, and his
instinct for words was a national surprise. . . . He is a
complete master of the rhythm and rhyme, the time
and accent, the pause, the balance, the flow of vowel
and clash of consonant that make the ' music ' for
which verse is popular and prized." His anapæsts
(Mrs Meynell loves only iambic and trochaic measures)
are " far too delicate for swagger or strut, but for all
their dance, all their spring, all their flight, all their
flutter, we are compelled to perceive that, as it were,
they *perform*." It is in the traditional metres that we
find his best dignity, and therefore his best beauty. His
exceptional faculty of diction led him to immoderate
expressiveness, to immodest sweetness, to jugglery,
prestidigitation and conjuring of words, to trans-
formations and transmutations of sound.

[1] The Oxford Dictionary suggests "rickets." It is an even less
attractive word than " Q's " " autoschediastic," on which the Dictionary
hrows no light.

" I believe that Swinburne's thoughts have their source, their home, their origin, their authority and mission in those two places—his own vocabulary and the passion of other men . . . he sustained, he fattened, and he enriched his poetry upon other men's passions ; what sincerity he has is absorbed in the one excited act of receptivity. He is charged with one man's patriotism, another's love of sin, a third's cry of liberty, a fourth's erotic sickness. . . .

" But by the unanimous poet's splendid love of the landscape and the skies, by this he was possessed, and in this he triumphed, . . . but this poet, who is conspicuously the poet of excess, is in deeper truth the poet of penury and defect."

We expect good criticism on Charlotte and Emily Brontë from so sensitive a member of their own sex as Alice Meynell, but anyone who has read May Sinclair's wonderful book on the sisters will almost certainly be dissatisfied with this essay. Mrs Meynell's controversy in this case is with those who admire Charlotte Brontë throughout her career. She altered greatly. There was a time when she practised such verbs as " to evince," " to reside," " to intimate," and " to peruse." She talked of " an extensive and eligible connexion," " a small competency," " it operated as a barrier to further intercourse," and of a child " for the toys he possesses he seems to have contracted a partiality amounting to affection."

" Encumbered," says Mrs Meynell, " by this drift and refuse of English, she yet achieved the miracle of her vocabulary. It is less wonderful that she should have appeared out of such a parsonage than that she should have arisen out of such a language." Later : " In alternate pages *Villette* is a book of spirit and fire, and a novel of illiberal rancour, of

ungenerous, uneducated anger, ungentle, ignoble.
In order to forgive its offences we have to remember
the immeasurable sorrow of the authoress's life.
It is well for the perpetual fellowship of mankind that
no child should read this life and not take therefrom
a perdurable scar."

Mrs Meynell finds occasion to extol her brief passages of landscape, and quotes excellent examples
of her success in this direction. She makes a good
point when she compares the sisters : " Whereas
Charlotte Brontë walked, with exultation and enter-
prise, upon the road of symbols, under the guidance
of her own visiting genius, Emily seldom or never
went out upon those avenues. She was one who
practised little or no imagery. Her style had the
key of an inner prose which seems to leave imagery
behind in the way of approaches. . . . She seems to have
a quite unparalleled unconsciousness of the delays, the
charms, the pauses of and preparations of imagery. . . .
Charlotte Brontë's noblest passages are her own speech
or the speech of one like herself, acting the central
part in the dreams and dramas of emotion that she
had kept from her girlhood—the unavowed custom
of the ordinary girl by her so splendidly avowed in
a confidence that comprised the world. Emily had
no such confessions to publish. She contrived to
remove herself from the world ; as her person left no
image, so her ' I ' is not heard in her book. . . . Emily
was no student of books. . . . Heathcliff's love for
Catherine's past childhood is one of the profound
surprises of *Wüthering Heights* ; it is to call her
childish ghost—the ghost of the little girl—when
she has been a dead adult woman twenty years that
the inhuman lover opens the window of the house on
the Heights. . . . Another thing known to genius

and beyond a reader's hope is the tempestuous
purity of those passions. This wild quality of purity
has a counterpart in the brief passages of nature
that makes the summers, the waters, the woods,
and the windy heights of that murderous story seem
so sweet. . . .Where are there any landscapes more
exquisite and natural than are to be found scattered
in these pages . . . the two only white spots of
snow left on all the moors, and the brooks brim-full ;
the old apple-trees, the smell of stocks and wall-
flowers in the brief summer, the few fir-trees by
Catherine's window-bars, the early moon. . . . None
of these things is presented by images ; nor is that
wonderful passage wherewith the book comes to a
close : ' I lingered under that benign sky : watched
the moths fluttering among the heath and harebells,
listened to the soft wind breathing through the
grass, and wondered how anyone could ever imagine
unquiet slumbers for the sleepers in that quiet earth.'

" Wild figure as she was, Emily Brontë vanished,
escaped, and broke away, exiled by the neglect of her
contemporaries, banished by their disrespect, out-
lawed by their contempt, dismissed by their indifference." It is pleasant to turn to May Sinclair
on the subject of the Brontës after this somewhat
scrappy diagnosis.

" Love of life and passionate adoration of the earth,"
says Miss Sinclair, " adoration and passion fiercer
than any pagan knew, burns in *Wuthering Heights*.
We are plunged, apparently, into a world of most
unspiritual lusts and hates and cruelties, into the very
darkness and thickness of elemental matter : a world
that would be chaos but for the iron necessity that
brings its own terrible order, its own implacable
law . . . but—and this is what makes Emily Brontë's

work stupendous—not for a moment can you judge
Heathcliff by his bare deeds. If there was never
anything less heavenly, less Christian, than this
drama, there never was anything less earthly, less
pagan. It is above all our consecrated labels and
distinctions. It is the drama of suffering born of
suffering, and confined strictly within the boundaries
of the soul. It is not (in spite of Madame Duclaux)
any problem of heredity that we have here. It is a
world of spiritual affinities ; never was a book written
with a more sublime ignorance of the physical. The
book stands alone, absolutely self-begotten and self-
born. It belongs to no school : it follows no tendency.
It is not ' Realism,' it is not ' Romance.' Redemption
is not its key-note. The moral problem never entered
Emily Brontë's head. She reveals a point of view
above good and evil. She is too lucid and too high
for pity. There is nobody to compare with her but
Hardy ; and even he has to labour more, to put in
more strokes, to achieve his effect. In six lines she
can paint sound and distance and scenery and the
turn of the seasons and the two magics of two atmo-
spheres. The book has faults, many and glaring.
It is probably the worst-constructed tale that ever was
written, and yet in style it stands far above anything
of her sister's. . . . She has no purple patches, no decorative effects. There are no angels in her rainbows :
her ' grand style ' goes unclothed, perfect in its naked
strength, its naked beauty. Nor does her dramatic
instinct ever fail her as Charlotte's so frequently does."
So much for an example of May Sinclair's critical
genius ; for 240 pages she can go on unfolding point
after point in each of the sister's work, which all make
that work clearer to understand, easier to appreciate.
To return to Mrs Meynell. Her last essay is an attack

on the prevailing conception of the eighteenth
century as " The Century of Moderation."

" After a long literary revolt against the eighteenth-
century authors, a reaction was due, and it has come
about roundly. We are guided back to admiration
of the measure and moderation and shapeliness of
the Augustan age. And indeed, it is well enough that
we should compare some of our habits of thought
and verse by the mediocrity of thought and perfect
propriety of diction of Pope's best contemporaries.

" If this were all ! But the eighteenth century
was not content with its sure and certain genius.
Suddenly and repeatedly it aspired to a ' noble
rage.' " She quotes example after example of such
extravagant essays in noble rage as :

> His eyeballs burn, he wounds the smoking plain,
> And knots of scarlet ribbon deck his mane.

" It was the age of common sense, we are told, and
truly ; but of common-sense now and then dissatisfied, common-sense here and there ambitious,
common-sense of a distinctively adult kind taking on
an innocent tone. . . . The eighteenth century matched
its desire for wildness in poetry with a like craving in
gardens. The symmetrical and architectural garden,
so magnificent in Italy, was scorned by the eighteenth-
century poet-gardeners because it was ' artificial,'
and the eighteenth century must have ' nature '—
nay, passion. There seems to be some passion in
Pope's grotto, stuck with spar and little shells.
Truly the age of *The Rape of the Lock* and the *Elegy*
was an age of great wit and great poetry. Yet it was
untrue to itself. I think no other century has
cherished so consistent a self-conscious incongruity."

Sound criticism, genial bantering, pleasing to read,

but set it beside May Sinclair's more robust stuff—
and what a world of difference.   Listen again to Miss
Sinclair on Charlotte Brontë :   " Shirley is modern
to her finger-tips, as modern as Meredith's great
women ; she was born fifty years before her time.
Shirley was literally the first attempt in literature
to give to woman her right place in the world."
Or again, of Emily :   " Her eye seeks, and her soul
possesses, the vision of life as she wishes it . . .
that was the secret of her greatness, of her immeasurable superiority to her sad sister's." Mrs
Meynell writes in the study of art for art's sake ;
Miss Sinclair in the market-place, also of art, for the
sake of erring humanity.

V

LAFCADIO HEARN

I

IT seems a curiously roundabout way of arousing
interest in our literature in the young people of
our own country, but I have proved by experience
that the best books of criticism on English literature
for beginners are Lafcadio Hearn's *Interpretations of
Literature,* and *Appreciations of Poetry,* lectures intended solely for Japanese students, put, for that purpose, into the simplest possible language. Extremely
modest about his own attainments, "I know very little
about English literature, and never could learn very
much "—he taught it as the expression of emotion and
sentiment—as the representation of life. He based it
altogether upon appeals to the imagination. He held
the chair of English in the University of Tokyo from
1896 to 1902. For six years he was the interpreter of
the Western world to Japan, and it is singularly
fortunate that the Western world had so dignified, so
broad-minded, so idealistic an interpreter. He used
no notes in his lectures, but dictated slowly out of his
head : knowing himself to be no scholar, and having
no belief in his critical powers, he did not think his
lectures worth printing : he spent no time in analysing
technique, but went straight to the heart of his
subject and treated it as an emotional experience, as
a total expression of racial endeavour, in which ideas,
however abstract, often control conduct, and in

which conduct often explains ideas : he was a devoted
Spencerian, and had a weird power of assimilating
books which he passionately loved. That is all that
we are told of him in the preface to these volumes : it
remains to be seen how far his lectures throw light on
his character.

He begins by explaining what he calls "the in-
superable difficulty," the understanding on the part
of the Japanese of the position of women in Western
civilisation. " The highest duty of the man is not to
his father, but to his wife . . . every man is bound
by conviction and by opinion to put all women before
himself, simply because they are women . . . in time
of danger the woman must be saved first : in time of
pleasure the woman must be given the best place ;
this first place is given almost religiously : so you
understand that woman is a cult, a religion, a god :
men bow down before women, make all kinds of
sacrifices to please them, beg for their good will and
assistance. The man who hopes to succeed in life
must be able to please the women—yet it is quite
possible to worship an image sincerely, and to seek
vengeance upon it in a moment of anger (hence wife-
beating) : this feeling of worship did not belong to
the Greek and Roman civilisation, but it belonged to
the life of the old northern races—in the oldest
Scandinavian literature you will find that women
were thought of and treated by men of the north
very much as they are thought of and treated by
Englishmen of to-day. Consider how the great mass
of Western poetry is love poetry, and the greater part
of Western fiction love stories. This feeling of worship has not originated in any sensuous idea, but in
some very ancient superstitious idea."

Having so far cleared the way for a perception of

our ideas, he proceeds to lecture on " The Question of the Highest Art." Art he defines as the emotional expression of life : " The highest form of art is that which makes you feel generous, willing to sacrifice yourself, makes you eager to attempt some noble undertaking. Moral beauty, as Spencer says, is far superior to intellectual beauty, as intellectual beauty transcends physical beauty : human love is a useful example : as the sudden impulse to unselfishness, to endure anything, to attempt anything difficult or dangerous for the person beloved, is one of the first signs of true love, so it is with art." " I should say that the highest form of art must necessarily be such art as produces upon the beholder the same moral effect that the passion of love produces in a generous lover. . . . Such an art ought to fill men even with a passionate desire to give up life, pleasure, every- thing, for the sake of some grand and noble pur- pose. . . . Drama, poetry, great romance or fiction, in other words, great literature, may attempt the supreme, and very probably will do so at some future time."

On the vexed subject of the interpretation of " Classical " and " Romantic " he has much that is useful to say.

" Classic work means work constructed according to old rules which have been learnt from the Greek and Latin masters of literature, . . . in other words the classicists say that you have no right whatever to choose your own forms of literary expression, while the romanticists urge that it is right and artistic to choose whatever form of literary expression an author may prefer, provided only that the form be beautiful and correct ; the great mistake which the champions of classical feeling made in England was that of considering language as something fixed and perfected, completely evolved ; so that the romanticist retorts that the classical people wish to stop all progress. It is only, however, out of the quarrelling of the two schools that any literary progress can grow."

He advises his audience to disregard the proverb *medio tutissimus ibis,* and plunge into extremes, to take sides vigorously in the conflict : " reforms are made by the vigour and the courage and the self-sacrifice and the emotional conviction of young men who do not know enough to be afraid, and who feel much more deeply than they think : feelings are more important than cold reasoning. It is a good sign in the young to be a little imprudent, a little extravagant, a little violent : too much of the middle course is a bad sign. It does not matter at all which side you choose : conservatism has done much, and liberalism has done still more : every alternation of the literary battle results in making the romantic spirit more classic, and the classic spirit more romantic : each learns from the other by opposing it." It is obvious that Hearn's own sympathies lie entirely with the romantic school, and he urges his hearers to attempt to write great books in the language of the common people. Reverting to Europe he shows them how the vested interests, the Universities, the Church, and Society, have always ranged themselves on the side of conservatism, and points out that the opposition to change was so great that only the most extraordinary man dared to break through : " Literary style means personal character : romanticism aims at developing a personality, while classicism represses it ; so the question resolves itself into that of Personality in literature : Personality in its highest form signifies genius, and so you will find that the vast majority of

great writers are Romanticists : but there are dangers :
the great genius can afford to dispense with any
discipline which impedes its activity : thousands of
young men want to be romantic mainly because
romanticism represents for them the line of least
resistance. Even to do anything according to classical
rules requires considerable literary training and literary
patience . . . so you will find that the same man
might very consistently be at one period of his life
in favour of classicism and at another in favour of
romanticism."

Having delivered judgment on these general themes
he turns his attention to individual writers, beginning
with Crabbe, of whom he writes more interestingly
than any other critic I have ever read. Hearn's most
potent faculty is that of driving us straight back to
read the writers of whom he speaks so engagingly.
He points out the realism of Crabbe, and shows us
that one of the first signs of realism is the absence of
variety in style : " What we like in him is his great
force and truth and pithiness of expression : he
depicts, in all its naked misery, the cottage of the
poor farm-labourer, the dirt, the misery, the disease—
the country girl, once pretty, then seduced, and
abandoned ; the strain of labour exacted in the fields,
the exhausted state of the men and women at nights;
the rapid decay of strength among them, their
inability to save money, the hopelessness of their old
age" : he quotes those well-known lines on a country
parson by a country parson which I cannot forbear
from repeating :

> A jovial youth, who thinks his Sunday's task
> As much as God or man can fairly ask ;
> The rest he gives to loves and labours light,
> To fields the morning, and to feasts the night ;

None better skilled the noisy pack to guide,
To urge their chase, to cheer them or to chide.
A sportsman keen, he shoots through half the day,
And, skilled at whist, devotes the night to play.

It is hard to account for the neglect into which a
man of such powers can have sunk. Hearn also
quotes the description of the bully at school, and
recommends his audience to begin their reading of
Crabbe with *The Tales* : " One of the reasons that
you will like it is the remarkable observation of
human nature everywhere shown." To whet their
appetites he narrates the plot of *The Frank Courtship*,
and adorns the tale by pointing the literary moral.

" How many of us who write, want to write only
about the things that please ? How differently did
Crabbe act. He did not like at all the conditions
under which he was obliged to live and work, but he
recognised that it might be of great use to record
them in literature, artistically, truthfully, and dispassionately. And he became a great artist by
writing about the things he detested : but he does
not intrude his own likes and dislikes : his business
as realist was to make pictures of life . . . to work
in this way requires more than self-denial : it requires
immense force of character."

He links up Crabbe with Cowper, " almost as much
a realist, but in another way." He brings out
very well Cowper's love of nature, his classicism, his
sense of colour, his hatred of Lord Chesterfield,
Public Schools, and ugliness, his love of love, his
gentle humour, his understanding of and sympathy
with animals, and his descriptive powers, quoting
and paraphrasing with great success passages calculated to make his students desire better acquaintance with this most sensitive of the precursors of the

Romantic Revival. It is significant, however, to note
that he omits to mention either his letters or his hymns.

In his lecture on Blake, by means of some very
clever paraphrasing he throws a good deal of light on
to the meaning of that much misunderstood word,
" mysticism." " Originally," he writes, " the term
was ecclesiastic : a mystic was a man directly inspired
from heaven to write of divine things. Later a
mystic came to mean a person who believed that
through religious faith and meditation it was possible
to obtain knowledge of things which could be learned
neither by reason nor through the senses ; latterly
mysticism is any form of belief in the possibility of
holding communication with the invisible world."
Blake is a mystic in all these three senses, influenced
primarily by the teaching of Swedenborg : he used
to see patriarchs and prophets and angels walking
about, and used to talk to them. It is interesting
to recall that he printed his own poems by an
expensive process which necessitated engraving the
whole of the text backwards on copper plates in
black and white, afterward colouring the pictures by
hand. He left behind him a hundred volumes of
illustrated poetry and prose which were burnt by an
" Irvingite " parson called Tatham on the ground
that they were all inspired by the Devil. Hearn
divides up Blake's poetic achievements into three neat
divisions : the first, written under the influence of the
Elizabethans ; the second, before he came to believe
that everything he wrote was the work of ghosts and
spirits ; and the last, when he lived in a continual
state of hallucination. Swedenborg had taught him
to search for revelation, and consequently we find
even in the simplest of his songs an ulterior spiritual
meaning which needs digging for. At the beginning of

his career he breaks loose from the school of Pope, and imitates Spenser, then he strives to express his philosophic views, which nearly always take a good deal of unravelling : but the important fact remains that his achievement was of such a sort as to make all the poets who came after him in a great degree his debtor : as Hearn says, " Every poet of importance makes a serious study of Blake, and there was no poet of the Victorian age who did not learn a great deal from him."

Our hearts go out to a critic who can begin an essay on Wordsworth by saying that " he is one of the most tiresome, most vapid, and most commonplace of English poets in certain respects, a poet who wrote an astonishing amount of nonsense. He wrote poetry as regularly and untiringly as a machine cuts or saws wood. The difference between his best and his worst is so great, so extraordinary, that we cannot understand it." He notes the influence of Crabbe and Cowper on Wordsworth, and dwells lovingly on the " generous, large, tolerant, and almost pantheistic " spirit of reflection that was so especially his : he rightly calls attention to his lack of a sense of humour, and then proceeds to show how exquisite are his happiest verses even when they dwell on the simplest things. " Of sexual love there is scarcely anything in Wordsworth : but love of children, love of kindred, and love of country and friends—these forms of affection have found in his verse the most beautiful expression which English poetry can offer." He is peculiarly helpful in pointing out the fallacies in Wordsworth's *Ode on Intimations of Immortality*, but does not even touch on his theory of poetic diction ; nor are his selections at all those which one would expect. That is perhaps one of Hearn's greatest charms : although he is only attempting to give the simplest account of our great writers, he never approaches them along the lines of stereotyped criticism ; consequently, even though we may imagine that we have heard the last word on a poet whom we have carefully studied, we shall do well to look up Hearn's comments before we conclude that there is no more to be said.

He draws a lurid picture of the sensitive, imaginative, emotional Coleridge wandering about, weak and erratic, begging charity and dying in a state of utter misery : he has, however, the justice to show the more lovable and beautiful side of the poet's nature, and shows how much of a helpless child he remained all his life : precisely the opposite of Byron (who was most manly in real life, but a child in thinking), Coleridge was a child in his life, a giant in his thoughts. " He was able to influence the whole intellect of England in matters of religious feeling": the Oxford Movement was very largely caused by Coleridge : German, Greek, and mediæval philosophy equally attracted him, and were equally absorbed by him. But all he ever did was done by fits and starts, in fragments, shreds, and patches. He only wrote about 2200 lines of good poetry, but those 2200 lines are such poetry that there is nothing greater in English past or present. *The Rime of the Ancient Mariner* takes up 1500 of these, *Christabel* 600, and *Kubla Khan* and *Love* the rest. Outside these there is scarcely anything of value as a whole. And yet no other modern poet has had so great and so lasting an influence. Scott wrote *The Lay of the Last Minstrel* in imitation of *Christabel*, and Byron, Shelley, Keats, Tennyson, Browning, and Rossetti all show traces of his influence. What Coleridge did was to invent a verse

which is the most flexible and most musical in which
a story can be told, the syllables of which may shrink
in number or expand, the rhymes of which may change
places and the cadences alternate between iambic
and trochaic : thus every possible liberty for which
a poet could wish for exists in this measure. There is
an amazing elasticity by means of which monotony
becomes impossible. But he also infused into poetry
something new in tone, in feeling, in emotional expression, which defies analysis : it is something ghostly
and supernatural.

Hearn explains the vogue for Byron by trying to
show that people were tired of the coldness and the
speculative tendencies of poetry. They wanted passion instead of philosophy, human characters instead
of ghosts, anything for a change : there had been
altogether too much talk about virtue and religion
and the soul : when the Satanic school began to
speak, the Love school ceased to interest. This essay
on Byron is one of his most brilliant feats : it explains
with admirable lucidity the reasons for Byron's
European popularity : it runs through the main
features of his life, emphasising very skilfully those
facts which went to the making of this peculiar
genius, his adulterous father, his passionate mother,
his cold, prudish wife, who represented in herself all
the convention and cant and hypocrisy of the age,
his instinct for fighting, his burning sense of injustice
at the way in which England treated him when his
wife left him : " There were two Byrons : one was
naturally reckless, selfish, and sensual ; the other was
generous, heroic, and truly noble." He traces his
poetic career briefly but effectively. He shows us
how the public went wild with delight in the years
1812–1814 over the *Childe Harold*, *Corsair* poems, and

idolised the man they were to execrate in 1815. The
best part of his work was written after this date. In
1823 he gave up poetry for ever in order to help the
Greeks, and in 1824 died for them.

" No poet ever had such a vast and sudden popularity, not only in England, but all over Europe : his
influence chiefly made the French romantic movement : German, Spanish, and Italian literatures were
all influenced by him, while the English student of
Russian literature cannot help being amazed at the
Byronic element in all their great writers . . . and
yet, within a generation, this popularity ebbed and
vanished : Byron is now scarcely read, the reason for
which is easy to see. Literature means hard work,
no matter how much genius is behind it : patient
self-control is an absolute necessity for the genius.
It is not merely a case of moral self-control : there
have been cases of a lack of right conduct in life
going hand in hand with splendid conduct in work.
The reason that his work is no longer read or valued,
except by the young, is that it is nearly all done
without patience, without self-control, and therefore
without good taste or the true spirit of art. Endowed
with a marvellous talent for writing in verse as easily
as other men write in prose, he poured out his poems
as a bird pours out its song, almost without effort.
He thought that passion was poetry . . . but to
utter one's feelings in verse is only the beginning of
poetry : after that there is the correcting, polishing,
and smoothing, which Byron could never do. Byron's
verse resembles lava by its heat and force, and also
in being full of dross. There is splendour, but
splendour always in the shape of ore. The great
genius never did its best, never tried to do its best,
never could have done its best, because there was no

power of patience or self-control to help it. The
success of *Childe Harold* was due to the subject : it
had all the charm of novelty : but it was also due to
the new style of character introduced : in all these
poems there was a spirit of revolt against God and
man : curiosity was aroused : everybody was shocked,
but everybody was pleased. In spite of its cynicism,
its evil eroticism, its rebellion, and its immorality it
made him the idol of the public because it exemplified
the universe-law that strength is the only important
thing. Any human being able to prove himself
superior to the moral, social, and civil law will be
greatly honoured in an European country. Byron
forced people to think in a new way. He made them
ask themselves whether it was really enough to be
simply good in this world, and whether what we
have been accustomed to call evil and wicked might
not have not only a reason for being, but a certain
infernal beauty of its own. He infused the whole of
European literature for a time with the Satanic spirit,
a spirit which signified a vague recognition of another
law than that of pure morality—the law of struggle,
the law of battle, and the splendour of strength even
in a bad or cruel cause. Remember that Byron never
intended to do this : he was not clever enough for
that : he did it in spite of himself, and this explains
his momentary power over literature."

He advises his hearers to read *Don Juan* in order
to see Byron at his best in satire, lyrical tenderness,
and descriptive splendour : in the meantime he culls
for them typical extracts to show that, though he
was no philosopher, Byron could yet express large
thoughts in a large and lasting way, that as a descriptive writer he could far surpass Scott or Wordsworth,
and that in two forms of verse, the Spenserian stanza

and ottavarima he showed extraordinary power : as an example of supreme narrative power he quotes *Mazeppa* at great length, and concludes with the wise words, " Any critic can find bad work in Byron : but scarcely any poet can show us, at certain splendid moments, the same strength and the same fire of emotional life."

He then turns to the second figure of the Satanic school, Shelley, " even more interesting, more of a rebel, more of an enemy of society than was Byron. Shelley was at once a very lovable man and a very great fool. His peculiar folly lay in trying to put into practice the mischievous teaching of Rousseau, that civilised men should live according to nature : now we know that nature is very cruel and not in the least degree estimable from the standpoint of pure morals." Tracing the main course of Shelley's life, he lays stress upon the boy's refusal to " fag " while at Eton, his hatred of Christianity, and all moral and social teaching, culminating in the publication of the tract which caused his dismissal from Oxford : having failed to secure his cousin, Harriet Grove, for wife he ran away at eighteen with Harriet Westbrook who was sixteen, and only married her to ensure legal protection for her : it was then that he came into contact with Godwin, the ex-clergyman atheist, novelist, and politician, and his queer circle, Fanny, Miss Clairmont, Byron's mistress, and Mary Godwin, the sixteen-year-old disbeliever in marriage with whom Shelley now threw in his lot, after telling Harriet that he no longer loved her at a time when she was pregnant, with the result that she drowned herself. Society somewhat naturally turned on him in spite of the fact that he was married to Mary, so he went to Italy, and was in his turn drowned at the age of thirty. As most critics have pointed out, it is impossible to understand Shelley's poetry unless we take into account these facts of his life. His mind may have been unbalanced, but his soul was supremely generous, and he bequeathed to us the finest lyrical poetry of his age : his direct influence was slight : there is but little " body " in his work : the voice is very sweet, and touches the heart : he created a new emotional utterance, but Lafcadio Hearn warns his pupils off the longer poems. " Very little of Shelley is truly great : *The Cenci* and *Prometheus Unbound* are grand, but his greatness must be sought in his lyrical poems, which are musically perfect, though it requires a good ear to perceive their supreme value : the melody consists of a peculiar, liquid, slow, soft melancholy, implied more by the measure than by the words." He proceeds to quote from and paraphrase in his own inimitable style some of the best-known lyrics, bringing out their truth to nature and the pure spirit of classicism which pervades them. Though his estimate cannot compare in brilliance with that of Francis Thompson or Professor Dowden, it can at least take rank with Bagehot's and Clutton Brock's, and helps us to understand and therefore love a rather difficult (because so disembodied) poet better than we did before.

On Keats he writes authoritatively and wisely. He stresses the significance of his exquisite ear for the music of words, his passionate Greek love of truth and beauty, the part played in his life by the unworthy Fanny Brawne, and attempts to account for his tremendous influence on Tennyson and Browning. " He is not a poet easily appreciated : he does not appeal to the young : this is because of the extraordinary finish and fullness of his lines, which demand constant effort of imagination and fancy to read correctly : there is, moreover, scarcely any story in the larger part of his works. He did not give us anything new in the way of form. The secret of his power lies in his quality—sonorousness of phrase, splendour of colour, and a sort of divine intuition in choice of words. He did this by studying and absorbing the best work of his contemporaries and fusing them together in a new form of expression. He summarised and utilised all the forces of the moment, and so taught the generations after him how to do the same thing. He was especially the eclectic poet of his time : he had the Greek gift of lucidity and is never vague, though he is given to over-elaboration, much ornament, too many images."

He advises his audience to read *Lamia, Isabella, The Eve of St. Agnes,* the Odes and Sonnets, and to omit the rest. He then quotes and paraphrases with wonderful skill the more famous odes, stopping to recommend his readers to read Apuleius's *The Golden Ass,* which he very rightly calls " one of the world's great books." " The faculty of instantly seizing the very centre and core of an emotional fact, and of setting it before the reader in one lightning-flash of dazzling verse is shown in the *Ode on a Grecian Urn.*" He has some excellent things to say on the subject of " pleasure-pain." " Certain effects of music give us pleasure or pain that can only be accounted for by the experience of millions of previous lives, transmitted to us by inheritance." He refers his readers to Spencer's *Origin and Function of Music* for further enlightenment. He concludes his study of Keats with a very minute and able analysis of each stanza of the *Ode to a Nightingale,* which he manages to make even more beautiful (if such a thing is possible) by the expanded prose version which he appends.

" In order to understand the spirit of a national
literature we must know what makes people laugh, as
well as what makes them weep." For this purpose
he chooses Hood as the subject of one of his lectures.
" Hood will be of use to you for another reason : the
great mass of his comic work consists of clever
punning : now many a student is quite at a loss
when he comes to deal with English conversational
idioms : they need a great deal of explanation : I
can think of no better way of learning familiar idioms
than by reading the comic poems of Hood . . . but
he had a double gift : he began by attempting serious
verse, but could not live by it, so he had to turn to
the comic muse, and immediately became popular.
*The Song of the Shirt, I Remember, The Dream of
Eugene Aram,* and *The Bridge of Sighs,* are immortal :
he had the gift for touching the sensation of fear, of
pity, of tenderness, of childish memories and of the
grotesque (in *Miss Kilmansegg and Her Precious Leg*)
in a very high degree."

In his essay " on the Philosophy of *Sartor Resartus* "
Hearn does something to counteract the tendency
of all modern critics to depreciate the teaching of
Carlyle. He realises that philosophers of Carlyle's
stamp are emotional rather than logical, have more
feeling than reasoning, " but they exert more influence
than the larger thinkers do because they are more
easily understood and more widely read." After
asserting that Carlyle's message is especially given in
Sartor Resartus, he confesses that up to the time of
reaching middle life he was unable to read the book
at all, but after that period each re-reading seemed
to make it appear " greater and wider and more
astonishing."

He then explains the general idea that Carlyle had

R

in writing a Philosophy of Clothes, in these words :
" Much had been written about the body as form, but
not about the body as the garment of the soul, as the
symbol of an infinite mystery. . . . The body of man
is worn out quickly like his clothes, and has in the
same way to be discarded. Death is our change of
clothes, nothing more. We have then the first great
statement, that all visible matter is but a garment or
manifestation of the invisible, and that man's body
is not a permanent reality, but only the symbol or
covering of him." Imagine humanity without clothes
—clothes are the Foundation of Society : universal
nudity would proclaim too powerfully the general
equality of all. The next point is the relation
between the development of society and civilisation
and clothes : all clothes are a mask, and so we get to
the stage when we ask ourselves whether naked truth
is always respectable, whether it is even always good,
whether it is not sometimes bad, whether falsehood is
sometimes not only good, but even divine : truth is
often wickedness, and falsehood pure love and goodness. So it is obvious that a mask is necessary, the
mask of clothes, of illusion. " Probably imposture is
of a sanative, anodyne nature, and man's gullibility
not his least blessing." The second part of the book
is autobiographical, and gives us the history of nearly
every man. In it we are made to see that even
religious fables have their worth, that through our
own suffering we learn what the suffering of mankind
is, that without evil there can be no good : in youth
we learn through pain, in adolescence comes a period
of scepticism during which we believe in nothing,
neither in love, friendship, religion, honesty, nor
truth. Later we learn to respect humanity because
we understand how bitter life is, and how bravely

mankind has borne the burden of it : in place of the
religion we lost, we win through to a larger faith ;
instead of the lost friendship, we gain a love for all
humanity ; and, finally, just as we discovered the
necessity for pain and evil, we begin to see that
falsehood, follies, and defections are of incalculable
value, and really form the husks or masks or visible
garments of invisible truth.

On finishing the autobiography we are led on
to discuss church clothes : what men commonly call
religion the philosopher calls the clothes of religion,
which wear out, and have to be thrown away and
replaced . . . so all forms and doctrines change.
The same is true of the clothing of military power :
its symbols of rank, its machinery of force, its trappings
of colour are only the outward signs : the forms
remain when the body is dead and the spirit vanished,
like the suit of clothes in Poe's *Masque of the Red
Death* : such a thing is an army without spirit, moral
discipline, or real reserve of power.

These few points serve, at any rate, to show how
Sartor Resartus stimulates thought and an interest in
life : " the worth of the reading is in its after-effect :
it forces big thoughts and compels the recognition of
new aspects of common things." Hearn concludes his
paper with a cogent summary of Carlyle's teaching
on obstacles to success. " The obstacles in life which
are really serious are not to be overcome, either by
energy or work or honesty or duty or faith or anything
purely good. For these obstacles are the wickedness
and folly and ignorance and envy and malice of other
men." He thinks it important that his pupils
should realise that " to be good in this world is very
difficult, not because of our own difficulty in being
good, but because other people make the difficulty for

us." To be good and strong . . . that is the final teaching of Carlyle.

He devotes two of his most interesting chapters to the study of nineteenth-century novelists, beginning with Sir Walter Scott, whose style he abuses. " The whole value of the Waverley novels is in the story-teller's way of telling his story : his characters sometimes *seem* alive, but they are often impossibly good : he achieves the appearance of life by piling up an enormous mass of detail : Shakespeare does not bother himself about the outer man : he gives you the real thought . . . then the soul that he made immediately covers itself with warm flesh and becomes alive. Scott bothers about nothing except the outer man . . . and yet he has a generous vivacity, a noble idealism, a fire of purpose which influenced all European literature for good."

He has not much that is good to say of Dickens. " A character did not appear to him the marvellously complex thing that it really is : he distinguished it only by some peculiarity : he was a marvellous caricaturist, a genius in the delineation of peculiarities, mostly of a small kind."

His attempt to revive an interest in Lord Lytton is timely, for few of us nowadays read him, but we learn from Hearn that no other great novelist ever wrote in so many different ways, upon so many different things ; he wrote fashionable novels, novels of crime, historical romances, novels of middle-class domestic life, and novels of the supernatural. He recommends *A Strange Story* as incomparably his greatest book : " No more terrible story was ever written : to read it is like an education in the supernatural." " The ornamental, rhetorical, highly coloured, and musical style reached its highest in him : do not believe

critics who tell you that Lytton's style is not worth
study." Hearn falls more into line with ordinary
criticism when he praises Thackeray as the very giant
of the art of novel-writing, but he seems to be unable to give any evidence for his statement beyond
the fact that his characters are all really alive. He
sums up Charlotte Brontë's achievement thus :
" What she did was simply to put into book form her
own experiences of love, despair, and struggle, but
this with the very highest art of the novel-writer,
with a skill of grouping incident and of communicating
vividness to the least detail, rarely found in English."
He gives a rather unnecessarily full life-history of
George Eliot, but wisely comments on the baneful
influence on her art which G. H. Lewes exerted : he
selects *Romola* as her greatest work, though he reserves
a place in his affections for *Daniel Deronda*. He passes
over *Westward Ho !* in favour of *Hypatia* in his estimate
of Kingsley, to whom he devotes much space as " one of
the greatest figures in nineteenth-century literature,"
an opinion based on little or no evidence. Trollope
" had an extraordinary imagination, but it was developed entirely in one direction, in that of character
types." Wilkie Collins he selects as the greatest in-
ventor of plots we have ever had : " he could make the
reader interested in bad characters." Stevenson he
likes for his short stories and his application of realism
to the romantic method. " By his style he belongs
to the very first rank of English prose-writers : he
has never had a real superior : the story charms,
but the value is in the author's manifestation of new
flexibilities and powers in the use of English, such as
before him were practically unknown." Meredith's
style, on the other hand, he finds " detestable, most
pernicious : it is colloquial, confidential, involved, and

often provokingly obscure " . . . yet as a novelist
" he is very great indeed—great as a psychologist,
as a student of the motives and acts of the most
complex and delicate waves of character : his special
force seems to be in the depiction of a contest between
two powerful characters. He is great in his exactness
—in his perfect mastery of all the details of the
epoch, the place, or the condition which he paints.
He is great in his skill of portraiture—in painting
for us a multitude of different characters with
such distinctness that we can see them and hear
them."

Over Kipling he gushes like a schoolgirl : " Without
any comparison the greatest writer of short stories
in English : he is all mind and eye. There is nothing
sensuous in his material : there is sensitiveness
extraordinary. He is supremely impersonal, he never
describes . . . no other writer is so terse : he never
says more than just enough to convey the idea desired,
never uses more adjectives than he can help, and never
uses a weak one. His sentences are hard, very short,
and very strong : he has the power to stir fear and
wonder as no other writer can, by the simple statement of the possible : he can explain some enormously
complex social condition by the selection of a few
powerful incidents which suggest all that cannot be
reported : immense self-control, energetic strength,
manly robustness show themselves in every line of
his work, but [we are astonished to hear it] he has
a defect . . . he is not only strong, he is brutally
strong, and manifests the pride of strength in unpleasant ways : he is nearly always cynical and very
often offensively so. There is but little of the tender,
or gentle, or touching, but much of the strange, the
horrible, the bloody, the morally terrible (cf. *The Light*

That Failed) . . . and yet he is capable of the most exquisite tenderness." It is curious that no mention should be made of his child studies, which are about the only things the modern remembers Kipling for at all ! His last choice among authors is Du Maurier, whose wholly forgotten novel *Peter Ibbetson* he recommends most strongly to his pupils.

After leaving the novelists, he breaks fresh ground by reviewing the philosophers, beginning with Omar Khayyam : " The immortal charm of this composition lies in the way that Omar treats the problem of the universe which he advises us not to worry about. The impermanency of existence, the riddle of death, the fading of youth, the folly of philosophy in trying to explain the unexplainable are all considered in the most winning and beautiful verse with a strange mixture of melancholy and of ironical humour. He preached a kind of Epicureanism and a kind of Pantheism which we cannot regard really seriously, but rather as an expression of one view of life in strong opposition to the fanaticism and hypocrisy of the age in which he lived." A chapter on the Pessimists includes a full study of " Owen Meredith's " *The Portrait*, an account of James Thomson's unhappy life, a criticism of *The City of Dreadful Night*, and remarks on J. A. Symonds, A. H. Clough, whose *Bothie of Tober-na-Vuolich* receives some praise, and on Matthew Arnold, whom he damns with faint praise as " reflecting the best of his own class of thought, a poet for the old and disillusioned rather than the young." Three philosophical poems are then reviewed at length, Browning's *Rabbi Ben Ezra*, Swinburne's *Hertha*, and Meredith's *Earth and Man*. Of Browning he says : " He becomes a poet-priest by virtue of that intense sympathy which he was able to feel and to express even for beliefs that were not his own " ; of *Hertha* that, as a poem, it is beyond praise as philosophy, but on mortality it is unquestionably thin and disappointing, being a medley of northern mythology, the Bhagavad-Gita, the Book of Job, old Greek and modern ideas, Paganism and Christianity, Paganism and individualism ; it is really just a beautiful song of the unity of life. But when he comes to Meredith he has much that is important to say. " Like Swinburne, Meredith preaches the unity of life, but he preaches it in a much vaster way. Like Swinburne, he would probably regard all gods and all religions as perishable phenomena : but he can find truth and beauty and use in all beliefs, in spite of their ephemeral forms. And like Swinburne, he regards all past and present and future existence as linked together. But when he comes to speak of the meaning of life in relation to ourselves he has much more to say than Swinburne. For Meredith Nature is indeed a god, a very terrible and exacting god, and our duty to her is plain enough. Life is duty : the character of that duty is effort : the direction of that effort should be self-cultivation of the highest human faculties at the expense of the lower. All sensualism, vice, cruelty, indolence, represent crimes against Nature. Meredith preaches a Nature-religion, very terrible, all the more so because we feel it to be true, because it is the religion of a thinking man of science, who is incapable of sentimental weakness. His moral poems are strangely awful : there is no pity, no syllable of mercy for human weakness. Nature gives us our body, but our inner life is beyond her power to make or unmake : she is only the nurse : for the rest we must help ourselves : we have to struggle and put aside fear. She will never tell us our lessons in advance : never tell us why we are hurt : we have to find that out for ourselves. She gives us power—but never what we ask for.

" The real purpose of Nature is to force man to develop himself until he reaches the divine condition : the first step is the conquest of animal passion, to subdue the very fierce temptations which she purposely puts in our way. She knows that only the strong can master their appetite. Goodness must be combined with intelligence, will, and strength ; goodness and weakness are of no use. Intellectual strength is the first acquirement. Strength of mind, capacity to govern one's passions independently of moral motives, is better than weakness of mind joined with the best of moral motives. Man is, up to now, only half master of himself, only half intellectually developed : it will be in a future universe that we shall understand Nature fully and be able to read her riddles, when other worlds have been evolved." From a consideration of Meredith's poetry he passes on to his prose in *The Shaving of Shagpat,* " a fable that will live after all his novels have been forgotten because it pictures something which will always be in human nature." It is in the style of *The Arabian Nights,* but *The Arabian Nights* are cold and pale beside it. " You cannot find in *The Arabian Nights* a single page to compare with certain pages of *The Shaving of Shagpat,* and this is all the more extraordinary because the English book is written in a tone of extravagant humour."

The plot is simple. Shagpat is a merchant who wears his hair long because his head contains a magical hair called the Identical, which has the power to make all men worship the man on whose head it grows. Shigli Bagarag is a barber who proposes to shave Shagpat : he meets a horrible, ugly old woman, who makes him promise to marry her because she can help him : on kissing her she becomes young and beautiful, and gives him the Sword of Aklis, with which he eventually shaves Shagpat. Hearn interprets the allegory thus : the sword of Aklis is the sword of science, Bagarag is the scientific reformer who sets out to cure abuses, Noorna, the maiden, is Science herself ; the hair is Error which persists so strongly in convention . . . and after it is destroyed what happens ? " The great sea of error immediately closes again behind the forms that find strength to break out of it." The concluding lecture of the first volume is devoted to an appeal to the youth of Japan to enlighten Western civilization as to Eastern ideas by giving them permanent expression in dramatic, poetic, or prose form : he felicitously cites the great Russian novelists as examples of his idea. " The great work of making Russia understood was accomplished chiefly by her novelists and story-tellers ; so that a total change of Western feeling toward the Russian people came about." National feeling cannot be reached through the head : it must be reached through the heart : the Western nations know nothing about Japan, and therefore distrust her : sympathy and understanding can only be evoked by giving them novels and stories written by the Japanese about Japanese life. In two or three years one great book would have the effect of educating whole millions of people in regard to what is good and true in Japan. " A man can do quite as great a service to his country by writing a book as by winning a battle."

II

The second volume opens with a most illuminating paper on Shakespeare. " No man can understand Shakespeare till he is old : and the English nation could not understand Shakespeare until it became old. In the sixteenth century Shakespeare was enjoyed only as schoolboys of fourteen years old now enjoy him—that is to say, he was read for the story only, without any suspicion of what an intellectual giant had appeared in the world. The first thing I should like to impress upon you is that Shakespeare was a phenomenon : he is not only the greatest, but also the most difficult of authors to understand. The difficulty lies in the comprehension of the depths of his characters—that is to say, the depth of his knowledge of human nature. Here is a man who created hundreds of living characters, every one of whom is totally different from every other, and all of whom are perfectly real, perfectly alive, perfectly interesting, never in any circumstances unnatural. It is more easy to forget living persons whom you have really known than it is to forget one of Shakespeare's great characters . . . the problem of Shakespeare is a psychological one : attributing his knowledge of character to purely personal experience, we should have to say that he had the power of representing with absolute accuracy every feeling that he had ever known in any situation . . . but the experience of fifty lifetimes could not account for them : he must have acted on intuition, from the experience of hundreds of thousands of lives : at any rate, he must have been a man of a most extraordinary and exceptional physical organisation . . . a more perfectly balanced character it is not possible to imagine : he had to encounter the most dangerous obstacle—pleasure and popularity, and keep his head : the cost of never allowing his feelings to drive him into extremes must have been terrible : his astounding power of abstract thinking must have gone hand-in-hand with great unhappiness, and yet he passed through life smoothly, triumphant, and calmly."

He just touches on the personal element in Shakespeare's work and goes on to define tragedy and comedy. " A tragedy should begin with a calm opening, and then gradually become more terrible : a comedy may begin in a tragical manner, but the progress must be a steady brightening." He comments at length on Shakespeare's lack of inventive power : " Genius does not need to invent, because it recreates anything which it touches. The sources show you better than anything the enormousness of his genius."

Again : " Questions of psychology never entered into his head : his art was unconscious, he never knew how wonderful his own work was : he only felt that it was true. He never had a fundamental idea : he never even had a theory of dramatic composition : the only limit he obeyed was that imposed by the dramatic necessities of the stage." A somewhat long analysis of Iago's character, " the most absolutely natural of his painful creations," is followed by a short disquisition on the heroines, and a plea for the study of Shakespeare through his situations.

It is interesting for us, professing Christians, to see how the non-Christian Eastern peoples receive our Scriptures : Hearn very concisely summarises the various phases through which the translations of the Bible ran, from the time when Tyndale and Coverdale " coloured

the entire complexion of subsequent English prose "
by taking the Greek text and not the Vulgate for
their model, through the 1535 compilation of the
Book of Common Prayer to the 1611 edition, for which
Lancelot Andrews did so much by overlooking and
correcting all the text. " It may be said without
question that even the mistakes of the old translation
were often more beautiful than the original." He
recommends his hearers to read Genesis, Exodus,
Ruth, Esther, the Song of Songs, and, above all, Job,
" the grandest book in the Bible." " Of the New
Testament there is very little equal to the Old in
literary value : indeed, I should recommend the
reading only of the Apocalypse." He then turns to
the simple power of the Norse writers, the force of
which he traces to their physical strength : they
use the economy of force, the basis of all grace,
discarding all ornament such as adjectives, and all
description : they used it in their verse, but had the
skill to avoid it in their prose. But it is necessary to
notice that skill is needed to make the incidents and
actions create the picture without the aid of definite
descriptive adjectives. The Norse writers are also
remarkable in eliminating emotion, partiality, and
sympathy : they evoke emotion by suppressing it
altogether in their narrative : " this is the supreme
art of realism," and certainly the extracts which he
selects for quotation would seem to prove his assertion.
It is clever of Hearn to present immediately after this
excerpts from Sir Thomas Browne to show the
extreme power of great classical culture, scholarship,
and reading which makes for a style " largely coloured
and made melodious by a skilful use of many-syllabled
words derived from the antique tongues." Sir
Thomas Browne was the first great English writer

to create an original classic style which affected not
only Samuel Johnson but all the eighteenth century.
Hearn takes *Hydriotaphia* as the best example of his
work because it displays best his learning and his sense
of poetry. " He quotes from a multitude of authors,
and would appear to have read everything that had
been written about science from antiquity up to the
middle of the seventeenth century : not only did he
remember what he had read, but he digested it,
organised it, and everywhere noticed in it beauties
that others had not noticed." He asks his readers
to notice how sonorous, how dignified, how finely
polished his rolling sentences are, how scholarly, how
mystic . . . " he is a great teacher in the art of
contrast, of compression, of rhythm, of melody. He
is the father and founder of English classic prose,
incomparably superior to Bacon."

Björnson is the subject of his third lecture on prose
style : he introduces his work with a dissertation on
the necessity of studying foreign writers in translation,
quoting Dumas, Hugo, and the Russians as examples
of foreigners who have influenced English literature.
Björnson is important because he casts back to the
ancient sagas for his style, and so influences all
European literature. He is the father and founder
of a new literature which we may call modern Norse.
The best of his fiction and the bulk of it treats of peasant
life : and this life he portrayed in a way that has no
parallel in European literature, with the possible
exception of the Russian work done by Turgenev
and others. He employs, for instance, exactness in
relating the succession of incidents : he has this in
common with the early Scandinavian writers, quick-
ness of eye and accuracy of perception.

Hearn's essay on Beaudelaire, which follows, is an

attempt to interest his readers in the charm of political prose as opposed to the stern stoicism of Björnson, but it is obvious that in this case his heart is not in his work, and he fails to convince us that Beaudelaire is worthy of our study, which is, perhaps, as well. A long essay on the supernatural in fiction is written with the idea of making us trust in our dream-life, " for dreams are the primary source of almost everything that is beautiful in the literature which treats of what lies beyond mere daily experience." On Ballads Hearn is not so good : he notices the essentials, the refrain or bur-then, the simplicity, the colloquialism, its persistence through all the ages, the tendency to dwell on faery lore, love, or war, and he recommends his hearers to read *Tam Lin, Thomas the Rhymer, Child Waters*, and *Sir Patrick Spens*, but he somehow fails to bring out the charm of balladry. On Herrick, however, he is very good : " He loved the pleasures of this world, good eating and drinking, out-of-door amusements, flowers, birds, and women. No man of his time wrote more love poetry or love poetry so good. He loved sports, country games, and dancing : much of his verse is vulgar, but the best of his poetry was of extra-ordinary beauty : it is evident that one who could write so simply and joyfully about life must have a good heart. He never took religion very seriously (though he was a parson), because he was too healthy, too energetic, too naturally happy. One reason for his continued popularity is that he reflects the love of English customs and manners, and always aims at simplicity : he felt the sadness of the impermanency of life, but being naturally joyous he stimulates his readers to enjoy life as much as possible. He is pagan : but his paganism is that of the Renaiss-ance : his philosophy is that of mother-wit, and he remained an Elizabethan at heart all his days, writing about bees and butterflies and honey and kisses of girls and the gods of Greece and Rome and the customs of Christmas and of May Day. In an age of corrupt hearts he kept the joyousness and simplicity of a child—sometimes of a naughty child, but never of a very bad child. A careful study of Herrick must do a student good, in the best of all directions, in the study of daintiness of feeling united with perfect simplicity and cleverness of expression."

He sums up (in a further lecture) the philosophy of Berkeley very clearly. " He was one of the most charming men who ever lived, Pope, Swift, Addison, and Steele all uniting to praise him. His great work was the destruction of materialism. Nothing exists except mind : sight, for instance, is unreal, because we see in the mind what we imagine to be outside of the mind. All that we imagine we perceive by the senses, we perceive really within the brain only : and we have no proof of any reality outside of ourselves in the material sense. What we call the Universe exists only in the mind of God, and what we know or feel is only the influence of His power upon ourselves. If we follow out Berkeley's reasoning to its conclusion, the result is pantheism. Again, it never occurred to Berkeley that the same reasoning might be used to prove the non-existence of mind. The work of Berkeley was like a generous thaw, freeing the European intellect from old trammels : he wrote English of great simplicity and clearness ; and he brought into it something very much resembling the fine quality of the beautiful strength and lucidity of Plato."

Hearn dwells at great length, in his essay on Poe's verse, on his value as a maker of sound, citing *The*

Bells as a proof of his argument. On the subject of
Longfellow he makes the useful suggestion that it " is
a very good test of an Englishman's ability to feel
poetry simply to ask him whether he liked Longfellow as a boy : if he did not then it is no use to
talk to him on the subject of poetry at all." " Of
all the poets of the age, none was so completely
romantic as Longfellow, so ideal, so fond of the
spiritual and the impossible. . . . Ever the favourite
poet of youth, without appealing to sense or passion,
his work yet remains in the memory : his heart and
his thought never growing, though his power as a
poet constantly grew. In his vast reading he was
eternally seeking and finding subjects or ideas in
accord with his beautiful youthfulness of spirit :
therefore, he remains the poet of young men, his
charm resting chiefly on his quality of ' ghostliness.'
We seldom find that he is really great : but he touches
the heart just as well as the great poets do and by
very much simpler means. Softness, dreaminess,
ghostliness, these are the virtues of Longfellow. He
is not a painter in oils : he is only a painter in water-
colours ; but so far as poetry can be really spoken of
as water-colour painting, I do not know of any modern
English poet who can even compare with him :
he perceived the beauty of the world in a quite special
way, feeling the ghostliness of Nature in all her mani-
festations, and reflecting it in his simple verse, without
calling to his help any religious sentiment."

Hearn next refers his readers to the ethical teaching
contained in the northern philosophies, quoting at
length passages of great beauty from the *Havamal*.
Men are warned to avoid three things above all :
drink, other men's wives, and thieves. It is also
full of sound advice on the virtue of silence, and the

folly of reckless talk : it shows that the happiest men
are those who know a little of many things and no one
thing perfectly : Hearn tries to prove to the Japanese
that the modern Englishman bases his whole code of
life on this philosophy : his distrust of book-learning,
his dislike of theories, his fortitude, his chivalry to
women, his caution, his moderation, his sense of
justice . . . " All European people regard the English
as the most suspicious, the most reserved, the most
unreceptive, the most unfriendly, the coldest-hearted,
and the most domineering of all Western peoples.
They speak highly of their qualities of energy, courage,
honour, and justice, and acknowledge that the
English character is especially well fitted for the
struggle of life : it is the best social armour and
panoply of war : it is not a lovable nor an amiable
character : it is not even kindly. But it is grand, and
its success has been the best proof of its value. The
great difference between English society and other
societies is that the hardness of character is very
much greater." But a study of the *Havamal* and of
English society leads to thoughts on society in general
and the warfare of man and man. " That is why
thinkers, poets, philosophers in all ages have tried to
find solitude, although the prizes of thought can only
there be won. After all, whatever we may think
about the cruelty and treachery of the social world, it
does great things in the end. It quickens judgment,
deepens intelligence, enforces the acquisition of self-
control, creates mental and moral strength, but it does
not increase human happiness." " The truly wise
man cannot be happy."

In an essay on " Beyond Man " he takes the opportunity of showing his contempt for Nietzsche :
" undeveloped and ill-balanced thinking " is the phrase
he adopts to sum up the Nietzschean philosophy.

His idea of the *Beyond Man* is something far nobler than Nietzsche's *Superman.* " Could a world exist," he asks, " in which the nature of all the inhabitants would be so moral that the mere idea of what is immoral could not exist ? " Look for a moment at ants. Their women have no sex : they are more than vestals : their soldiers are amazons : their males small and weak, suffered to become the bride-grooms of a night and then to die : this suppression of sex is not natural, but artificial : it is voluntary : by a systematic method of nourishment ants have found that they can suppress or develop sex as they please. It vanishes whenever unnecessary : when necessary, after a war or calamity, it is called into existence again. Ants have entirely got rid of the selfish impulse : even hunger and thirst allow of no selfish gratification. The entire life of the community is devoted to the common good and to mutual help and to the care of the young. They have no religion, no sense of duty : but their whole life is religion in the practical sense. They have a perfect community, in which no one thinks of property except as a state affair, no ambition, no jealousy, no selfishness. " Go to the ant, thou sluggard, consider her ways." The question that is raised is " Will man ever rise to something like the condition of ants ?"

There then follows a succession of essays that are peculiarly Japanese in arrangement : no English critic would ever think of grouping all the poetry about tree-spirits, all the poems about insects, birds, night, and so on in separate, self-contained lectures, but the result of this method is eminently satisfactory : Hearn lightly touches on and explains all the mythological legends like those of Itylus, Philomela, Procne, and Arachne, and shows how English poets have dwelt lovingly on nightingales, larks, swallows, hamadryads, butterflies, dragon-flies, bees, grass-hoppers, crickets, spiders, ants, May-flies, doves, cuckoos, larks, sea-gulls, hawks, and all the host of beautiful living things that fly and crawl about us. In this way he introduced scores of poems which he would otherwise not have been able to bring before the notice of his pupils, and these essays though long, well repay careful reading. His lectures close with a farewell address, in which he again implores the adolescent Japanese student, however busy he may be, to devote some portion of every day to the creation of literature. " Even if you should give only ten minutes a day, that will mean a great deal at the end of a year. I hope that if any of you really love literature you will remember my words and never think yourselves too busy to study a little, even though it may be only for ten or fifteen minutes a day."

It would be hard to over-estimate the enormous influence which such an inspiring teacher and idealistic interpreter exercised over the minds of those who heard him. To the growing English boy, with a leaning towards literature, I can think of no books which could be more useful, for Hearn not only shows us what to read, but what is far more difficult, how to set about reading : he gives us the incentive, and he attunes us to the right mood. To read great masters in the spirit of Hearn is to be uplifted to an astonishing degree : he makes everything clear, he helps us to wrest the secret from out of the heart of even the most obscure : he removes completely the terror with which so many of us approach writers of the stamp of Berkeley and Locke ; he makes us concentrate always on the ulterior meaning behind the mere music of poetry, and under his guidance we find a straight path to the heart of a writer and the soul of a people.

VI

SIR EDWARD COOK

IN *Literary Recreations* Sir Edward Cook touches
on a most important point in criticism when he
states that one of the only reasons for a man
daring to write a book about books is his desire or
power of communicating to his readers the very
sincere pleasure he has found in them himself. "My
desire," he says, " is the sole reason for my undertaking
so Herculean a task" : his power is obvious from the
first page of his book to the last.

His first paper, on "The Art of Biography," teems
with brilliant ideas. A good biographer must have,
like Boswell, an instinct for what is interesting and
characteristic, and know how to arrange, select, plan,
and present. The rules to be observed are "Brevity
and Relevance," to keep the man in the foreground,
to make him stand out as a person from the background of event, action, and circumstance (which is
why the best biographies are more often of men of
letters than of men of action). A book which pro-
claims itself the *Life and Times of Somebody* is a
hybrid, little likely to possess artistic merit as biography. The true biographer will similarly beware of
Somebody and His Circle. His work is to be relevant
to an individual.

Sir Edward Cook finds the conventional first
chapter on Ancestry "as tiresome as the introduction
to a Waverley novel." Researches into hereditary
influences are too often a snare to the biographer;

he " tends to see significance in everything : characteristic carelessness if the hero drops his pipe :
and characteristic carefulness if he picks it up again."
How much worse to trace back characteristics to
ancestors ! Another danger of irrelevance lurks in a
Life and Letters. Again, the man who writes a biography full of irrelevant good things will have them
picked out by others who will fit them into their proper
places. He does but open a quarry. " He who writes
with strict respect for the conditions of his art may
carve a statue."

Next to Relevance come Selection and Arrangement : it must be understood that not everything
that is relevant can be included : it is, however, just
as easy to err by leaving out as by putting in.

" To tell ' sacred ' things aright requires the nicest
tact, but to leave them altogether untold is to strip
the biography of the things best worth telling. It
is to turn the key on the heart of the subject."

Arrangement again calls for very great care. In
the case of a full and varied life, the severely chronological method, consistently applied throughout, is
almost certainly the worst. It becomes worse if
letters, too, are given in mere chronological order.
The object of the biographer is to produce an ordered
impression, not the effect of a kaleidoscope. Again,
he must be honest. Sir Edward Cook rightly finds
fault with Dowden's *Life of Shelley* as savouring of
a partiality passing the bounds of common sense.
" The sugar-candied mood is as dangerous as the too
candid."

A good subject is a *sine qua non,* but moral goodness
is not in itself a sufficient recommendation. There are
excellent biographies and autobiographies of rascals,
and there are very dull books about saints. The

first qualifications of a good subject are that the life
of the man or woman should be really memorable,
that there should be a marked personality behind
the actions, that the character should be distinctive
and interesting.

A second element in the goodness of biographical
subject is the existence of material of self-expression,
clothed in attractive and intelligible language. Such
material may exist in the shape of diaries, memoranda,
letters, or recorded conversations.

Again, contrasts and foils are often useful : a hero
postulates a villain : it is one of the ironies of the art
of biography that the lives which, from some points
of view, are best worth writing are those which
nobody will read and which, therefore, are seldom
written, for as George Eliot said : " the growing good
of the world is partly dependent on unhistoric acts :
and that things are not so ill with you and me as they
might have been, is half owing to the number who
lived faithfully a hidden life and rest in unvisited
tombs."

As Ruskin's most able editor we should expect Sir
Edward Cook to write well on Ruskin's style, which
is the subject of his second paper. First he cites other
men's views : Mr Asquith's epithets of " intellectual
independence," " spiritual insight," and " golden-
tongued eloquence " : Lord Morley's " one of the
three giants of prose style in the nineteenth century,"
and Lord Acton's " doubled the opulence and significance of language and made prose more penetrating
than anything but the highest poetry."

" The secret of Ruskin's style at bottom," says Sir
Edward Cook, " nearly all comes to this : that he had
something to say, that he said it in the way that was
natural to him, and that nature had endowed him

with exquisite sensibility." The essential features are underived and incommunicable : the style is the man. His gift was of nature : the glow, the colour, the music, the exuberance of language are found in his notes and diaries no less than in his finished books. Throughout his working life he saw with his own eyes, he felt with his own heart, and what he learnt was knowledge at first hand. He read widely and discursively, but always in the original texts, which accounts for some of his waywardness and ingenious perversity although it preserved his intellectual independence. In his autobiography he tells us that his literary work was done as quietly and methodically as a piece of tapestry, but he took infinite pains in getting the stitches right. His command of language was due to the constant habit of never allowing a sentence to pass in which he had not considered whether, for the vital word in it, a better could be found in the dictionary. There is an interesting story of Ruskin's father telling his son's publisher to send in a separate account for corrections to him. " Don't let my son know : John must have his things as he likes them : pay him whatever would become due, apart from corrections, and send in a separate bill for them to me." Paragraphs and chapters were written over and over again before they satisfied him. There is, however, as Sir Edward Cook notices, a danger in taking overmuch thought over one's style : " The mischief comes, not from taking pains about the manner of saying a thing, but only when the manner begins to be of more moment than the matter, a mischief from which Ruskin, in his earlier work, did not escape. ' All my life,' he says, ' I have been talking to the people, and they have listened, not to what I say but to how I say it.' "

Too much attention was called to the manner of his style by palpable display, but later " he became master not more of rhetorical pomp and of the long rolling sentence than of concentration, closely packed with thought. He revised and elaborated in order to clarify, to chasten, to deepen, and to impress." It is the very number of his gifts that so astonishes us in Ruskin. " Not only was he possessed of acute sensibility and of a most original mind, but he had a great mastery of language ; he was something of a botanist, geologist, and mineralogist, and I doubt whether he ever sat down to describe anything with the pen which he had not spent hours in drawing with the pencil." Sir Edward Cook finishes his most suggestive critical study of the great stylist by recommending five examples of his prose style as especially worthy of our study : the chapter on " The Region of the Rain Cloud," the description of the narcissus fields on the mountain-side about Vevay, the description of the old tower of Calais Church, all in *Modern Painters*, the description of an old boat at the beginning of *The Harbours of England*, and the description of the Rhone at Geneva in *Præterita*.

The Art of Indexing is to me the most charming of these papers. " There is no book," he begins, " so good that it is not made better by an index, and no book so bad that it may not by this adjunct escape the worst condemnation." He rightly goes on to assert that the importance of the art of indexing is little understood : " Many people do not even know that it is an art at all."

Two classes of books in particular should always have a good index—the best books and the most unreadable books. " The best books, because there is so much in them that a reader will want to find again :

the worst books, because lacking an index they are
without any reason for existing at all." He even
urges, as Doctor Johnson did to Richardson, apropos
of *Clarissa Harlowe*, that novels should have an
index. His argument for this departure is ingenious.
" A biography cannot be considered complete without
an index. Why not also a novel ? The great characters of fiction are much more worthy of memory,
and do, in fact, live much longer, than the subjects
of most biographies." For the life after death it is
not necessary that a man or a woman should have
lived. But Sir Edward Cook does not suggest that time
must be allowed to set its seal on a novelist's work
before the day comes for an index. He then goes on to
define what he means by an index. " An index is
meant to be a pointer and to serve as a time-saving
machine. It should enable a reader, first, to find
readily the place where the author has said a particular thing, and, secondly, it should enable him to find
all that the book has said on a particular subject."
In applying these principles he lays down as the first
rule, one book one index. One index alphabetically
arranged is the only right plan. The next point is to
settle what to include in the index. Proper names,
of course, are the first essential ; then, every subject on
which the indexer finds any substantial discussion : he
is working for an unknown future, and for readers whose
tastes and interests he cannot know. He must, for
this purpose, exercise discrimination. A good index
will have a great many titles : then comes the question
of arrangement. The most frequent and heinous
vice is the practice of following a subject-heading by
long strings of page numbers without any indication
of what you will find on the several pages : this is to
fob you off with an index which is no index. . . .

Where then a book contains many mentions of a person or a subject, the indexer must analyse them and tell you not only on what page each mention will be found, but also what is the subject of the mention on each page. This is the most difficult and least mechanical part of an indexer's work. If the reader thinks that anybody can do it, let him try his hand and he will learn better. It needs much time, thought, and judgment to seize the true sense of a passage, to decide what description will best facilitate reference, and then to make the entry with the concision required in an index. He quotes the classic example of how not to do it, which is alleged to occur in a law book :

BEST, Mr Justice, his great mind, p. 101.

On turning to the page one is supposed to have found the statement that " Mr Justice Best said he had a great mind to commit the man for trial." Sir Edward Cook takes advantage of this delicious story to press home the point that the indexer should be impartial. His business is to be a signpost, not a critic. " Let no damned Tory index my History," said Macaulay.

How, next rises the question, is the indexer to arrange the entries under each heading after he has sorted them out under proper names or subjects ? The plan generally adopted is to arrange the entries in the order in which the passages indicated by them occur in the book, but Sir Edward Cook brings forward several grave objections to this, and suggests that in every long heading in an index there should be sub-headings, and the order of arrangement under each should be alphabetical. It greatly adds to the labour of the indexer, but it also greatly helps facility of reference. The number and kind of sub-heads must depend on the nature and volume of the matter in

hand. It may be helpful sometimes to divide references to general subjects into (1) leading ideas or
principal passages, and (2) general references. In (2)
entries should be alphabetical, but in (1) the order may
well be explanatory and logical. Should the author
do his own indexing ? Sir Edward Cook thinks that
he should where possible because " there is nothing
like making an index for discovering inconsistencies
and needless repetitions : few authors have the
patience, but those who have not should recognise the
importance of the art and make due acknowledgment
so that indexing might be established as one of the
minor literary arts." " Index by So-and-So in the
forefront of a book would be at least as reasonable as
' Wigs by Thingummy,' on the programme of *Hamlet*."
A list of statistics on the scale for an index follows,
Lord Morley's *Recollections* holding the record of
1 to 10. The book takes up 760 pages and the index,
in small print and double column, 76. He ends on a
note of general comment of very great value.

" A perusal of the pages of an index, and even the
process of making it, are not dull, dead things. I
confess that when I look into a new book, especially
if it be one which I have not yet bought, I turn first
to the index. There is no better way of sampling a
book. From reviews you can never tell. The reviewer's taste, if he blames, may not be yours ; and
if he praises and gives you specimens you may find
that he has picked out all the plums and that the rest
is leather and prunella. An index gives you a taste
of the quality at once, which, perhaps, may be why
some authors and publishers are so shy of it. It is
not an easy art, but if you persevere you may find the
same sort of satisfaction that a good housewife is said
to find in a spring-cleaning or a scholar in rearranging

his books. . . . A master of worldly wisdom gave
this among other injunctions to his pupils : ' Never
drudge.' The scholar, when trial is made of his
patience, acts on a different precept : ' Never grudge.' "

An extremely effective description of the inception
and progress of the *Cornhill Magazine* is the subject of
Fifty Years of a Literary Magazine. " Thackeray's
latest books, the last pages of Charlotte Brontë, the
first appearances of many a poem by Tennyson,
Browning, Mrs Browning, Meredith, and Swinburne,
and many a collected volume by Matthew Arnold,
J. A. Symonds, Leslie Stephen, Robert Louis Stevenson, and a host of other ' writers of eminence ' are
all to be found in the back numbers of the *Cornhill*."
Mr George Smith, the only begetter of the magazine,
was the first man to combine the monthly review and
the serial publication of novels in one magazine to be
sold at the price of the then cheapest monthly periodi-
cal. Thackeray was made editor, and though Trollope
accuses him of too thin a skin and of being un-
methodical, he made a great success of it. It is
startling to-day to think that " Mrs Grundyism "
was powerful enough to prevent Mrs Browning,
Thomas Hardy, and Ruskin from continuing certain
contributions, which must have hurt Thackeray very
much, but he must have been compensated by the
thought that he secured for his venture a circulation
of 100,000 copies a month almost at once, as well as
by the thought that he set a tone and a standard of
high humane culture which has never left it. The
Thackeray touch can still be traced in it to-day.
Leslie Stephen, James Payn, and Reginald Smith
each succeeded in turn to the editorship, and kept up
the tradition by ripe judicious selection and high rates
of pay. A single number of the magazine once cost

George Smith £1183, and in four years he paid £32,280 to literary contributors alone, and £4376 to artists for illustrations. Thackeray was then getting twelve guineas a page and George Eliot £583 for a single instalment of *Romola*.

" To-day the greatest circulations belong to periodicals of a very different kind. We hear much in this connexion about a decadence in the popular taste. I do not believe it. The fallacy consists in an implied assumption that persons who, fifty years ago, would have read *Cornhill* now read the more frivolous magazines. The fact is that the latter class of readers were, fifty years ago, reading either nothing or periodicals far more rubbishy. There is another side of the case. The market for good literature, whether in books or in periodicals, is larger to-day than it has ever been, but the supply is provided by many more competitors. There are fewer literary magazines, but in the magazines there is as much literature." He then passes on to *Literature and Modern Journalism*, a noble defence of the art and craft of writing for the newspapers. He notes how all the great writers combine to ridicule the mere journalist, from Dickens (himself once editor of *The Daily News*) in *The Eatanswill Gazette*, and Thackeray in *Philip*, to Lord Morley, who dismisses the newspaper Press in trenchant phrase as " that huge engine for keeping discussion on a low level," Ruskin, who talks of " so many square leagues of dirtily-printed falsehood," Leslie Stephen, who defines journalism as " writing for pay upon matters of which you are ignorant," and Thomas Hardy, most merciless of all, who, in a lecture, once said : " While millions have lately been learning to read, few of them have been learning to discriminate ; and the result is an appalling increase every day in slipshod writing that would not have been tolerated for one moment a hundred years ago . . . writing is now done by men, and still more by women, who are utterly incapable of, and unconscious of, that grin of delight which William Morris assured us comes over the real artist, either in letters or in other forms of art, at a close approximation to, if not an exact achievement of, his ideal."

" The journalist," retorts Sir Edward Cook, " seems to me to stand in a middle position between the expert and the complete ignoramus. When he starts upon a subject he often knows very little about it, but he sometimes picks up much as he goes along." " When I want to learn a subject," said Disraeli, " I sit down to write a book about it. . . ." " The connexion between literature and journalism has been and is still close, and there is certainly as much good writing in the Press as at any earlier time. The spirit of literature invades journalism to-day, and the publication of a great book is recognised as an event not much less important than the affairs of a cinema artist." " *The Literary Supplement of ' The Times '* seems to me to show a higher and more evenly sustained level of literary merit than I can remember in any newspaper of my time." The tone and manners of the Press reflect those of the world it mirrors, and these are certainly an improvement to-day on what they were a hundred years ago. " The idea that modern journalism is harmful to literature because its scrappiness encourages triviality and desultoriness is founded on a misconception." " The *Tit-bits* journalism is not entirely occupied with the diffusion of useless knowledge : the ' Home Journals ' owe their success to the dissemination of comforting moral platitudes which are, after all, only crude and prosaic echoes of Tennyson." " But perhaps the best that can be said for scrappy journalism is that it affords to millions of people an innocent pastime . . . it is a delusion to suppose, when one sees, say during the luncheon hour in the City, boys and girls in St Paul's Churchyard devouring their favourite *Scraps* or *Cuts* that they would otherwise be immersed in contemplation of the Cathedral or the study of Philosophy. It is probable that the newspapers are schoolmasters which bring a certain number of the great public to read other things. It is certain that the extension of the popular newspaper press has synchronised with an extension of cheap editions of classical literature, and it is unlikely that the publishers put these reprints upon the market solely from a disinterested love of good literature." After all, " journalese " is not so terrible as " officialese," and it must be remembered that there are millions of people who read nothing except what the journalists write. Having concluded his defence, Sir Edward Cook makes an appeal to all writers.

" There is nothing which a journalist should cultivate more scrupulously than the craftsman's conscience, and there is no better training in this than the study of good literature." " If my manner of speaking is good," said John Bright, " it may have become so from reading what is good, so that the eye and the ears and the mind may become familiar with good language."

The writer, however humble may be his sphere, who has some knowledge and appreciation of good literature, may always keep an ideal before him. He will be able then to achieve that grin of delight of which William Morris speaks as coming over the real artist on achieving his ideal.

His essay on *Words and the War* will increase in interest as the years go on, for some of the words coined since 1914 would be in danger of being forgotten were it not for their preservation in books of this sort. " A page of history may be summed up in a new word or phrase or in the altered sense of an old one." It would be indeed ungrateful if our children were allowed to forget the origin of such heroic names as Anzac, Waacs, and Wrens. What will the youth of a hundred years hence be able to make of such sentences as " stalled his bus and pancaked thirty feet, crashed completely, put a vertical gust up me . . . just as I was starting my solo flip in a rumpty " ? Is there ever likely to be a term of endearment quite so soul-satisfying as to supersede " Blighty " ? A history of the war in little might be written out of the words it has brought into common use.

His seventh essay, *A Study in Superlatives*, is in some ways the most charming in the book. It has, at any rate, the very great merit of sending the reader back to re-read many of the masterpieces of literature in order to make up his mind afresh as to which is the finest line in poetry, the world's greatest ode, and so on. We all know, as Lord Morley said, " that we are not called upon to place great men as if they were collegians in a class-list." We are not called upon, it is true, but we all do it, and, after all, there is much to be said in favour of good lovers and good haters of books. It is this characteristic that so pleases us or infuriates us in Swinburne, for instance, as when he says of a certain piece that it is " so much the noblest of sacred poems in our language that there is none which comes near it enough to stand second," a piece, by the way, which one need scarcely say, is not to be found in any

T

hymn-book. " It is a disgrace," says Sir Edward
Cook, " of long standing to the English Church that
with so great a wealth of religious poetry at choice,
so much doggerel should be used in places where they
sing " ; a sentiment with which most of us would
cordially agree.

Ruskin talks of the epitaph of Simonides on the
Spartans who fell at Thermopylæ as " the noblest
group of words ever uttered by man." It is useful
that we should be betrayed into stating our favourites,
for a man is known by the company he keeps in his
reading, by the authors he loves, by his preferences
and aversions. It is, for instance, enormously helpful to us to know that Samuel Butler regarded
Handel and Shakespeare as our greatest achievements. With regard to favourite lines, Mr Gladstone
plumped for " Or hear old Triton blow his wreathed
horn " and

μηδέ τι χείρονος ἀνδρὸς εὐφραίνοιμι νόημα.

Tennyson chose " Whose dwelling is the light of
setting suns," and Lord Morley as " the most melting
and melodious single verse,"

After life's fitful fever he sleeps well,

The anthologist of prose and verse extracts would do
well to study famous authors' selections of the best
passages. Homer, Horace, Burke's panegyric on
Howard, Carlyle, Charlotte Brontë's description of
Rachel as Vashti in *Villette*, and Virgil are among the
most commonly selected. " Amusement may be
gained," says Sir Edward Cook, " in placing the five
great odes of Keats in order of merit. Swinburne,
in this instance, gives a first to each." " Perhaps,"
he says, " the two nearest to absolute perfection,
to the triumphant achievement and accomplishment

of the very utmost beauty possible to human words, may be that to *Autumn*, and that on a *Grecian Urn*; the most radiant, fervent, and musical is that to a *Nightingale*; the most pictorial and, perhaps, the tenderest in its ardour of passionate fancy is that to *Psyche*; the subtlest in sweetness of thought and feeling is that on *Melancholy*." The game, as Cook says, has, at any rate, the advantage of making the players refresh their memory of pieces of which it has been said that " Greater lyrical poetry the world may have seen than any that is in these, lovelier it surely has never seen nor ever can it possibly see." I, for one, demur from Hallam's judgment in pronouncing Milton's *Ode on the Nativity* as the finest in the English language. Sir Edward Cook allows that it may be true of regular odes, but among irregular odes is any finer, he asks, than Tennyson's *On the Death of the Duke of Wellington*?—an ode which was almost universally depreciated by the critics on its appearance on account of its unconventionality and un-Tennysonian note. In choosing the best work of any poet, Sir Edward Cook suggests that it is a tribute to Tennyson's genius that opinion is still divided as to whether his best piece was written when he was 26, 38, or 76, while it is universally admitted that all Wordsworth's best work was done between the ages of 28 and 38, and that nobody would choose anything written by Browning after he was 56, or Swinburne after he was 42. *Don Quixote, The Vicar of Wakefield, Heart of Midlothian, Les Misérables, Persuasion,* share the honours of the greatest novel ever written, as Thucydides, Tacitus, and Gibbon have still to fight for premiership among historians.

His penultimate paper on *The Poetry of a Painter* deals with J. M. W. Turner's failure to become a poet, in spite of the utmost industry and diligence and a very highly developed imagination. As a public lecturer Turner failed in spite of the great pains that he took . . . his notebooks are full of verses and contain even more poetry than drawings.

He was, at any rate, able to appreciate good poetry when he met it ; he takes as mottoes for some of his pictures exceedingly apt lines from Milton and Thomson, the favourite poet of the great public at the time. He fell under Thomson's spell and imitated him. Akenside, Ossian, Scott, and Byron were all used by him to illustrate his pictures, and his sympathy with the last of these is obvious. The queer thing is that Turner was really the Shelley among painters, though the poet never saw the pictures and the painter did not know the poems. " In both there is a strain of pensive melancholy joined to a sense of the material beauty of the universe which finds expression in a love of iridescence, colour-depth, and soft mystery. The vast landscapes of Turner's later manner, melting into indefinite distance, recall many passages in Shelley's *Prometheus*." One example out of many very apt ones given by Sir Edward Cook may be cited :

> Half the sky
> Was roofed with clouds of rich emblazonry,
> Dark purple at the zenith, which still grew
> Down the steep west into a wondrous hue
> Brighter than burning gold.

The colouring is that of many a sky of Turner's. It is curious, too, to notice the dates : the production of *Alastor*, *Prometheus*, and *Julian and Maddalo* synchronise with the transition to Turner's second and more aerial period. The more Turner read, and

the more his art of painting developed, the greater
became his desire to write poetry. He occasionally
hits on a good line, but he was never able to keep at
one level for more than a line or two : he persistently
tried and he persistently failed. Sir Edward Cook
attempts to explain why a consummate master in
one art should strive so continually after expression
in another. Something was due, no doubt, to his
obstinate pride and constant ambition, something to
mere love of mystification. He was shy, sensitive,
secretive, ill-favoured, of humble birth, destitute of
the graces, and wished to be recognised as a " literary
gentleman." Browning's

> Does he paint ?   He fain would write a poem . . . .
> Put to proof art alien to the artist's,
> Once, and only once, and for one only,
> So to be the man and leave the artist,
> Gain the man's joy, miss the artist's sorrow,

may explain matters more fully. Turner, we learn,
missed the man's joy : he found no woman of sympathetic soul to love him, but the instinct to escape
the artist's sorrow, the interest of self-expression, was
strong within him. In his own art he was open to
unsympathetic criticism. " What is the use of them
except together ? " he asks. He turned to poetry in
the hope of finding a medium that should all-express
him. The hope failed him. " Indistinctness is my
forte," he says of his pictures. The same is true of
his poetry ; and in poetry indistinctness is a fault.
He lacked the logical faculty, the feeling for beauty,
and even for coherence, in words : he had the imagination of a poet, but his thoughts travelled faster than
his language could follow. So the double gift that was
Blake's and Rossetti's was denied to him. He never
succeeded in explaining his pictures, all of which

require many, many pages. His persistence in attempting verse suggests another remark. According to Pater all art aspires towards the condition of music, a theory that pleased Whistler because it irritated his critics. A rival theory contends that all art tends to pass into the condition of poetry, and it was to this view that Turner inclined. On the technical side his pictures were studies in colour, in his mind and intention they belonged to the domain of the poets. He painted his impressions, and these were largely coloured by thoughts on the fates and fortunes of men and states.

Sir Edward Cook's last essay, on *The Second Thoughts of Poets,* is also his longest and most ambitious. It shows more, perhaps, than any of the other papers how happy has been his reading, how discursive, how deep and how careful. It is as well from time to time that some one should remind us of the commentator's art, and it is even better that we should be shown how poets revise the first draft of their impressions: "Shelley's manuscript might have been taken," says Trelawny, " for a sketch of a marsh overgrown with bulrushes, and the blots for wild ducks." A study of poets' second thoughts makes us realise that some of their happiest phrases were not " inevitable " inspirations, but were, in reality, second thoughts.

> Far from the fiery noon, and *eve's one star,*

read originally,

> Far from the fiery noon, and evening.

> *And on the bosom* of the deep
> The smile of Heaven lay

was first printed

> *And on the woods* and on the deep.

The classic instance of revision is, of course, *The Ancient Mariner*, which was re-written in three ways : Coleridge altered the archaic style : he omitted some grisly passages : and he altered several things to make the story clearer :

> One after one, by the horned moon
> (Listen, O stranger, to me),
> Each turned his face with a ghastly pang,
> And cursed me with his e'e,

becomes

> One after one, by the star-dogg'd moon,
> Too quick for groan or sigh,
> Each turn'd his face with a ghastly pang,
> And cursed me with his eye,

which is a very obvious improvement in every way, caused by the necessity of having to change " e'e " to " eye." It is interesting to think that " It ate the food it ne'er had eat " originally ran " The Mariners gave it biscuit-worms " ! and that " a thousand thousand slimy things " is merely a declension from " a million million slimy things." " The first editions are the worst editions," says Tennyson, and it certainly did his verse good to be grossly abused in the *Quarterly*, for it checked the publication of any fresh verse by the poet for nearly ten years, and was not Horace " the wise adviser of the nine-years ponder'd lay " ? At any rate, Lockhart's gross attack made Tennyson alter for the better many verses ; examples are given from *Oenone* and *The Lady of Shalott* and *In Memoriam*, which are well worth comparing. It is hard to imagine that there could ever have been lines in Fitzgerald's *Omar Khayyam* calling for revision, but there is no question that " Alas, that spring should vanish with the Rose "

is much improved by the substitution of " Yet Ah "
for " Alas." It is worth, in this instance, preserving
all the editions, for many valuable stanzas were
ultimately deleted. " Two of the loveliest of modern
poems owe much of their perfection to second
thoughts." It is excellent to think that Sir Edward
Cook selects *Love in the Valley* as worthy of the epithet
" loveliest." But which of the two versions, 1851 or
1878, is it that you mean when you think of it ? The
later version has the greater following, but Tennyson
preferred the earlier. Meredith found the excellent
swinging cadence in a song by George Darley, but
the 1878 version gives instances of maturer artistry
in the very first lines.

Under yonder beech-tree $\begin{cases}(1851) \text{ standing}\\(1878) \text{ single}\end{cases}$ on the green-
    sward.

Couched with her arms behind her $\begin{cases}(1851) \text{ little}\\(1878) \text{ golden}\end{cases}$ head.

A comparison of two famous stanzas makes interesting study. Here is the 1851 edition :

Shy as the squirrel and wayward as the swallow ;
Swift as the swallow *when athwart the western flood*
Circleting the surface *he meets* his mirrored winglets,—
Is that dear one in her maiden bud.
Shy as the squirrel *whose nest is in the pine-tops ;*
Gentle—ah ! that she were as jealous as the dove !
Full of all the wildness of the woodland creatures,
Happy in herself is the maiden that I love !

But good as this is, how much more inevitably right
is this, of 1878 :

Shy as the squirrel and wayward as the swallow,
Swift as the swallow along the river's light
Circleting the surface to meet his mirrored winglets,
Fleeter she seems in her stay than in her flight.

Shy as the squirrel that leaps among the pine-tops,
Wayward as the swallow overhead at set of sun,
She whom I love is hard to catch and conquer,
Hard, but O the glory of the winning were she won !

"The love poem of 1851," says Sir Edward Cook,
"was transformed upon revision into the most
beautiful of poems and lyrics of the joy of earth."
Compare again Rossetti's early version of *The
Blessed Damozel* with that of 1870 and after :

The blesséd damozel leaned out
From the gold bar of Heaven ;
Her blue grave eyes were deeper much
Than a deep water, even,

is not comparable with :

The blesséd damozel leaned out
From the gold bar of Heaven ;
Her eyes were deeper than the depth
Of waters stilled at even.

It is queer to think that Rossetti thought it necessary
to cancel two such beautiful lines as :

Fair with honourable eyes,
Lamps of a pellucid soul—

because Browning afterwards talked of "lustrous and
pellucid soul" in *The Ring and the Book*, and he feared
the charge of plagiarism. "This instance," says
Sir Edward Cook, "should be a warning to critics
who, in all ages, have been over-fond of seasoning
their discovery of parallel passages with suspicion of
plagiarism."
Matthew Arnold made a very happy alteration in
The Scholar Gipsy when he changed "Pluck'd in shy
fields and distant *woodland* bowers" to "Pluck'd
in shy fields and distant *Wychwood* bowers." This

alteration may serve as the poet's answer in advance to one of the most perverse criticisms ever made by a man of taste. Dr Garnett thought that, though the charm of Arnold's pieces may be " enhanced for Oxonians," yet " the numerous local allusions which endear the poem to those familiar with the scenery, simply worry when not understood," to which Professor Saintsbury has retorted : " One may not be an Athenian, and yet be able to enjoy the local colour of the *Phaedrus*."

Keats vastly improved a famous ode by substituting " magic " for " the wide," and " perilous " for " keelless " in the following lines :

> The same that oft-times hath
> Charm'd *the wide* casements, opening on the foam
> Of *keelless* seas, in faery lands forlorn :

Was it his own unhappy passion that induced him to change

> O what can ail thee, *knight-at-arms*,

to

> O what can ail thee, *wretched wight* ?

His second thoughts were not always the better, though his final revision of his sonnet *To Sleep* is infinitely finer than the earlier versions.

" I have never made," says Sir Edward Cook, " a close study of Wordsworth's own second thoughts : but such as I have chanced to note are seldom improvements. After all, Wordsworth is of all great poets the most unequal, and his happiest things came by grace and not by reflection."

" Beauty and truth," he concludes, " may come together and find the exactly right words in the flash of a moment, or after many attempts : yet Tennyson's saying should be remembered : ' Perfection in art is, perhaps, more sudden sometimes than we think, but then the long preparation for it, that unseen germination, *that* is what we ignore and forget.' Wordsworth wrote best when he revised least . . . one thing alone is certain—that poetry is an art, and that art is long."

VII

SET DOWN IN MALICE

MR GERALD CUMBERLAND seems to have set out with the idea of treating the living as Mr Lytton Strachey in *Eminent Victorians* set out to treat the dead. That is to say, he seeks to earn some notoriety as an otherwise unknown man by lampooning his betters. But there is a marked divergence between the two men. Mr Strachey is pre-eminently the eclectic, the fastidious scholar, well-read, magnificently equipped with the historic sense, with an exact knowledge of what is grain and what is chaff, able to sift and weigh evidence, almost a genius at discarding irrelevancies and retaining minute features which illuminate and bring into prominence the side of the character he wishes to revivify. Mr Cumberland is just a precocious schoolboy indulging in scandalous chatter : fascinating us with saucy tit-bits cleverly retold, but, nevertheless, just a witty schoolboy cheeking his masters when he ought to be getting on with his work.

It is significant that he begins with Shaw, himself a master craftsman in the same school. He says nothing about him that is worth putting on to paper ; in fact, twenty-seven pages of twaddle have to be waded through before we arrive at any statement which could possibly mean anything more than the paragraphs in *Society Snippets*. Then we find something definite about . . . Lloyd George of all men !

" He has a wonderful gift of making you feel that

he thinks you are the most interesting and most
intelligent person he has ever met." I rather imagine
that somebody's leg was being pulled when Mr
Cumberland called on Lloyd George, and it was not
the Prime Minister's. Anyway, why *Set Down in
Malice*? Perhaps Mr Cumberland aspires to an
O.B.E. Doctor Walford Davies is (forsooth) to be
judged by his stock of adjectives in an after-dinner
speech, which included " pernicious," " poisonous,"
" naughty," " unlicensed," and " immoral." Frank
Harris has a whole chapter to himself, and is enthusiastically praised : no malice here, only a vague
impression of a great genius, greatly generous, a
lover of delicacies " from whom no gastronomic
secrets were hid." There is a grotesque picture of
Stanley Houghton, after closing his ledgers, jumping
gymnastically on to a passing tram every night,
bound for Alexandra Park. After a hurried meal,
out with the MSS., the notebooks, the typescript, and
to work ! And how hard he did work ! " He was
hard ; he was unimaginative ; he was unromantic.
But he was extraordinarily apt, and he had a neat and
tidy brain. . . . He was not modest, and he could not
feign modesty. His vanity was neither charming
nor aggressive ; it was cold and distant, without
geniality, without humour. . . . He had no genius :
there was not a trace of magic in him : he was merely
extraordinarily clever, closely observant and possessed
of an instinctive sense of form and of literary values."
One remark in an interview Mr Cumberland had
with Houghton sticks in my brain : it is a good
illustration of his critical ability : " Only G. H. Mair,
Willie Yeats and high-school girls think Synge
great, Houghton."

It is not until page 69 that Mr Cumberland really

wakes up, but Arnold Bennett rouses him to active
irony.

" Bennett was rather short, thin, hollow-eyed,
prominent-toothed. He wore a white waistcoat and a
billycock hat very much awry, and he had a manner
of complete self-assurance. . . .

" ' I notice,' said I, ' that you continue writing for
The New Age in spite of their violent attacks on
you."

" ' Yes,' he answered laconically, and he looked
dizzily over my left shoulder." The account of the
breakfast given in Manchester by G. H. Mair to Arnold
Bennett and Houghton is very well told : the whole
hour was spent in a tedious and protracted discussion
about a cabman, a very large trunk, and strangulated
hernia. "A great writer," concludes Mr Cumberland :
" no doubt, a very great writer : but you might gaze
at him across a railway carriage for hours at a time
and never suspect it."

There is a delightful story of G. K. Chesterton
emerging from Shoe Lane, hurrying into the middle
of Fleet Street, and abruptly coming to a stand-
still in the centre of the traffic. " He stood
there for some time, wrapped in thought, while
buses, taxis and lorries eddied about him in a whirl-
pool and while drivers exercised to the full their art
of expostulation. Having come to the end of his
meditations he held up his hand, turned round,
cleared a passage through the horses and vehicles
and returned up Shoe Lane." When Mr Cumberland
lies, he lies like Falstaff, for which I love him. Of
Masefield, too, he has something interesting to tell us.
" He has an invincible picturesqueness : he is tall,
straight, and blue-eyed, with a complexion as clear
as a child's. His eyes are amazingly shy, almost

furtive. His manner is also shy . . . He speaks to
you as though he suspected you of hostility, as
though you had the power to injure him and were on
the point of using that power. You feel his sensitiveness and you admire the dignity that is at once
its outcome and its protection. . . . His mind is cast
in a tragic mould, and his soul takes delight in the
contemplation of physical violence. . . . I believe he
is intensely morbid, delighting to brood over dark
things, seeing no humour in life, but full of a baffled
chivalry, a nobility thwarted at every turn."

It is pleasing to think that A. A. Milne, whose
judgment in these things most of us respect immensely, did not find Mr Cumberland at all to his
liking. It is amusing to hear that Mr Cumberland
considers his own English prose style more correct,
more lucid, and more distinguished than that of
Newman in the *Apologia*.

On the subject of "Intellectual Freaks" he is
quite worth reading : he starts by making fun of
certain members of the Theosophical Society: "they
were cultured without being educated, credulous but
without faith, bookish but without learning, argu-
mentative but without logic. The women, serene and
grave, swam about in drawing-rooms, or they would
stand in long, attitudinising ecstasies, their skimpy
necks emerging from strange gowns, their bodies as
shoulderless as hock bottles." These ladies talk like
the Duke in G. K. Chesterton's *Magic*.

He is equally contemptuous of "the vast throng of
people who arise at eight or thereabouts, go to the
City every morning, work all day, and return home at
dusk ; who perform this routine every day, and every
day of every year ; who do it all their lives ; who do
it without resentment, without anger, without even a

momentary impulse to break away from their surroundings.

"All these people are freaks of the wildest description : yet they imagine themselves to be the backbone
of the Empire.   Perhaps they are. . . .

"I know a man still in his 'twenties' who keeps
hens for what he calls 'a hobby.'   Among his hens
he finds all the excitement his soul needs. . . . I
should esteem this man if he kicked against his
destiny; but he loved it, until the Army conscripted
him.   God save the world from those who keep hens."

When he comes to enlighten us on Fleet Street,
Mr Cumberland has some shrewd comments to make
on journalism, as for instance :   "If an editor is in
want of a dramatic critic, a musical critic, or leader
writer, or a descriptive reporter, he never advertises for
one.   He always knows some one who knows somebody
else who is just the man for the job."   On the other
hand, we learn that "money-making in Fleet Street up
to about seven hundred and fifty pounds a year is the
easiest thing in the world for a man who has any talent
at all for writing, especially if that talent be combined
with versatility . . . if you have proved yourself by
inducing a number of editors of repute to take your
stuff, go in and win."   On the other hand, "no man
by taking thought can add a thousand pounds a
year to his income, for money is not made by thought
but by intuition."

Of Orage, for whom he has a profound admiration
and certainly no malicious word, he writes : "he has
the all-seeing, non-rejecting eyes of a child.   He has
also the eternal spirit of youth."   His paper, *The
New Age*, "reverences neither power nor reputation ;
it is subtle and unsparing ; and if it is sometimes cruel,
it is cruel with a purpose."   Famous men write for it

because "they can tell the unadulterated truth and because they are proud to see their work in that paper."

Coming as he does from Manchester, one would expect Mr Cumberland to be interested in music, and the truth is that the major portion of his book is filled with gossip about musical people because he was himself primarily a musical critic.

"I would rather," he writes, "be a musical critic on £150 a year than a stockbroker earning £1500."

It is only natural that he should rate Ernest Newman highest among his fellow-craftsmen.

"Here we have a first-rate intellect functioning with absolute sureness and with almost fierce rapidity. As a scholar, no man is better equipped ; as a writer, he ranks with the highest : for fearlessness and inflexible intellectual honesty, he has no equal. . . . He is highly strung, imaginative, rationalistic ; he believes little and trusts not at all, loves intensely and hates bitterly."

His estimate of Manchester and Mancunian people is trite and dull : he wakes up again, however, in his description of Chelsea and Augustus John, for which and for whom he has praise.

"The essential thing about Augustus John is the quiet, lazy exterior which, in some peculiar way, contrives to suggest hidden fires and volcanic energies. . . . He has the mystery of Leonardo. One feels that his personality hides a great and important secret, but one feels also that that secret will remain hidden for ever. Sombre he is, sombre yet vital, sombre and full of humour."

"Chelsea men and women," we read, "are keen-witted, level-headed, and experienced people of the world."

U

He is rude about Mr Henderson's face, patronising on the subject of Lord Derby, and thinks Elizabeth Robins the greatest of living British female writers : " her temperament is not dissimilar to Charlotte Brontë's, that great little woman whose sense of the ridiculous was so great but whose power of expressing it was so small."

One of the rare occasions in the book when Mr Cumberland is bearable (on a first reading he charms by his freshness, his cheek, and his courage ; a second and further readings show him as striving for effect at any cost : he does not, as I expected, so much irritate one as fill one with depression and boredom), but as I was saying, one of the rare occasions when he actually pleases is the time when he talks of Pachmann. I like the hyperbole in this appreciation : none but a Manchester man would have indulged in it : but the *Manchester Guardian* correspondent would have quoted Aristotle and spoken above our heads, using archaic words and new-coined phrases : not so, Mr Cumberland ; he is nothing if not plain-spoken : nothing if not extravagant : . . .

" Cities have been sacked and countries ravaged ; Babylon, Nineveh, Athens, and Rome have bloomed flauntingly and wilted most tragically : and the most exquisite thing that has been produced by all this suffering, all this unimaginable labour, is the Chopin-playing of de Pachmann. The world has toiled for thousands of years and has at last given us this thing, more delicate than lace, more brittle than porcelain, more shining than gold. . . . " This is not criticism, but it makes one begin to think that Mr Cumberland must have been almost human when he wrote it, as he certainly was when he wrote : " In listening to noble music, I invariably feel much greater than, and curiously irritated by, the presence of other people." I also feel drawn to a man who talks of organists having as much imagination as the *vox humana* stop.

On theatrical people he is unconvincing : one hears something about Beerbohm Tree's memory, Henry Arthur Jones's self-importance, Temple Thurston's sensitiveness, Gerald Cumberland's slavish devotion to Janet Achurch, and Miss Horniman's detestation of Romance and Mancunian hardness, but there are no brilliant thumb-nail sketches of actors and actresses whom we have learnt to love or hate. On the other hand, I did not realise before how much music is regarded in Berlin as a trade. "A musician does not go to Berlin to get money : he goes to get a reputation." Unless you were known in Berlin, you were everywhere considered a second-rate kind of person, a mere talented outsider. Few artists have gone to sing or play in Berlin except for the purpose of obtaining favourable Press Notices. It may cost a couple of hundred pounds, but it is counted money well spent, well invested. The story of the concert-agent who required £325 to provide hall, printing, advertisements, invitations, preliminary paragraphs, audience, critics' articles, and so on is probably like most of the rest of the book, pure or impure fabrication, but is delightful.

After much that is irrelevant about Grieg, whom he calls " Griegkin," Richter, " the great disciplinarian ", the " polished, emotional " Landon Ronald, and other musicians, he picks out two names as of vital importance in British creative music—Sir Edward Elgar and Granville Bantock : Elgar, " conservative, soured with the aristocratic point of view, super-refined, deeply religious ; Bantock, democratic, Rabelaisian, free-thinking, gorgeously human." Of the two it is obvious that he prefers the latter. Among the people whom Mr Cumberland would like to meet (a quite neat idea, well worked out), W. B. Yeats is given pride of place on account of his " lack-lust " nature : He wants to satisfy himself as to what precisely is wanting in this lily-fingered, effeminate poet. These are not exactly his words. The versatility of Hilaire Belloc also attracts him : " Even now, on the border-land of middle age, I cannot pick up a new book of Belloc's without a little thrill : he is so clean, so bravely prejudiced, so courageous. He is a lover of wine and beer, of literature, of the Sussex Downs, of the great small things of life : a mystic, a man of affairs, a poet. What, indeed, is he not that is fine and noble and free ? "

It is when he writes like this that all our prejudice against Gerald Cumberland suddenly vanishes : the only true criticism, said some one, is that which appreciates : it seems as if this man might have been a true critic, but has misunderstood or ignored this axiom, and so queered his pitch. On the other hand, there are times when it is necessary for the critic to speak plainly, and no one is so well fitted to say what we all feel about D. H. Lawrence as Cumberland. Lawrence is one of the men he would like to meet for reasons which he does not state : but he does realise that here was a genius who in *Sons and Lovers* and *The White Peacock* (which Mr Cumberland, in his perversity, calls *The Red Peacock*) gave the world something entirely new. He could so easily have been the leading novelist of the day : instead, he allowed himself to be overwhelmed by the passion of sex, and then ran away out of the ugly chaos we call life : there was no riband of silver in his case : it was just

sheer funk . . . we feel the same sort of sense of loss
that we felt when Richard Middleton and John
Davidson killed themselves. These things are not
done.

For some rather obscure reason there is a good deal
of talk about night clubs in this book, but as it all
leads up to an exceedingly cunning suggestion about
their reconstruction much dull description may be
forgiven. I, for one, am quite willing to subscribe to
Mr Cumberland's establishment if it comes up to his
vision :

" A night club is never for the old. There should be
no card-playing. Dancing one would have, of course,
and music of the best. And wine, and many pretty
women, and a perfume of roses . . . and above all,
a big room set apart for the hour that comes after
dawn. At dawn we would all go into another room,
a room coloured green, with narcissi and jonquils and
hyacinths on the tables : a room with open windows :
a room with fruit spread invitingly : a room where
one could still be gay and in which one need not feel
sordid and spiritually jaded and spiritually unclean."

Set Down in Malice is altogether a most curious
book. It certainly satisfies a craving that we all
feel to know something about our more famous
contemporaries, but I cannot, for the life of me,
think why he should search for something nasty to
say about most of them. It is as false a method as
that of the headmaster's testimonial to his assistants
when he wants to get rid of them : to be fulsome in
eulogy iscertainly no worse, except that it is commoner,
than to be blatant in one's rudeness. Mr Cumberland
has certainly met some most interesting people, but it
is doubtful whether any of them will ever speak to
him again : he seems to have wantonly infringed one of

the severest unwritten laws of society : he has broken
the confidence which was not asked.   In his endeavour
to achieve perfect honesty he has tried to evade
another natural law which cannot lightly be broken,
that of compromise, and has succeeded in giving us a
false and quite dishonest portrait.   He is like popular
caricaturists who emphasise Lord Northcliffe's hair
and G. K. Chesterton's *embonpoint.*   Even Lytton
Strachey did not stop at Manning's " Hat."

No.   Gerald Cumberland's book ought to have
been worth a place on one's permanent bookshelf, but
isn't.   In a year it will be as dead as this week's
Bystander.

VIII

THE HUMOUR OF "SAKI"

Reginald
Reginald in Russia
The Chronicles of Clovis
The Unbearable Bassington
When William Came
Beasts and Super-Beasts
The Toys of Peace

IT was in the Christmas vacation of 1905 that I
was presented with a copy of *Reginald* by a fellow-
undergraduate. There are some debts that one
can never repay in full; it is perhaps something
that we never forget the friend who introduces us to
an author who ultimately becomes a favourite: I
shall feel that I have, in some degree, repaid him in
this case if I can entice any reader of this chapter who
may have missed Munro's work to love it as I do, for
he who brings before our notice what exactly suits
our temperament is a private benefactor of a very
high order. "Saki's" humour—let it be admitted
at once—is not for all tastes. There may be some
who look upon such playing upon phrases as "There
are occasions when Reginald is caviare to the Colonel,"
or "We live in a series of rushes—like the infant
Moses"—as unworthy. These are they who refuse
to laugh at the nimble-witted Nelson Keys, and prefer
to reserve their merriment for an abstruse Shakespearean pun about "points" and "gaskins."

Again, it may be urged that such a jest as the following may be found every week in the comic papers :

" There is my lady kitten at home, for instance : I've called it Derry : then if there are any unseemly noises in the night, they can be explained succinctly —Derry and Toms." Whether or no that is a good joke I don't profess to judge. All I know is that I have remembered it for nearly fifteen years, and I have no memory whatever for stories of any kind. I am not ashamed to say that I laugh whenever I think of it. That is the type of humour that exactly appeals to me. How we laughed too over the deft, ironic touches that we afterwards came to regard as Munro's choicest gift, from the simple " Reginald considered that the Duchess had much to learn : in particular, not to hurry out of the Carlton as though afraid of losing one's last bus," or " she was one of those people who regard the Church of England with patronising affection, as if it were something that had grown up in their kitchen gardens," to the crisper, unforgettable " never be a pioneer : it's the Early Christian that gets the fattest lion," " the frock that's made at home and repented at leisure," " the stage can never be as artificial as life ; even in an Ibsen drama one must reveal to the audience things that one would suppress before the children or servants " ; " in a few, ill-chosen words she told the cook that she drank : the cook was a good cook, as cooks go ; and as cooks go, she went " [1] : " *c'est le premier pa qui compte*, as the cookoo said when it swallowed its foster-parent," " a young man whom one knew instinctively had a good mother and an indifferent tailor—the sort of young man who talks unflaggingly

---

[1] This has now received the supreme honour of being introduced into a *revue* as an original joke !

through the thickest soup, and smooths his hair, dubiously as though he thought it might hit back " . . . and so on. I am tempted to go on quoting, as we used to in those far-off days of youth . . . but with me, at any rate, *Reginald* has stood the test of time. I read it to-day with just as many involuntary guffaws of mirth as I used to : it is no book for the railway carriage, if you are constituted as I am.

The sketch of Reginald, who is forced to spend Christmas at an intolerably dull house, planning some diversion (a favourite trick of Munro's), is almost a test example.

" I had been preceded [to bed] a few minutes earlier by Miss Langshan-Smith, a rather formidable lady, who always got up at some uncomfortable hour in the morning, and gave you the impression that she had been in communication with most of the European Governments before breakfast. There was a paper pinned on her door with a signed request that she might be called particularly early on the morrow. Such an opportunity does not come twice in a lifetime. I covered up everything except the signature with another notice, to the effect that before these words should meet the eye she would have ended a misspent life, was sorry for the trouble she was giving, and would like a military funeral. A few minutes later I violently exploded an air-filled paper-bag on the landing, and gave a stage moan that could have been heard in the cellars. Then I went to bed. The noise those people made in forcing open the good lady's door was positively indecorous ; she resisted gallantly, but I believe they searched her for bullets for about a quarter of an hour, as if she had been an historic battlefield."

I find it impossible to copy that story down without

laughing ; to me, at any rate, it is irresistibly funny, and it is in Munro's peculiar vein : he is better at this practical-joke sort of fun than any man I know : you may legitimately urge that such a sense of humour connotes cruelty, and " Saki " seems to me to be, on occasion, one of the " hardest " writers I know.

After all, so far as I understand him, he sets out to scourge the foibles of Society : he is a sort of prose Pope : at times he is just as polished and his arrows are quite as well-barbed. " He died quite abruptly while watching a county cricket match : two and a half inches of rain had fallen for seven runs, and it was supposed that the excitement killed him." " Isn't there a bishop who believes that we shall meet all the animals we have known on earth in another world ? How frightfully embarrassing to meet a whole shoal of whitebait you had last known at Prince's ! I'm sure, in my nervousness, I should talk of nothing about lemons." " Whether the story about the go-cart can be turned loose in the drawing-room, or must be told privately to each member of the party, for fear of shocking public opinion." " She must have been very strictly brought up, she's so desperately anxious to do the wrong thing correctly. Not that it really matters nowadays, as I told her : I know some perfectly virtuous people who are received everywhere." " There's Marian Mulciber, who *would* think she could play bridge, now she's gone into a Sisterhood—lost all she had, you know, and gave the rest to Heaven." As you may, by this time, have gathered, Reginald is one of those flippant young men about town (not very common) who are as neat in their speech as they are in their clothes. I visualise Munro as very like his own Reginald in his youth, sardonic and rude at garden parties, never losing an

opportunity of revenge on his enemies, conversa-
tionally brilliant in a way that unfortunately reminds
one of Wilde at very rare intervals as in " That is the
worst of tragedy, one can't hear oneself talk," and
" Beauty is only sin deep," but he escapes from the
sterile artificiality of the Wilde school very quickly,
and Wilde never could have hit on the sort of humour
one finds in such a sentence as : " Never be flippantly
rude to any inoffensive, grey-bearded stranger that
you may meet in pine forests or hotel smoking-rooms
on the Continent. It always turns out to be the
King of Sweden."

Reginald stage-managing a Sunday-school treat by
depriving the choir-boys of their clothes and compelling them to form a Bacchanalian procession
through the village with a he-goat and tin-whistles,
but no covering beyond a few spotted handkerchiefs,
provides us with an inexhaustible theme for mirth ;
Reginald telling tales about Miriam Klopstock,
" who *would* take her Chow with her to the bath-room,
and while she was bathing it was playing at she-
bears with her garments. Miriam was .always late
for breakfast, and she wasn't really missed till the
middle of lunch " ; Reginald refusing to accept
invitations from a sort of to-be-left-till-called-for
cousin of his father on the ground that " the sins of
the father should not be visited by the children " ;
Reginald " ragging " the Major who was for ever
reminding his fellow-guests of things that he had
shot in Lapland, " continually giving us details of
what they measured from tip to tip as though he
thought we were going to make them warm under-
things for the winter " ; whatever he is doing he is a
sheer delight. What I cannot understand is why
such a scintillating book should have so far failed to

attract the public that a second edition was not called
for until a year after publication, and a third edition
was not printed until six years had passed. To me,
this little book of 118 pages contains the cream of his
work. True, it contains no example of his essays in
the tragic muse, some of which are no whit inferior to
his best in the comic vein, but in *Reginald* we see him
at his most ingenuous, most naïve, and most youthful.

Before considering his other books it will be as well
to give such facts of his life as may help to illustrate
his work. He was born in 1870 in Burmah, the son
of a Colonel. His mother died young, so he was
brought up by two maiden aunts, with old-fashioned,
Scottish ideas of discipline, who lived in North Devon,
near Barnstaple. One cannot help thinking that
Sredni Vashtar, by far his most powerful story, owes
something to reminiscences of early life. He knows
nearly as much about children as Kenneth Grahame
and Eric Parker know. Like all boys destined
to become writers he read widely : he was devoted
to animals and nature, as might be expected from an
impressionable child brought up in such exquisite
surroundings. In spite of delicate health, he was
always working out ingenious, mischievous schemes,
as is only too evident from his books. He must have
been a constant thorn in the side of his aunts and
anyone else who, for the moment, was responsible
for him. On the return of his father he accompanied
him to Davos, Normandy, Dresden, and Austria :
museums and picture galleries became his educators.
Eventually the boy joined the Burmese Mounted
Police, but loneliness, combined with seven attacks
of fever in eleven months, necessitated his return to
England. He then came to London and plunged into
journalism by writing political satires for *The West-*

minster Gazette. In 1902 he went to the Balkans for *The Morning Post,* and during the Revolution of 1905 was the correspondent of that paper in Petrograd.

After removal to Paris, he came back to London in 1908, to find that a brilliant future as a man of letters awaited him. He lived very simply in lodgings in Mortimer Street, and refused to adapt his style in order to appeal to wider circles, preferring to occupy a permanent niche in our literature which, in the opinion of many good judges will be lasting, rather than make an ephemeral reputation and probably much money by prostituting his genius. In spite of his age, he managed to enlist in the 2nd King Edward's Horse shortly after the outbreak of war, but had to exchange into the 22nd Royal Fusiliers on account of his health. He was offered a commission twice, but refused, just as he refused many " cushy " jobs that were offered to him. He fell in the Beaumont-Hamel action in November 1916.

We may now return to our criticisms of his other books. *Reginald in Russia,* as so often happens in the case of sequels, was most disappointing and need not detain us.

The Chronicles of Clovis (1912) is, in the opinion of most of his admirers, his best book. It is certainly his most characteristic work. In it we see his understanding of and love for animals, his almost inhuman aloofness from suffering, his first-hand knowledge of house-parties and hunting, his astounding success in choice of names for his characters, his gift for epigram, his love of practical jokes, his power of creating an atmosphere of pure horror, his Dickensian appreciation of food and the importance of its place in life, his eerie belief in rustic superstitions, and his never-failing supply of bizarre and startling plots.

Clovis is, of course, only Reginald re-christened : he supplies the epigrams and is the prime instigator of most of the practical jokes.

For originality of theme it would be hard to beat *Tobermory*, the story of the cat who suddenly assumed human speech at a house-party and began to regale a drawing-room full of guests with precise extracts from the private opinions of each of those present about the others.

" ' What do you think of human intelligence ? ' asked Mavis Pellington lamely.

" ' Of whose intelligence in particular ? ' asked Tobermory coldly.

" ' Oh, well, mine, for instance,' said Mavis, with a feeble laugh.

" ' You put me in an embarrassing position," said Tobermory. ' When your inclusion in this house-party was suggested, Sir Wilfred protested that you were the most brainless woman of his acquaintance, and that there was a wide distinction between hospitality and the care of the feeble-minded. Lady Blemley replied that your lack of brain-power was the precise quality which had earned you your invitation, as you were the only person she could think of who might be idiotic enough to buy their old car. You know, the one they call "The Envy of Sisyphus," because it goes quite nicely up-hill, if you push it.' "

Once given the idea, which is brilliant, it is easy to see how, in the hands of an artist, there is no limit to the humour to be derived from it. It is like *Gulliver's Travels*.

There is a simplicity about his plots that makes one gasp at their effectiveness, as in the case of Lady Bastable, in whose house Clovis did not wish to stay longer, and so obtained permission to leave by the

ruse of playing on Lady Bastable's weak spot. She
was always in dread of a revolution : Clovis only had
to rush into the servants' quarters and shout : " Poor
Lady Bastable ! In the morning-room ! oh, quick ! "
and lead the butler, cook, page-boy, three maids, and
a gardener still clutching a sickle, rapidly to the room
where she was seated quietly reading the paper, to
make her fly through the French windows in igno-
minious retreat.

The Unrest Cure is in much the same vein : Clovis,
in this case, manages to disturb the even tenor of
the existence of a " groovy " middle-aged bachelor
and his sister by a " fake " massacre of the Jews in
their neighbourhood.   The plot, as usual, is ingenious
and convincing.

But the story that stands out in this volume is
the gruesome *Sredni Vashtar*, which tells of a delicate
small boy (living under the strictest surveillance of a
religious aunt), who managed to keep a Houdan hen
and a great ferret in the recesses of a tool-shed
unknown to his tyrannical overseer.   The hen was
found and destroyed.   Other gods were suspected,
and the woman made a personal investigation to
discover the ferret while the boy prayed for vengeance,
his face glued to the window which overlooked the
garden and the tool-shed.   After an interminable
interval he saw a long, low, yellow-and-brown beast
emerge with dark wet stains around the fur of jaws
and throat . . . and, after a lull, during which he
happily made himself some toast, he heard the scared
sobbings and the shuffling tread of those who bore a
heavy burden into the house.   The atmosphere is as
tense and awe-inspiring as it is in *Thrawn Janet* or
Markheim, or the mysterious tales of Richard Middleton.   It is a relief to come down to the antics of

Adrian of Bethnal Green, who amused himself by
transferring the bath-room label in a German hotel
to the adjoining bedroom-door belonging to Frau
Hofrath Schilling, who, from seven o'clock in the
morning onwards, had a stream of involuntary
visitors. We rise to the purer regions of irony again
in *The Chaplet*, where the chef of a famous restaurant
plunged the head of the conductor of the orchestra
into the almost boiling contents of a soup tureen
because the guests had allowed his consummate dish
of *Canetons à la mode d'Amblève* to grow cold on their
plates while they listened to the strains of *The Chaplet*.

One begins to think that advertising agencies must
have lost a gold mine by the death of " Saki," after
one has read *Filboid Studge*, the story of the penurious
young man who wanted to marry the daughter of a
patent-food seller. Mark Spayley, the prospective
bridegroom, steps in to save his future father-in-law
from ruin. As " Pipenta " the food had failed to
" catch on." Spayley re-christened it " Filboid
Studge," and designed one huge, sombre poster
depicting the damned in Hell suffering a new torment
from their inability to get at the Filboid Studge,
which elegant young fiends held out just beyond
their reach. The scene was rendered more gruesome
by a subtle suggestion of the features of the leading
men and women of the day. The poster bore no
fulsome allusions to the merits of the new breakfast
food, but a single grim statement in bold letters
along its base : " They cannot buy it now."

Spayley had grasped the fact that people will do
things from a sense of duty which they would never
attempt as a pleasure. Needless to say, he loses
the wife he wants owing to the startling success
of his poster. As Clovis said : " After all, you have

this doubtful consolation, that 'tis not in mortals to countermand success."

From *The Music on the Hill* we learn that " Saki " held in very considerable awe the power of the great god Pan : his lonely life as a boy in North Devon must have led him to realise that the forces of Nature are relentless and terrible. This fact must have been seared into his heart, for he recurs to it again and again. The doing to death of the young city-bred wife by the hunted stag because of her disbelief in the power of the wood-gods is horribly effective in its irony. *The Peace of Mowsle Barton* is intended to prove that London may very well be more restful for the nerves than the depths of the country, where old women seem to have retained their witchcraft and possess some remnants of their legendary powers of magic and cursing.

The Hounds of Fate is exactly in the vein of Masefield's long narrative poems, and shows the slow, unchanging steps of doom tracking down the miscreant who thinks to escape vengeance. There is a quite sufficient sprinkling of the terrible in this book, which is, perhaps, all the more hair-raising by reason of its juxtaposition with the light and airy persiflage of Clovis. One word on his choice of names : a mere catalogue will suffice to show how perfectly they are invented. As an exercise in imagination, I would suggest that you try to visualise the appearance and characteristics of each, and then compare your results with the reality. In every case you will, I think, very nearly approximate to his conception. I will begin by helping you.

Constance Broddle (a strapping, florid girl of the kind that go so well with autumn scenery or Christmas decorations in church).

The Brimley Bomefields (depressed-looking young women who have the air of people who have bowed to destiny and are not quite sure whether the salute will be returned).

Septimus Brope (the Editor of *The Cathedral Monthly*).

Groby Lington (a good-natured elderly man of recluse habits who kept a pet parrot).

Now try a few for yourself:

Bertie Van Tahn, Odo Finsberry, Agnes Resker, Mrs Riversedge, Mrs Packletide, J. P. Huddle, Aristide Saucourt, Rose-Marie Gilpet, Duncan Dullamy, Betsy Croot, Mortimer Seltoun, Cocksley Coxon, Loona Birnberton, Martin Stonor.

Which is the witch, the unorthdox Dean, the chef, the old-fashioned hostess, the man who was reading for Holy Orders, the youth who was so depraved at seventeen that he had long given up trying to be any worse, the Christian Scientist, the Company Promoter, the solid, sedate man who discussed the prevalence of measles at the Rectory ? . . . I maintain that their names fit them so exactly that you ought to be able to " spot " each of them at a glance.

I do not propose to dwell on *The Unbearable Bassington*, in which joy and pain are blended so inextricably that we find ourselves laughing through our tears at one moment, and weeping through our laughter the next. " Saki " was not a great novelist, even though we may claim that *When William Came* was a magnificent *tour de force*. If anything could have roused England to the menace of Prussian militarism in those days before the war this bitingly ironic fantasy should have succeeded ; but we were too far sunken in our torpor, and the squib fizzled out. As propaganda this novel deserves lasting fame, but from the artistic point of view " Saki's " reputation will rest solely on his manipulation of the short story, in which branch of letters he was, as I am trying to show, a past master.

In *Beasts and Super-Beasts* he sometimes excels even the most witty chapters of *The Chronicles of Clovis* : as can be seen from the title, he specialises in animal stories, and by a queer trick now attributes his more effective practical jokes to the inventive genius of sixteen-year-old flappers instead of to young male " rips " of the Reginald-Clovis type.

His choice of beasts is as queer as his choice of names : they bear something of the same resemblance to ordinary animals and ordinary names as Heath Robinson's drawings do to the usual machine diagram. Just as Heath Robinson ridicules absurd inventions, so does " Saki " burn up with the white flame of his scorn all pretenders to occult powers : the man whose aunt averred that she had seen him actually turn a vegetable marrow into a wood-pigeon before her very eyes gets a very thin time at the hands of Clovis, " whom he would gladly have transformed into a cockroach, and stepped on had he been given the chance." Munro was probably all the more bitter against the charlatan because of his own belief in unaccountable phenomena : he casts a wonderful air of verisimilitude over the story of Laura, who, at the point of death, declares that she is coming back as an otter to worry her friends, and does so : having been hunted and killed in that capacity, she next reappears in the guise of a naked brown Nubian boy, intent on mischief as ever.

Even the hoaxes in this book seem to depend on animals : there is the story of how the flapper kept the parliamentary candidate from brooding over

politics at night by committing to his care a gamecock
and a pig, on the plea that the outhouses had been
flooded owing to the bursting of the reservoir : there
is the delicious tale of the man in the train who
always failed to capture the attention of any of his
fellow-passengers until, at the instigation of a friend,
he launched the following at their heads : " A snake
got into my hen-run yesterday morning and killed
six out of seven pullets, first mesmerising them with
its eyes, and then biting them as they stood helpless.
The seventh pullet was one of that French sort,
with feathers all over its eyes, so it escaped the mes-
meric snare and just flew at what it could see of the
snake and pecked it to pieces." From that day his
reputation as the Munchausen of the party was
assured. The story of the tame otter that had a
tank in the garden to swim in and whined restlessly
whenever the water-rate was overdue, was scarcely an
unfair parody of some of his wilder efforts. And
then came Nemesis. His wife followed the example
of her mother and great-grand-aunt by dying immediately after making a " Death's Head Patience "
work out. At last something had really happened in
the romancer's life. He wrote out the full story only
to find that he was disbelieved in every quarter.
" Not the right thing to be Munchausening in a time of
sorrow " was the general verdict, and he sank once more
to conversation about canaries, beetroot, and potatoes,
a chastened and lonely man.

There is irony enough and to spare in the story of
how the family of Harrowcluff came to figure in the
Honours' List. Basset, at the age of thirty-one,
had returned to England after keeping open a trade
route, quietening a province, enforcing respect . . .
all with the least possible expense. He was likely

to be thought much of in Whitehall : his elder half-
brother, Lucas, was always feverishly engrossed in a
medley of elaborate futilities, and bored him sadly
with his constant discoveries of ideas that were
" simply it." On this occasion the inspiration came
to Lucas while he was dressing. " It will be *the*
thing in the next music-hall revue. All London will
go mad over it. Listen :

> Cousin Teresa takes out Caesar,
> Fido, Jock, and the big borzoi.

A lilting, catchy sort of refrain, you see, and big-
drum business on the two syllables of bor-zoi. It is
immense." It was : to the surprise of his family the
song caught on, the name of Harrowcluff became
more and more famous until at length, under the
heading of " Merit in Literature," Colonel Harrowcluff had the satisfaction of seeing his son's name in
the List of Honours. But it wasn't Basset.

The story of Cyprian, who preferred to accompany
his aunt on a shopping expedition without a hat and
was seen by her at intervals to be deliberately pocket-
ing the money for various articles from buyers who
mistook him for a salesman, is in the best Reginald
manner, as is the story of the young man who, having
gambled all his own possessions, staked his mother's
peerless cook and lost.

The Story-Teller, in which Munro shows his complete
understanding of children, ought to prove invaluable
to those who want to know how to hold the attention
of small boys and girls : the flick of the satiric whip
at the end of the story when the aunt stigmatises the
stranger's fable as " improper " is delightful.

" ' Unhappy woman,' said the bachelor to himself,
' for the next six months or so those children will

assail her in public with demands for an improper story.' "

There are tales of wolves (a favourite animal with " Saki "), elks, hunters, boar-pigs, whitebait, honey-buzzards, a most hilarious picture of a cow in a drawing-room, and of two Turkestan camels climbing a grand staircase : one begins to think that " Saki " must have felt some affinity with one of his own characters, an artist who always represented some well-known place in London, fallen into decay, populated with wild fauna. " Giraffes drinking at the fountain pools, Trafalgar Square," " Vultures attacking dying camel in Upper Berkeley Street," " Hyænas asleep in Euston Station," and " Sand-grouse roosting on the Albert Memorial " are some of his happiest titles, and it is not hard to think of " Saki " visualising some of his scenes in much the same way. His love for animals was great, his love of the incongruous even greater : a combination of these two passions would account for much of the merriment his animal stories cause us.

His last book, *The Toys of Peace*, published post-humously, is not so sustainedly successful as his earlier collections of short stories. He was so ardent a soldier that writing for *The Morning Post*, *The West-minster Gazette*, and *The Bystander* must have seemed but toying with life in comparison with the great vocation to which he was suddenly called to con-secrate his time. His first story, ironic as ever, shows us parents of a pacific turn of mind endeavouring to divert their children's taste from blood-lust to the excitements of peace, from guns to ploughs, from toy soldiers to toy city councillors, by giving them figures supposed to represent Mrs Hemans, John Stuart Mill, and models of the Manchester branch of the

Y.W.C.A. The result can easily be guessed. " Peeping in through the doorway Harvey observed that the municipal dustbin had been pierced with holes to accommodate the muzzles of imaginary cannon, J. S. Mill had been dipped in red ink and apparently stood for Marshal Saxe.

" Louis orders his troops to surround the Y.W.C.A. and seize the lot of them. ' Once back at the Louvre and the girls are mine,' he exclaims. ' We must use Mrs Hemans again for one of the girls : she says " Never ! " and stabs Marshal Saxe to the heart.' "

As I said before, " Saki's " understanding of the psychology of childhood is profound. His old trick of happy simile returns with as good effect as ever, but on rarer occasions.

" Nowadays the Salvation Army are spruce and jaunty and flamboyantly decorative, like a geranium bed with religious convictions."

His brain never lost its cunning in coining perfectly fitting names : " Eleanor Bope " brings before us at once a realistic picture of the aunt with freak ideas about " peace " toys. " Crispina Umberleigh " could only be a woman of martinet habits, born to sit in judgment. " Octavian Ruttle " could not be other than amiable ; you would expect Waldo Orpington to be frivolous and chirrup at drawing-room concerts ; we know exactly the kind of novel to expect from Mark Mellowkent, while the home life of Mr and Mrs James Gurtleberry can be guessed without much explanation.

How far it is permissible to search for a serious design in the work of a humourist it is hard to say, but one story so far stands out from the rest of his work as epitomising his attitude to life, that one is tempted to base a theory on the ideas contained in it.

Why, we ask ourselves, does " Saki " so frequently have recourse to hoaxes for his plots ? Why does he take an almost indecent delight in those of his characters who are fluent liars, who exercise their imagination at everybody else's expense ? The reason, I think, will be found in *The Mappined Life*, which might almost have been written by Tchehov.

" We are able to live our unreal, stupid little lives on our particular Mappin terrace, and persuade ourselves that we really are untrammelled men and women leading a reasonable existence in a reasonable sphere : we are trammelled by restrictions of income and opportunity and, above all, by lack of initiative. Lack of initiative is the thing that really cripples one, and that is where you and I and Uncle James are so hopelessly shut in. There are heaps of ways of leading a real existence without committing sensational deeds of violence. It's the dreadful little everyday acts of pretended importance that give the Mappin stamp to our life. Take my case : I'm not a good dancer, and no one could honestly call me good-looking, but when I go to one of our dull little local dances, I'm conventionally supposed to ' have a heavenly time,' to attract the ardent homage of the local cavaliers, and to go home with my head awhirl with pleasurable recollections. As a matter of fact, I've merely put in some hours of indifferent dancing, drank some badly-made claret-cup, and listened to an enormous amount of laborious light conversation. A moonlight hen-stealing raid with the merry-eyed curate would be infinitely more exciting."

That is " Saki's " secret. Behind the mask of the satirist and the elegant buffoon we can trace the features of one who so loved life that his affections always swayed his more sober reason, of one whose favourite companions were the Reginalds and Clovises of this world, because they, at least, could never grow up and worship at the shrine of routine.

" Saki " was not only a child-lover, he was a child himself, with all the imagination, the irresponsibility and the harsh cruelty of children fully developed in him : there is nothing sweet or mellow or restful in his genius : he surprises us just as " O. Henry " surprises us by turning a complete somersault in his last sentences after astonishing us with all manner of gymnastic capers in each paragraph before. It reminds one of music-hall acrobats who, after taking our breath away several times during their " turn," make their adieux by performing some incredible antic that leaves us too shattered even to applaud.

Such is the humour of " Saki," which never descends to caricature like so much of Dickens, is never aimless like that of W. W. Jacobs, is often bitter like his masters, Pope, Dryden, Swift, and (at times) Wilde, always verbally brilliant, polished, and cold : his exaggerations are all marked with a restraint which, of course, makes them all the more grotesque and mirth-provoking : his accents are as precise as those of the most prim governess or the most literal Scotsman :

" ' There is a goat in my bedroom,' observed the bishop.

" ' Really,' I said, ' another survivor ? I thought all the other goats are done for.'

" ' This particular goat is done for,' he said, ' it is being devoured by a leopard at the present moment. That is why I left the room : some animals resent being watched while they are eating.' "

It is here that he differs from Stephen Leacock, his transatlantic counterpart : both are prolific in verbal felicities, but Leacock is far less subtle : where

" Saki " is giving full play to a wonderfully developed imagination, Leacock is confined by the bounds of his terrestial fancy ; where " Saki " soars into the highest regions of the truly comic, Leacock is content with the slow, earth-borne car of Parody ; the barbs of irony which " Saki " employed were aimed at foolish humanity straying pitiably from paths where they might be happy, while Leacock's sarcastic darts are levelled at a particular failing of foolish " cranks." Leacock has intermittent flashes of great brilliance, but his intellect is that of a highly talented professor ; " Saki," like "O. Henry," rises quite frequently beyond cleverness into that inexplicable, rarefied atmosphere where only the genius can survive.   Like " O. Henry," and only too many other geniuses, he escaped recognition in his lifetime : " Saki " had only an eclectic public : but the passion of the devoted few always keeps the reputation of great men burning until the time comes for posterity to acknowledge the master, and there is no doubt whatever that the time will come when " Saki " will be given his niche among the great humourists.

IX

WOMEN

THERE is no subject so constantly in man's thoughts as some member of the opposite sex. Wherever two or three men are collected together gossiping, in the end some generalisation about women will set them off : this is not to say that Englishmen, as a race, talk so incessantly about them as Frenchmen do : nor do I suggest that men give the same amount of time to talking about women as women do about men : it is rather in his thoughts that women take precedence with a man. He is able to concentrate on his work or his games when occasion demands, but in his leisure moments, at the theatre, in church, in the train, in the streets, at fashionable restaurants, he likes to delight his eyes with the sight of pretty women : in books he gluts himself with vicarious love-making, he wallows in sentimental affection for fictitious heroines. If he is unmarried he is always more or less in love : if he is married he is either preposterously in love with his own wife or some one else. All this in spite of the fact that most women make men miserable, that men despise them as a sex, that as companions their own sex is in nearly every way superior. All bachelors suspect their married friends because they unite invariably in urging them to do as they have done : whereas no successful barrister, journalist, or prince of commerce ever yet did anything but try to put off all his acquaintances from taking up the profession in which he has made good.

331

Women are in so many cases a fascinating mystery
or a horrible enigma that it is with a sense of having
discovered the sesame to their nature that we pick up
a betrayal of the sex by one of their number.[1]

Women, published by Martin Secker, by an anonymous author, is one of the most provocative books
I have ever read. True or not, it is good that man,
sentimental man, should learn what one woman
thinks of her sex. First there is her attitude to the
war, commonly designated as " splendid." There
is no question in the author's mind that the women
liked the war : it immediately gratified their instinctive hunger for emotion : " not Lord Kitchener,
but the women of England, made the new armies."
" It was the women who sent the men out to fight by
cajolery, bullying, ridicule . . . the woman pacifist
has yet to be born. Having sent the man to fight, the
women found that England was theirs. War became
glorious fun : it was an excuse for wearing uniforms
and acquiring power : it gave birth to a sex-hatred
which may now be permanent. Owing to her lack
of imagination, the average woman is unable to have
anything more than a shallow sympathy with suffering, principally physical suffering. Just as they
dote on physical strength and fear intellectual ability,
so do they understand, to a certain degree, wounds
of the body without being able to realise the more
poisonous and lasting wounds of the mind. The
emotional excitements which every woman must have,
have led to an amazing moral laxity during the last
five years. They are much more completely and
continuously sensual than men, living as they do in
a marvelling delirium of the senses : life has become

---

[1] I am only, of course, guessing when I attribute the authorship of
Women to a woman.

a precarious business at best : we are all fatalists : consequently, we have snatched at happiness and secured, in too many cases, misery : this is the outcome of the ' splendid ' behaviour of women." So much for the thesis of Part I.

In Part II we are told something of the characteristics of women. There is the love of physical strength mentioned above, the faculty of imitativeness . . . and the passion of cruelty : at all costs a girl will conform to the prevailing fashion, however unsuited she may be : in the principal affair of their lives, the business of love, they are past masters : they sedulously cultivate the myth that all women are mysterious in order to cover the nakedness of their souls and to render themselves more attractive : that is why a woman instinctively dreads a man with brains : he may, at any moment, probe the veil and mortally wound her legendary self, " the offspring of vanity out of vacuum." Just as the dominant interest in all novels written by women is sex so is sex the obsession of all women. Novel-writing is the outcome of repressed sexual emotions.

Part III is devoted to the question of " Why Men Love Women." Leaving out of account all the minor stages in love-making, it is interesting to read that " affairs " with unmarried women subside more normally than those with married women. The married woman, having endured a disappointment, having had distaste aroused, and having had developed within her a desire for revenge upon the cause of her disappointment, becomes more quickly reckless. She counts the cost less : she knows as nobody else can do the sweets of stolen intercourse. Men like something stable. They wish to feel that love and company await them through life. The happily-married man exults in a condition for which his heart has all his life secretly yearned.   There comes a time in the life of man when he can no longer endure amorous uncertainty.   The game has lost its first savour.   He wants to be sure of one woman for ever. It is a dream.   All men of character are extremely lonely and long for rest : that is their first desire : that is what prepares them for love.   Apart from very exceptional men, the sexual instinct can be appeased without love.   In ordinary courtship the sexual appeal obviously counts for a good deal, because most people have nothing to give in marriage but the sexual relation : they have no spiritual communion. With the best types of men the sex relation is secondary to the relation of the spirit.   They ride for ever, seeking understanding and sympathy.   To rest and to confess, to be made whole and to be comforted, to be understood, to have a wife who, knowing all our weakness, has yet the strength to love us and to be proud of our love, these are the love aspirations of men.   They are rarely more than aspirations, because women also require comforting : and when women appeal to men for comforting, the breakfast must have been intolerably bad, or the day quite too distressingly exacting, if, during the first year of married life, married sympathy is not forthcoming.   Afterwards, no doubt, with puzzled disappointment upon both sides drying up the wells of tenderness and longing, both are harsh.   Neither then, perhaps, struggles to adjust the differing rhythms of mood.   But at first, when the flush of rapture is still warm, only inarticulateness, only cowardice, can account for the failure of unity in mood. There is no peace, because men and women alike are egoists when they are in emotional conflict.

It is not through the senses, first of all, that man

loves—if he is capable of loving. It is through imagination and humour and pity and admiration.

See the exchanged glance of true lovers—what is there ? On the girl's side a glance for reassurance, quick, side-long : on the man's side a puzzled questioning scrutiny. He suddenly realises just exactly how frightened of her he is. He will never stop being afraid, because she is physically weaker than himself. As long as women are physically the inferior sex they will be compelled to be mysterious. Their determination may be much stronger than that of men. It is certainly more unquiet and assertive. But it can only be combated by physical force : and physical force is the one weapon which most men will never apply to their wives. They will be strangers to each other for the rest of their lives ; the lover will stand regarding the woman he loves, seeing through her ; seeing her vanities, her angers, her discomforts and triumphs, cajoleries and inexpressible reliefs. He sees her a child and a woman, a coward and a heroine, a human heart that lives in a world of illusion . . . but he must never tell : women are far too serious to endure the true picture. They have too much of the " heroic " in their temperament. To see life and character clear, and to laugh without cruelty or pain, is a power denied to all but two or three women. If it were a widespread gift we should all laugh ourselves into apoplexies.

" Women in Love " is the subject of Part IV. We are first shown the phenomenon of hate following hard upon love, of married men being " caught on the rebound," of very young men crying off on the day after a proposal and acceptance. All men have a deep-seated conviction that women are tricksters. Distrust of or a contempt for all women is more common than genuine love for one woman : this is because she has made the sexual act her lifelong preoccupation. To a man it is a moment of dread and anxiety, a moment of unsettlement—almost of demoralisation . . . there comes brutality between married people : the impulse to cruelty towards the beloved is common : in women it often takes the form of a frigidity that is expressively known as " sulking."

Think of the novels women most admire : they are novels of feminine surrender : they are novels in which the heroine at last succumbs to the urgent wooing of the hero, or the desires of her own physical nature : among modern novels it is the erotic tale that finds most readers among women : any novel which contains a marriage at first left unconsummated, with the ugly intrigues of the wife to indicate her willingness for cohabitation forming its subsequent *motif*, is infallibly a success with women : their savage curiosity in following the theme is unmistakable : it is an index to their predilections : a study of marriage which does not dwell on the physical relation is to them intolerable. To the man, then, the period of love-making is a time of emotional turmoil, of active distress : to the woman it is a time of engrossing delight and triumph. Later they are always trying to import into their too restricted imaginings some of that excitement of which they can get so little in celibate or monogamous life. That is why women thrive on crises. When she no longer is jealous of her husband, she no longer loves, which means that she loves another man.

In the act of love itself women are more sensual than men. She is at peace, half-swooning, absorbed in sensation. It is for men to think, to regret, to fear, with a comical mixture of startling associations

and questionings. It is the case that many men,
if they are inexperienced in love, are astounded at
the abandonment of the beloved. They are excited
and exultant, but they are ashamed and afraid :
the woman is neither ashamed nor afraid. Love is
really and actually woman's whole existence. Defrauded by some dreadful accident of a love upon
which he had set his heart, a man continues soberly
to perform his task in life. He goes from day to day,
wearily, until passion cools, and his knowledge of
things inexpressible deepens and grows more clear.
He is full of grief : but his soul remains unscathed.
Though the endurances of the hours be indescribably
those of agony unappeasable, yet he retains his hold
upon other realities and is reinforced by his own
steadfastness. If a woman be defrauded of the love
she covets it is as though she were at sea, weeping
and helpless, in contrary winds : she may long cling
despairingly to the illusion that all is not lost : her
morbid fancy may continue to picture secret joys
which will never be hers. Finally, anything may
happen. She is no longer controlled by habit or
obedience to the laws of society.

In the last section of the book we are asked to
consider " The Best of Both Worlds."

The modern girl has not changed in essentials :
the only alteration lies in the use of fresh armaments
and the development of a new offensive : the decay
of religious acceptance has led to a rise in the respect
given to intellectual attainments : her aggressiveness
is a bluff : she still strives to impress the male ;
there is no real, though much pretended, equality :
there is bound always to be constraint in intellectual
relations between men and women, due to the fact
that a woman is incapable of thinking originally, that

she is incapable of thinking or arguing disinterestedly,
from pure love of truth, that she is always half-
consciously and guiltily bluffing herself and trying to
interest her auditor in her own ego.

Women demand education, not for its own sake, but
rather as if it were a new costume : the sense that
marriage awaits them robs them of incentive to work
at a task for which they have no natural impulse :
that is why they are intellectually unambitious :
but all women cannot hope to marry : they will have
to adapt themselves if the returned soldier adopts a
truculent attitude to the women who try to oust him
from jobs. But from those women who will be
unable to adapt themselves we may expect a fierce sex
war to begin.   They will find that they are absolutely
dependent for moral support upon the other sex.
" On the whole," one hears, " women are admirable
workers, but never capable of continuous self-
reliance.   They go to pieces suddenly : they cannot
take a blow : they lack physical stability :   they
become weak, vicious, and despondent when consideration for them is removed.   At all times and in
all circumstances, they are predominantly sexual.
They cannot be both masters and mistresses.
Triumph in the sex war. for women would mean
sterility in all the arts and enterprises of the modern
world.   Compromise is the only solution : nature
will be too strong for women : the lack of power to
create is due to physical causes which cannot be
overcome : all efforts to escape from the consequences
of it are the workings of hysteria, the frustration of
the sexual impulse."

Such, in essence, is the main contention of this
remarkable book.   Exaggerated, bitter, and lacking
in humour, it may be ; but, at least, it tends to send

the reader back to first principles to decide quite what
woman means to him.   It is inevitable that one should
take the standpoint of a man in this case.   In early
youth we discover how comfortable and necessary
to our happiness are a mother's arms, a mother's
lap, and a mother's bosom.   The schoolboy finds to
his horror, a little later, that there are things which
he cannot tell his mother simply because she cannot
understand his point of view.   If he has sisters he
will be horrified at a woman's code of honour : the
years pass and, as a prefect at school or an undergraduate, he will fall in love with many women, all
much older than himself.   This love will be platonic
and pure : he may easily, at this period, feel that he
has contaminated himself beyond all hope of redemption by having illicit relations with girls of his
own age in a lower station of life.   He will never
quite recover from this feeling if he falls.   Earlier in
life it satisfied him to kiss girls at dances or at pic-
nics . . . now he may be sexually aroused and given to
furtive low bursts of passion at irregular rare intervals.
Not many men, however, succumb to this sort of temptation.   But the next stage is common to nearly every
man : suddenly, without warning, he will find that one
girl so attracts him that he will be acutely miserable
whenever he is parted from her, exceedingly jealous
if she casts a favourable eye on any other of his sex :
he will blurt out a proposal of marriage, and, to his
amazement, she will accept him : and in the months
that pass before they are married he will be still more
astonished at her calmness and lack of passion.   At
length comes the nuptial day, and he will, for a little
time, find the changed conditions a little arduous, a
little disappointing : then he will settle down for
good or ill.   And here comes the great divergence

between the happy and the unhappy. In a great number of cases each of the two parties will satisfy the other's wants, physically, mentally, and spiritually: they will fuse excellently and merge into one spirit, one body : life will become a magnificent thing, and each will strengthen the other to bear any adversity . . . but many marriages are not made like this, in heaven : little rifts within the lute begin to appear : one of the two begins to " nag," the other to sulk : they shut themselves up into watertight compartments, and existence becomes a misery. How to avoid such a catastrophe is one of the most necessary things in life to learn.   " By mutual understanding and forbearance " comes the answer pat.   But are there not instances where the husband or wife scents in the other a determination wilfully to misunderstand, wantonly to go his or her own way ?   There are secrets in a woman's nature which no power, not even a good man's love, can wrest from her : there are compartments in a man's heart which he feels that even his best beloved would only defile if they were laid bare to her view.   It is in spite of obvious weaknesses and vices that we love one another : Shakespeare's " Sonnets to the Dark Lady " are a wonderful revelation of the power of love to destroy the critical faculties. Even when we realise that we have mistaken a harpy for an angel we are unable to escape from the toils : the married man is like a cat : he cannot contemplate change with any feeling but profound aversion : that is why so many quite rational beings submit to being " hen-pecked " by their wives when they would die rather than endure an insult from their fellow-man.   That is why one reads of lurid tragedies in the newspapers of men who have been driven to murder other men who have attempted to interfere in their

domestic affairs by trying to capture their wives'
affections. Happily-married couples more nearly approach man's highest conception of heaven than they
themselves can ever realise. Others, less fortunate,
gaze hungrily at these ideal soul-companionships
and curse their own lot : at any rate, no hell can ever
compare with the ever-gnawing hopeless longing of a
man who loves his wife, knowing that whatever he
does she will have no love for him. He seeks consolation in drink, in sport, in male companionship, even in
other women, but he never finds contentment, but
wanders, half-crazy, his outlook on life poisoned, his
early promise of genius or talent or business capacity
ruined, a mere husk of a man, fit only to be scrapped
—and all through the fault of one woman. There
is nothing to be gained by pretence. All men realise,
even if they refuse to confess it, that they are completely under the thumb of the other sex, once they
have given their hearts away. It is possible to
eliminate the whole trouble if you refuse ever to have
any dealings with them, but once married, there is no
hope for you, if you make a mistake. The use,
therefore, of a book like *Women* would seem to be
that it should make men pause before sliding into
matrimony, before choosing their life-mate. It
would seem to advocate later marriages, to suggest
that we should arrive at years of discretion before
allowing ourselves to succumb to charms which may
only be temporary. We are told that there is much
wrong with the marriage and divorce laws : there
certainly is, but there is far more wrong with the
attitude with which men regard women and women
regard men. This is an extremely difficult age :
it was enough in the past to seize your woman and
mould her to your requirements by brutality and

bullying : woman has become emancipated : she
is now man's equal and ought to be a far finer creature :
at present there are not lacking instances of her
abusing her new-won privileges. She understands
being beaten : not always does she understand the
man who prefers to recognise her rights and give her
the chance to mould herself. She regards such a
husband as lacking in conviction, if not in passion :
the truth is that the time has not arrived when the
man can lay all his cards on the table and expect the
woman to know enough of the game to play fairly.
Her code is so entirely different from his : man so
idealises the other sex that he is blind to its deficiencies
until it is too late, and then, horribly tortured, turns
cynic or reverts to a state of primitive savagery.
It is a horrible impasse, for this is what happens :

If a couple are mutually happy there is no need for
argument : their case is settled. If the man's ardour
cools while his wife remains faithful and loving, he
may form sporadic illegal unions, but he will eventually
return to his wife if he finds that his cruel thought-
lessness is driving her to despair : not only will he
return, but his love will be re-born through the agency
of pity ; but if it is the wife's passion that cools while
the man remains faithful, there is the devil to pay.
For she will seek an outlet for her thwarted desires
elsewhere, the husband will become a prey to jealousy
and be driven almost mad . . . he may plead with
her never so rationally, abase himself before her never
so pathetically in a way that would wring tears from
a devil's eyes, but she will pursue her wanton way
regardless of all his misery, stony-hearted to his plea
for pity, more cruel and icy than any villainous
inquisitor of fiction, more malignly mischievous even
than Iago.

It would be well if men were educated to differentiate the true from the false : a woman's whole early training is spent in learning to sum up a man's qualities. Man goes into the race blind and handicapped through ignorance : it isn't fair, and no amount of reading novels or juggling with marriage laws can make it so.